Assessing and Guiding Young Children's Development and Learning

Second Edition

ORALIE MCAFEE
DEBORAH J. LEONG
Metropolitan State College of Denver

ALLYN AND BACON
Boston London Toronto Sydney Tokyo Singapore

Series Editor: Frances Helland
Marketing Manager: Kathy Hunter
Production Administrator: Deborah Brown
Editorial-Production Service: Mary Young, Omegatype Typography, Inc.
Composition and Prepress Buyer: Linda Cox
Manufacturing Buyer: Suzanne Lareau
Cover Administrator: Suzanne Harbison

Library of Congress Cataloging-in-Publication Data

McAfee, Oralie.
    Assessing and guiding young children's development and learning /
Oralie McAfee, Deborah J. Leong.—2nd ed.
        p.   cm.
    Includes bibliographical references (p.   ) and indexes.
    ISBN 0-205-26332-1 (pbk.)
    1. Early childhood education—United States   2. School children—
Rating of—United States.   3. Educational tests and measurements—
United States.   4. Classroom management—United States.   I. Leong,
Deborah.   II. Title.
LB1139.25.M4   1996
372.12′64—dc20   96-32717
                                                                 CIP

Printed in the United States of America
10 9 8 7 6 5 4 3   01 00 99 98

Photo Credits: All photographs by William Harvey, Jr.
Graphics: Morgan Graphics, Evergreen, CO

*This book is lovingly dedicated to
John, Rob, and our families*

CONTENTS

PART II: Assessing and Teaching

Chapter 3:   Why, What, and When to Assess?   27

PREFACE

Authentic assessment, done in the familiar context of the classroom, is at the heart of teaching and learning in the early childhood classroom. Only through knowing children's current knowledge and understandings, their skills, interests, and dispositions, can we develop curriculum that builds upon their strengths and provides experiences that support their continued development and learning. The purpose of this book is to show how to do authentic, alternative, classroom-based assessment, and then how to interpret and use the information to plan curriculum that is responsive to and supportive of children's learning. The second edition of *Assessing and Guiding Young Children's Development and Learning* has been extensively revised and updated to reflect the rapidly developing concepts of appropriate assessment, educational outcomes, and the way young children develop and learn.

Underlying Themes

The underlying themes that have guided us are congruent with national trends in early childhood education and in assessment at all levels.

Assessment as Classroom-Based and Authentic

The book's focus is "alternative" assessment—ways of finding out about and keeping track of children's development and learning that are an authentic part of ongoing classroom life and typical activities of children. We explain and describe how to do this in nontechnical language. These assessment procedures can be used by people working with young children in varied early childhood settings. They do not depend on group or individual standardized tests.

Assessment as a "Work in Progress"

The text presents assessment as a growing, developing aspect of teaching and learning, one that is by no means ever finished. The extensive section on portfolios reflects their popularity with teachers, children, and parents. We guide teachers in setting up and using portfolios, and address practical questions frequently omitted in other discussions. New sections on standards, benchmarks, and rubrics define and show how these concepts relate to assessment. Guides and examples show how teachers can be sensitive to sociocultural and individual diversity. We describe teachers' roles and responsibilities in assessment related to inclusive education. Current best thinking is incorporated throughout.

Assessment as a Process

Assessment is treated as a flexible, practical process. The process begins with the "why, what, and when" of assessment, progresses through data collection and recording, and then shows how to compile, interpret, and use the results. Numerous examples from different developmental and curriculum areas show how each step is carried out with young children.

Assessment as a Professional Activity

Assessment is treated as a highly professional activity, not something done casually or haphazardly. The book is designed to help teachers improve "the conceptual and procedural foundations for assessment" (Hiebert & Calfee, 1989, p. 50). There are suggestions for improving the reliability and validity of alternative assessment, for meeting ethical and legal responsibilities, and for communicating with others about assessment results. The concepts and procedures that are presented are grounded in sound conceptual and scientific bases. They meet all of the guidelines for appropriate classroom assessment outlined by the National Association for the Education of Young Children (Bredekamp & Rosegrant, 1992, 1995).

Philosophical Orientation

Although the assessment procedures presented can be used with any approach to early childhood education, the examples reflect the authors' convictions about young children's growth. We see development and learning as an integrated process that fuses the universal yet variable process of human development with an individual child's personal encounter with the social and cultural world. We see adults and other children as active participants in that development and learning—responding, modeling, guiding, assisting, and scaffolding in developmentally appropriate ways. We see learning "processes" and "products" equally important as children co-construct ever more complex learnings in a supportive, responsive environment.

Organization

Topics and chapters are organized to provide readers maximum flexibility in meeting their own learning needs. Chapters can be read in order: Part I (Chapters 1 and 2) prepares teachers to approach assessment professionally; Part II (Chapters 3 through 9) takes them through the steps in the assessment process; Part III (Chapters 10 and 11) takes assessment beyond the classroom—to communicating with parents and other professionals, and addressing contemporary assessment concerns. Each part and chapter can also stand alone, so that readers may select chapters to meet their own needs.

Features

Assessment and Analysis Guides

Easy-reference assessment and analysis guides present steps in the development and learning sequence for major child development and curriculum areas. These are ready for readers to use as references for interpreting assessment and for curriculum planning in response to assessment.

"Red Flags"

A listing of developmental "red flags" alerts teachers to patterns of behavior that signal the need for a closer look.

Study, Discussion, and Reflection Aids

Questions and exercises are designed to promote complex thinking and reflection. The first question at the end of each chapter is specifically designed for readers who are keeping a reflective journal to foster their own growth and development.

Glossary

The glossary defines currently used assessment and curriculum terminology in clear, nontechnical language.

Summaries and Suggested Readings

Summaries highlight important points in each chapter; suggested readings related to the subject of that chapter show readers where to find additional information.

Examples and Applications

Numerous charts, figures, forms, and illustrations make clear what is being discussed and link it to the real world of children and schools. Many forms are ready to copy, adapt, and use. Examples of children's work from the range of early childhood—ages 3 through 8—show how assessment is carried out at all these ages.

This book is grounded in our own teaching and learning experiences. These include teaching young children and working with parents from all socioeconomic levels and diverse cultures. We expanded that teaching and learning to preservice and inservice early childhood personnel in a variety of settings, helping them learn about assessment and curriculum and how to create classrooms that are responsive to children. The examples and illustrations are "real," although names and places are fictitious. To avoid the problems presented by the lack of a gender-neutral pronoun for *child* and *teacher*, we use both *he* and *she*, since children and teachers come in both genders.

Acknowledgments

Our work has been enriched by the young children and college students we have taught and learned from, our colleagues throughout the country who have shared their insights with us, and preschool and primary teachers, administrators, and agency personnel in the Denver metropolitan area and throughout Colorado who let us share assessment practices in the real world.

Metropolitan State College of Denver has supported our work in many ways for both the first and second edition of this book. For the second edition, we particularly thank President Sheila Kaplan, Dean Joan Foster, Dr. Lyn Wickelgren, Carolyn Schaeffer, Brenda Byrne, Gay Cook, Dr. Dmitri Semenov and our colleagues in the psychology department.

Special thanks go to Jeremy Leitz and Leslie and Brian Fauver for letting us see the world as they see it, and to Dr. Elena Bodrova for her insights on Vygotsky.

In addition to our colleagues who reviewed the manuscript and made helpful suggestions for the first edition of this book, we wish to thank the reviewers for the second edition: Leah Adams, Eastern Michigan University; Mary-Margaret Harrington, Southern Illinois University at Carbondale; and Linda Pearl, Eastern Michigan University.

*Assessing and Guiding
Young Children's
Development and Learning*

CHAPTER ONE

Assessment in Early Childhood: A Work in Progress

Preschool and primary teachers throughout the country are studying children's learning and development in new and rewarding ways—ways that are embedded in instruction, thereby guiding it (Airasian, 1994; Stiggins & Conklin, 1992). These teachers are systematically observing children at work and play—"kid-watching" (Goodman, 1978). They are asking children to explain and describe their work and their thinking processes. They are collecting and analyzing samples of children's work. They and the children are developing portfolios to showcase children's learning in one or more developmental or curriculum areas. They are developing, using, and recording results from performance assessments—appraisals that ask children to perform a real task or solve a problem to demonstrate their learning. They are "keeping track" (Engel, 1990) and "documenting" (Chittenden & Courtney, 1989) children's ongoing learning through checklists, participation charts, written records, photographs, sketches, and other means. They are teaching children to document and assess their own learning through journals, reading logs, the editing and revising of their own writing, and reflecting on their own work, interests, and needs. The result is a rich and comprehensive description of an active, developing, and learning child—one that concentrates on what a child knows and can do, but that also helps teachers plan future learning.

The broad term *assessment* refers to almost all forms of measurement and appraisal, including tests, observations, interviews, and reports from knowledgeable sources, recorded and integrated in an organized manner and used in planning for further instruction (Mendelson & Atlas, 1973). The term is sometimes used to refer to one appraisal or one measure, or to avoid the negative connotations of the terms *test, testing,* and *evaluation.* To distinguish the new assessment approach from developmental screening; readiness, achievement, and diagnostic testing; unit tests; and the many other instruments and procedures typically called assessment, it is referred to as *classroom assessment, alternative assessment,* or *authentic assessment. Classroom assessment* includes the innumerable and complex ways in which teachers appraise children's learning in the classroom. *Alternative assessment* refers to almost any type of assessment other than standardized tests and similar developmental inventories and achievement tests.

Performance assessment refers to a specific type of alternative assessment in which children demonstrate a skill or create a product that shows their learning (Stiggins, 1995). Authentic assessment conveys that good assessment captures children's development and learning in their on-going daily activities. The term *curriculum-embedded assessment* points up that assessment should be an integral part of teaching and learning, in contrast to tests that require children to perform "on-demand." All the terms mentioned so far have slightly different meanings, but are frequently used interchangeably.

Authentic and performance assessment evaluate the child in tasks that are as close to "bona fide practical and intellectual challenges" as possible (Finn, 1991, p. 10). Assessment tasks are "instances of complex performances that directly represent the ultimate goals of education" (Shepard, 1991b, p. 235). For instance, instead of underlining a picture or "bubbling in" a circle to indicate if they can match, classify, and sort pictures of objects, children actually match, classify, and sort objects. Instead of counting dots or pictures on a page, children count to solve a classroom or individual problem.

There is a distinction between performance assessment and authentic assessment (Meyer, 1992). Performance assessment refers to the type of pupil response. If motor coordination is being measured, the child performs an appropriate action. If writing is under consideration, the child writes. In authentic assessment the child "not only completes the desired behavior, but also does it in a real-life context" (Meyer, 1992, p. 40). Authentic assessment takes place as part of ongoing life and learning in the classroom, playground, hallway, lunchroom, and other typical school and center settings.

Factors Contributing to Current Changes in Assessment

Several social and educational factors contribute to current changes in assessment practices. These include changing concepts of the purpose of assessment and of how children develop and learn; changing educational goals, curriculum, and teaching strategies; the changing nature of the population in schools and centers; and the limitations and inadequacies of traditional testing.

Changing Concepts of the Primary Purpose of Assessment

Assessment should be "used to help the individual in his efforts to learn" (Tyler and Wolf, 1974, p. 170). It should result in "benefits to the child such as needed adjustments in the curriculum or more individualized instruction and improvements in the program" (National Association for the Education of Young Children and National Association of Early Childhood Specialists in State Departments of Education, 1991). Assessment is not meant to determine whether children pass or "flunk," to decide whether or not they are "ready" or eligible for a given program, or to assign them to a fixed group or class. Assessment for individual learning and development provides information that supports teachers' planning and children's learning. "A number of trends in American education have converged in the 1990's. . . . One key trend is a shift in what the public expects from schools. No longer is it enough to give children the chance to learn. Schools are now expected to ensure that children actually learn" (Northwest Regional Educational Laboratory, 1991, p. 1). Authentic assessment is part of the process of ensuring that children actually learn. Although assessment results are also used for other purposes, such as reporting to parents and children what has been learned, communicating with other educators, and in some cases reporting to funding agencies and the public, their primary purpose is to guide and support children's learning.

Changing Concepts of How Children Develop and Learn

We are reaching a better understanding of how children develop and learn, and the roles that parents, teachers, and other children play in that process. Children actively construct knowledge within a social context that affects what and how they learn. They do not acquire knowledge and skills all on their own, automatically developing qualitatively more complex skills, ideas, and understandings as they mature. Neither do they simply learn what is taught and "reinforced"—the behaviorist psychology that once dominated learning theories. Learning and teaching are viewed as complex enterprises in which children, adults, the things children work and play with, language interactions, and all aspects of the child's life—in and out of school—interact to influence that learning (Bodrova & Leong, 1996; Seifert, 1993). Children don't just learn more and more discrete facts and skills. Rather, they try to organize this information, develop theories, see relationships, and "develop their own cognitive maps of the interconnections among facts and concepts" (Shepard, 1989, p. 5).

Assessment practices should mirror the dynamic learning processes implied in this constructivist and holistic view of child development and learning.

Changes in Educational Goals, Curricula, and Instructional Strategies

Curriculum goals and content (what children should know and be able to do), learning processes (how children learn), instructional strategies (how to teach), and assessment (how to determine what children have learned) are interrelated (Bredekamp & Rosegrant, 1992). All are receiving critical scrutiny in the search for better ways to educate children.

Curriculum goals have been broadened to include competencies that cut across all developmental and curriculum domains, such as problem solving, self-regulation, creative thinking, decision making, reasoning, and learning how to learn. Educational outcomes are being reexamined by national, state, and local groups representing the various curriculum content areas (mathematics, science, the arts, physical education, and others) and shaped into broad, yet specific standards that identify what children should know and be able to do in each of the content areas (see Chapter 3). Learning processes and instructional strategies to achieve those standards are frequently suggested or implied, such as active "hands on" learning in science; working with manipulatives as well as symbols, and problem solving as well as computation in mathematics; and integrated language arts teaching that capitalizes on children's emerging reading and writing abilities. All emphasize that children should apply what they are learning to real-world situations and problems (Education Week, 1995; Marzano, Pickering, & McTighe, 1993). Traditional measures are not adequate to assess children's progress toward many of these outcomes, nor are they compatible with the learning processes and instructional strategies being used (Stiggins, 1995). For example, reading readiness and achievement tests may include items that children using whole language approaches are not taught. Skill and knowledge those same children have about expressing themselves through writing may never be tapped.

Many early childhood schools have mixed-age and multi-age groupings instead of traditional age and grade groupings. Children may move from a "family grouping" in preschool and kindergarten to a nongraded primary (first and second grades). Teachers are experimenting with a less formal, more developmentally appropriate curriculum organized around integrated thematic units (insects, keys and locks, friends and family), projects, or investigations (how houses are built, the school bus, water, the river) to make children's learning meaningful. Whole language approaches to reading and writing are replacing or supplementing traditional basal readers and workbooks. The importance of free exploration and play to young children's development is being reaffirmed—even for children with disabilities. These trends call for careful and thorough documentation of what experiences children have had, what they know and can do, and how they are developing in relation to expected learnings—in short, better assessment.

The Changing Nature of School and Center Populations

The need for assessment strategies appropriate for all children in our increasingly diverse school and center populations has added new insights to the whole assessment enterprise.

Children in early childhood programs mirror the racial, ethnic, cultural, linguistic, urban/rural, socioeconomic, and educational diversity of the larger society. The number of children in the United States from culturally and linguistically diverse backgrounds has increased. Diversity among children younger than age 6 is even greater (Zill, Collins, West, & Hausken, 1995). Traditional testing and measurement approaches are often ill suited to these children; this is explained in the next section. As diversity increases, efforts to develop and use assessment procedures that give a truer picture of what children from diverse backgrounds know and can do take on greater urgency. Alternative assessment procedures offer promise (Bowman, 1992).

There is enormous variation in the type and number of planned educational experiences children have. Some children entering kindergarten or first grade may have been in a group child care setting since infancy. For others, kindergarten or first grade may be their first experience in a group. Some children will have attended every "enrichment" experience available—swimming classes, soccer teams, science workshops, and music lessons. Others will have none of these experiences.

Inclusion of children with special needs increases the diversity in early childhood classrooms. As a group, "young children with special needs are . . . tremendously diverse" (Wolery, Strain, & Bailey, 1992, p. 95). Assessing their strengths and needs requires flexible assessment practices that include a child's functioning in everyday life (Bagnato & Neisworth, 1991; Wolery, Strain, & Bailey, 1992).

The Limitations and Inadequacies of Traditional Testing

Standardized tests are the focus of much of the criticism aimed at inappropriate assessment. Standardized tests specify testing conditions and directions so that testing situations are alike from one setting to another. They are usually published, widely distributed, multiple-choice, norm-referenced (MC/NRT) measures. Some states and school districts have developed or adopted standardized tests that they use for a variety of purposes. Standardized tests include achievement tests, developmental inventories, academic readiness tests, and prekindergarten and developmental screening tests, as well as individual and group intelligence and achievement tests. Critics target the tests themselves, their overuse and misuse, their unsuitability for a diverse population, and their undue influence on education.

Technical and Educational Inadequacy. Many tests for young children do not meet technical standards set by the American Psychological Association (1985) (Goodwin & Goodwin, 1993; Meisels, Steele, & Quinn-Leering, 1993; Shepard & Graue, 1993; and others). They may not reliably measure what they purport to. Developers may promote the tests for inappropriate uses, such as deciding whether or not children are ready for kindergarten or first grade. The populations on which the tests were "normed" may not be appropriate. In some cases, information regarding the psychometric properties of the tests is not available. In addition, tests may be based on an outmoded theory of what and how children learn. For instance, academic readiness tests may focus on skills that may or may not have any relation to future success in reading or mathematics (Stallman & Pearson, 1990). Items may be poorly constructed, ambiguous, and open to various interpretations, only one of which is deemed "right" (Kamii, 1990).

Overuse and Misuse.   Educational institutions and individuals spend enormous amounts of time and money on tests and testing—money that might be used in other ways to benefit children. Misuse of the results of those tests costs children and society even more. Measures designed for one purpose may be inappropriately used for another, such as when a test or developmental inventory designed to give information to teachers on children's "readiness" for school or reading is used to delay children's entry to kindergarten or first grade—a "high-stakes" placement decision the test was not designed for. The tests cannot accurately predict children's performance in the year or years to come, even when they claim to (Shepard & Graue, 1993). Issues of retention and readiness are complex and intertwined with many other social and educational forces, including the escalation of early childhood curriculum. Legally, public schools cannot keep age-eligible children out of kindergarten or first grade because they are not "ready." More important, mounting research provides evidence that retention "goes against the best interests of the vast majority of students who are left back" (Gage & Berliner, 1992, p. 660). A meta-analysis of 44 independent studies of retained versus promoted students showed consistent results—children who were retained did not gain significant advantages by being held back a year (Holmes & Matthews, 1984). In addition, retention had a negative impact on self-esteem and child motivation.

Test results may be misused in deciding eligibility for special programs or ability grouping. Test results may be misused by making them the sole or primary criterion for decisions affecting educational opportunity, when they should be only one of many factors (National Association for the Education of Young Children, 1992). Testing may result in children's being placed in categories or labeled in ways that do not enhance their development and learning.

Unsuitability for the Population.   Evidence is strong that many tests and testing procedures are unfair to poor children, youngsters from any racial/ethnic background other than the middle-class majority, children whose first language is not English, divergent and creative thinkers, and just about any group one might wish to investigate (FairTest, 1990; Kamii, 1990; National Association for the Education of Young Children, 1988; Perrone, 1991; and many more).

Young children have problems taking tests of any kind, even individual tests administered by skilled psychologists (Bagnato & Neisworth, 1991).

They may see no point in playing adult "games," especially with strangers in a strange situation (Kamii, 1990). They have particular trouble with group-administered paper-and-pencil tests, as young children are easily distracted, bored, or made uneasy; they also have trouble following directions and marking or "bubbling in" the response. They may act silly or refuse to participate. Traditional tests may be particularly inappropriate for young children with special needs, the very population with which they are used the most (Bagnato & Neisworth, 1991).

One-shot testing is poorly suited to the way children grow. Children's development and learning proceed unevenly, with spurts and regressions. Some children may suddenly "put it all together" and achieve unexpected insights. Some children progress in tiny increments that few tests are sensitive enough to detect, yet the progress is real and significant for that child.

Undue Influence on Education.   Knowing they will be judged on how well children score, teachers may teach and shape instruction to fit the test, not necessarily the content of greatest worth. This practice, often unconscious, may narrow and distort the curriculum to items most amenable to testing or to those that fulfill the purposes of the test (Meisels, Steele, & Quinn-Leering, 1993; Shepard & Graue, 1993). Tests intended for national distribution may not be congruent with local curriculum. At the least, teachers have to take extra time to teach children test-taking skills such as keeping their place and making precise markings. In some schools, whole days of instructional time are devoted to taking tests.

All too often tests are used as the primary approach to accountability—the way schools and centers report to their patrons what and how well they are doing. Well-publicized scores from tests are used to compare schools, districts, and states; racial and ethnic groups; and the current year with previous years—as a way of judging quality and effectiveness. Such comparisons lead to distortions and misunderstandings of the properties of tests, as humorously exemplified by the "all above average" children of the mythical town of Lake Wobegon.

Few people would abolish the use of all tests, even with young children. Early screening and identification of correctable physical problems, developmental delays, or other factors that place children at high risk for school failure enable many children to receive appropriate treatment (Meisels, Steele, & Quinn-Leering, 1993). Individual clinical tests provide valuable information to guide important decisions, such as whether or not a child has special needs (Cronbach, 1990). In addition, tests may be the best way to assess certain kinds of learning, such as basic knowledge about a particular topic (Stiggins, 1995). Most early childhood educators advocate delaying use of group-administered, standardized, multiple-choice, norm-referenced tests until children are in third or fourth grade, and discontinuing tests that lead to delayed entry to kindergarten or first grade (Bredekamp & Rosegrant, 1992).

The selection and use of standardized tests, inventories, and diagnostic procedures are beyond the scope of this book. The theoretical and statistical bases underlying such measures, and the many considerations in evaluating, selecting, and using them, call for focused education. We recommend a specialized course or one of the many excellent books on tests and testing.

Expectations of Teachers

Current expectations of teachers as assessors of children's learning and development are high. Professional organizations, other teachers, specialists, parents, and the general public contribute to those expectations.

Professional Organizations

Professional organizations and teacher education leaders expect teachers to be competent in assessment. The National Association for the Education of Young Children specifies that since early childhood teachers are the child's primary assessor (Bredekamp & Rosegrant, 1992), they should have "theoretical and research knowledge and practical skills in . . . observation and recording of children's behavior for purposes of assistance in achieving goals, providing for individual needs, and appropriately guiding young children" (1982, pp. 4–5). A 1990 statement issued jointly by the National Education Association, the National Council on Measurement in Education, and the American Federation of Teachers identified seven standards for teacher competence in educational assessment.

Teachers should be skilled in the following areas:

1. Choosing assessment methods appropriate for instructional decisions
2. Developing assessment methods appropriate for instructional decisions
3. Administering, scoring, and interpreting the results of both externally produced and teacher-produced assessment methods
4. Using assessment results when making decisions about individual students, planning teaching, developing curriculum, and school improvement
5. Developing valid pupil grading procedures which use pupil assessments
6. Communicating assessment results to students, parents, other lay audiences, and other educators
7. Recognizing unethical, illegal, and otherwise inappropriate assessment methods and uses of assessment information (Standards for Teacher Competence in Educational Assessment of Students, pp. 3–5)

Accountability

The public, parents, funding groups, and governing boards hold schools and teachers responsible for children's school-related achievement. Educators are expected to say what they are doing and what the results are. In the past, large-scale accountability reports depended heavily on test scores. Now, states such as Arizona, California, Maryland, and Vermont, as well as many school districts, are using authentic, performance-based classroom tasks to provide the broad information needed for accountability (Stiggins, 1995;

Valencia, Hiebert, & Afflerbach, 1994). Procedures used in these projects are still being developed and tested. Teachers are involved in many ways: conceptualizing the framework, developing assessment tasks and evaluation guides, documenting children's learning by using the agreed-upon procedures, ensuring trustworthiness of the data, and scoring student work from other teachers and schools. Even when tests continue to be the primary accountability measure, they are frequently augmented by alternative assessment results. Like authentic assessment itself, its use for accountability is still a work in progress.

In addition to accountability information, which applies to many children, parents expect systematic, timely, well-documented reports of their own children's progress. Any substantive recommendations must be thoughtfully made and supported by appropriate documentation.

Working with Other Professionals

Expectations that teachers exchange or report information may require a change in record-keeping strategies. The short notes that teachers take as reminders to themselves may not be sufficient information for people unfamiliar with the context, task, or child (Valencia, Hiebert, & Afflerbach, 1994). For example, teachers must have well-documented information ready to present if they are going to make a contribution to a team that assesses and makes recommendations about a child with special needs.

Teachers may be expected to provide information to help overcome the lack of communication, linkages, and continuity among the various levels and programs in early childhood education. A child may go from a program for 3-year-olds, to one for 4-year-olds, and on to kindergarten and first grade with little or no communication among the teachers or schools involved. Even health and testing records may not be transferred. Children may be "pulled out" of class for special programs with little or no coordination and communication among teachers. In highly mobile populations, children may move from one school or center to another several times during the school year, going back to "start" each time. Reliable information transmitted from one setting to another can ease transition and help teachers in the new setting be more responsive to a child's needs (Administration for Children, Youth, and Families, 1986; Love, 1991).

Challenges

Assessing young children's development and learning by using nontraditional, authentic, or performance procedures is not without challenges. The major concerns are credibility, feasibility, and need.

Credibility

Tests, testing, and all the statistical analyses and reporting procedures that accompany them took many years to develop and gain the power they now have. The psychometric concepts (such as mean, percentile, standard deviation—even IQ) surrounding them are well accepted, if not always well understood. The scores and statistics derived from testing have assumed awesome power in the minds of many people. More informal authentic measures as a means of large-scale assessment may not be credible to the public, parents, researchers, and policy makers. Parents used to traditional ways of measuring achievement—test scores, grades, ratings, rankings, years in school—may be reluctant to accept other approaches, even for reporting individual achievement.

Authentic measures do not have specified safeguards similar to those that psychologists have developed for tests. Ways of ensuring validity and reliability (does the procedure consistently measure what it claims to?), objectivity, and freedom from bias (Goodwin & Goodwin, 1993) are yet to be developed. There is great variation in the quality of classroom assessments at all age and grade levels (Stiggins & Conklin, 1992). Chapters 4 and 5 address concerns about quality in assessment.

Feasibility

Authentic classroom assessment takes thought, effort, time, and commitment. Teachers are expected to carry out assessment responsibilities concurrent with their existing workload. If teachers also participate in school- or districtwide committees to develop alternative assessment strategies, demands on their time and expertise can become too great. Schools and teachers should have realistic expectations about how much they can do and carefully select those assessment approaches that best suit their needs and resources. It takes time to develop the knowledge and skill to assess well, time to integrate sound assessment practices into instruction, and time to actually assess and determine the implications of results.

Need

Schools and centers must help a larger proportion of pupils reach high standards of performance; assessment is central to that effort. Sound appraisals are essential if teachers are to plan appropriate learning activities and experiences and chart children's progress. Children's individual strengths and needs are too diverse for a "one size fits all" curriculum, within which students are ranked from highest achiever to lowest achiever.

Adults working with children need to understand that no magical testing or assessment technique will tell them all they need to know; there are, however, many ways to increase the amount and quality of information we have about children. Increasing use of authentic assessment may help teachers and parents regain faith in their own educational judgment and wisdom and in their ability to sensitively appraise, understand, and assist the development of young children (Eisner, 1995). "More than new forms of assessment, what is needed is a refusal to accept bondage to any single technology . . . [but to thoughtfully select] different kinds and mixes of assessments for different purposes" (Haney & Madaus, 1989, p. 687).

The purpose of this book is to help teachers learn to use those "different kinds and mixes" of appraisals to help children develop and learn.

Summary

Teachers, schools, and centers throughout the United States are devising better ways of finding out and recording how children feel, behave, and think; what they know and can do; their physical well-being; and their interests, attitudes, and dispositions. This effort will help them to guide, assist, and participate in children's growth, development, and learning—not just to grade, rank, sort, or group children. The process, called alternative assessment, authentic assessment, classroom assessment, or performance assessment, is underway but far from complete in either broad concept or specific details. Factors contributing to current developments in assessment include changing concepts of the primary purpose of assessment, and of how children develop and learn; fresh thinking about educational goals, curricula, and instructional strategies; increasing diversity of school and center populations; and the limitations and inadequacies of traditional testing.

Teachers are expected to be competent in assessment. Professional organizations have set high standards for assessment literacy and professional practice. The general public and policy makers expect teachers to be accountable in their work with children, and to provide information needed for large-scale assessment, as well as that designed for classroom use. Communicating with other professionals requires that teachers be able to document and explain assessment results.

Challenges facing early childhood educators as they use authentic assessment in the classroom include the possible lack of credibility and acceptance of alternative assessment, the feasibility of having time and resources to accomplish such assessment, and the challenge of linking appropriate, quality assessment with appropriate instruction so that all children can achieve their potential.

For Further Study, Discussion, and Reflection

1. Most adults have taken many types of tests and assessment measures. Reflect on your experience with them. Do you consider any "unfair"? If so, why? Which measures do you consider an adequate evaluation of what you had learned or not learned? Why? In what ways could evaluation of your learning have been improved?
2. Demographic, social, educational, and political forces influence assessment practices. In what ways are these forces influencing assessment in education in your community? Substantiate your conclusions with current evidence from newspapers, radio or television news, school newsletters, or personal experience.
3. Interview a kindergarten teacher about kindergarten entrance policies. Are any formal or informal tests used to determine children's readiness? If so, what are they? What other considerations go into determining "readiness"? In what ways do these policies conform to or deviate from current research and recommendations regarding school entrance and retention?

4. Explore the diversity of the young children in your state, town, or community. If you need to, visit some classrooms. Explain the implications of your findings for assessment.

5. A study of teachers' assessment practices showed that the assessment's primary purpose was "judging students' achievement for assigning grades" (Stiggins & Conklin, 1992, p. 47). Discuss this finding, relating it to current thinking about the primary purpose of assessment.

Suggested Readings

Bodrova, E., & Leong, D. J. (1996). *Tools of the mind: The Vygotskian approach to early childhood education.* Englewood Cliffs, NJ: Merrill.

Bredekamp, S., & Rosegrant, T. (Eds.). (1992). *Reaching potentials: Appropriate curriculum and assessment for young children* (Vol. 1). Washington, DC: National Association for the Education of Young Children.

Bredekamp, S., & Rosegrant, T. (Eds.). (1995). *Reaching potentials: Appropriate curriculum and assessment for young children* (Vol. 2). Washington, DC: National Association for the Education of Young Children.

Gough, P. B. (Ed.). (1993). Feature section on alternative assessment. *Phi Delta Kappan, 74*(6), 444–479.

Herman, J. L., Aschbacher, P. R., & Winters, L (1992). *A practical guide to alternative assessment.* Alexandria, VA: Association for Supervision and Curriculum Development.

Kamii, C. (Ed.). (1990). *Achievement testing in the early grades: The games grown-ups play.* Washington, DC: National Association for the Education of Young Children.

CHAPTER TWO

Legal and Ethical Responsibilities in Assessment

"Fairness, the rights of all concerned, and professional ethical behavior must undergird all student assessment activities, from the initial planning for and gathering of information to the interpretation, use, and communication of the results" (American Federation of Teachers, et al., 1990, p. 5). To do this, teachers must know what "professional ethical behavior" in assessment means, have the skills to carry it out, and develop the habits and dispositions to do so. Chapter 2 presents basic knowledge and skills to apply and practice in all aspects of assessment.

Even though assessment is done primarily to guide classroom activities, teachers collect and record important and perhaps sensitive information about children. Decisions and recommendations based in part on that information can influence children's opportunity to learn, and are thus considered "high stakes." A recommendation for inclusion in a program for gifted or talented learners, for the special help that a learning-disabled youngster needs, or that a kindergartner be retained or promoted relates to that child's opportunity to learn and must be made with the greatest of care. Even decisions about instructional methods and goals have an impact on children's opportunities to learn. For example, overemphasis on drill and practice may deprive children of opportunities to apply knowledge to practical problems. Reports to parents and other school personnel must be fair and factual. In assessing young children, teachers should do the following:

1. Know and abide by laws and court rulings pertaining to assessment information and its use
2. Know and abide by school and center policies
3. Be fair and impartial
4. Increase the trustworthiness of the information they collect
5. Use assessment information and results in appropriate ways

Know and Abide by Basic Rights, Laws, and Court Rulings

Classroom practices and instructional decisions may seem far afield from the courtroom and legal processes, but they are not. Legal issues relating to assessment and its use revolve around three rights of individuals: equal protection under the law, due process, and privacy (Sandoval & Irvin, 1990). Laws and court interpretations change, but basic principles and rights and their implications for teachers, schools, and programs do not.

The Right to Equal Protection under the Law

Equal protection under the law means that in actions by the government, including school personnel, "an individual should enjoy the same rights and receive the same benefits or burdens as all other citizens," unless there is a valid reason (Sandoval & Irvin, 1990, p. 86). Information that is used to assign a child to a specific treatment, such as special education, must be justified and valid. If one group disproportionately receives or doesn't receive benefits, there is a possibility that the equal protection principle is not being upheld.

Most of the court decisions relating to "equal protection" have to do with the placement of ethnic minority children in special education (usually in classes for the educable mentally retarded) or in lower academic "tracks" on the basis of tests and other measures (*Diana* v. *California State Board of Education et al.*, 1970; Mercer, 1972). P.L. (Public Law) 94-142—the Education for All Handicapped Children Act of 1975, and P.L. 101-576—the Individuals with Disabilities Education Act of 1990, prohibit the use of tests that are discriminatory and mandate measures that are valid for the proposed use.

Language differences present special concerns in assessing young children. Court decisions (*Lau* v. *Nichols*, 1974) and laws (P.L. 94-142, 1975) have established children's rights to assessment in their primary language. If teachers of non-English-speaking children do not speak a particular child's primary language, they will need to seek help from someone who does.

The Right to Due Process

Due process means that people have "the right to protest and be heard prior to any action taken" with respect to them (Sandoval & Irvin, 1990, p. 86). They have a right to a hearing before any action and cannot have their rights and privileges as citizens arbitrarily, unreasonably, or capriciously removed. Two major laws spell out the responsibilities of educational institutions to parents and children relating to due process: P.L. 94-142, the Education for All Handicapped Children Act, and P.L. 93-380, the Family Educational Rights and Privacy Act of 1974. Together, they require that parents or guardians of young children be notified of their rights in advance of any major decisions or procedures. Parents or guardians have the right to submit evidence; to have appropriate legal representation; to cross-examine witnesses; to examine all school records and challenge those they do not agree with; and to receive an independent psychological evaluation provided by the state. Schools and centers have worked to meet these requirements in staff and family conferences—"staffings"—where all concerned with a major decision about a child confer and consider evidence and options.

Parents of children who attend a school that receives federal assistance may see all information in the official files, including portfolios and other assessment documentation, notes on behavioral problems, family background items, attendance and health records, class rank, test scores, grade averages, psychological reports, and all other records except personal notes made by staff members solely for their own use.

The Right to Privacy

Although the right to privacy is less clear-cut than equal protection and due process, it involves an individual's right to choose "whether, when, and how behaviors, attitudes, beliefs, and opinions are to be shared with others" (Sandoval & Irvin, 1990, p. 87). The same laws that provide for due process require that parents give permission before any testing or release of information to someone other than the parent or the educational institution. P.L. 93-380, the Family Educational Rights and Privacy Act of 1974, requires that parents give written consent before school officials release records to unauthorized persons or institutions. Schools must keep a written record of who has seen or requested to see a child's records.

In addition, there are ethical constraints. When you work with children all day, it is easy to carry incidents, frustrations, or interesting observations into a teachers' lounge, nearby restaurant, or social gathering. Don't. Share information about children only with people who have a need and a right to know. Never make potentially damaging oral or written remarks. Keep written notes, checklists, or other records—even those that are in progress—in a place where they are not readily accessible to adults or other children who might casually read them. Place private information in the appropriate file, and discuss it only on a professional basis. Teachers are in a position of trust. In this privileged role, they know many things about children and families that may never appear on paper, much less arise in casual conversation. Teach this and other ethical behavior related to confidentiality of information to any classroom assistants or volunteers.

Sensitive information about family background or children's problems should be kept in confidential files. Children's portfolios that consist primarily of work products are usually all right in open folders in the classroom. However, if you share classroom space with other community groups, find a lockable cabinet to slide the folders into. Portfolios that contain information usually considered private, such as performance results or summary reports, should be kept confidential. Children's journals present a special case. Although they are done as part of classroom work, they sometimes contain children's feelings, concerns, and problems, including ones from home. Make a distinction between journals that simply report on a child's project or class work and those that may be more personal. Young children can seldom make a distinction between what is private and what is to be shared with other children and teachers. Teachers may have to do some screening.

Notes, full or partly completed checklists, rating scales, or other forms should be placed in a file folder or drawer or slipped to the bottom of the stack on a clipboard, away from casual reading by anyone.

Major Legislation

Legal responsibilities relating to assessing and planning educational services for young children are contained in several federal laws providing for children with special needs. They build upon basic civil rights accorded to all citizens.

P.L. 94-142 (1975) established national educational policy for children with disabilities from ages 3 to 21. The Education for all Handicapped Children Act specified appropriate safeguards for testing and measurement, and formalized use of the Individualized Education Program (IEP).

P.L. 99-457 (1986) effectively mandated the provisions of P.L. 94-142 for children with disabilities ages 3 through 5 and provided incentives for serving younger children. The law required an Individualized Family Service Plan (IFSP) for families of infants and toddlers.

P.L. 101-576 (1990) renamed the Education for All Handicapped Children Act (P.L. 94-142) as the Individuals with Disabilities Education Act (IDEA) and reauthorized its basic provisions.

P.L. 101-336 (1990), the Americans with Disabilities Act, requires equal access and reasonable accommodation for individuals with disabilities, including equal access to enrollment in early childhood facilities (Wolery & Wilbers, 1994).

Together, these laws, their amendments, and regulations establish that

- Tests and measures used to identify, classify, and place children in special needs programs must be nondiscriminatory. They must be used for the purpose for which they are intended and administered by qualified individuals. All assessment practices must be free from bias.
- Parents must have appropriate prior notification and give informed consent before administration of any measures for classification, planning, and placement.
- Parents may request an evaluation or reevaluation of their child and an independent evaluation.
- Parents may have children assessed in the language they know best.

- Parents may review their child's records, obtain copies, challenge questionable information, and have it withdrawn.
- Young children with disabilities, preschool through primary, are entitled to free, appropriate public education.
- Parents can question and challenge actions related to their child's education taken by a school.
- Young children with disabilities must have an IEP. Families of infants and toddlers must have an IFSP. Parents have a right to be involved in their children's educational plans. (ERIC Clearinghouse on Disabilities and Gifted Education, 1994)

Individual states have their own laws and requirements specifying how they will comply with federal legislation.

Know and Abide by State, School District, and Center Policies

Follow state, school district, and center policies about assessment, record keeping, and reporting. Find out what is in cumulative files, personal files, and health records and who sees the files for what purposes. Determine policies and recommendations about what teachers and children put in classroom portfolios. Secure information on policies and procedures for referral of children for further assessment. Know procedures for documenting and reporting information about children and families that state and local policies require you to report, such as suspected child abuse and neglect.

Some policies may undergo change as greater effort is made to transfer records from one early childhood setting or program to another. Some information will be required in transfer records; some will be optional. As primary-school children move to the intermediate grades, what reading and writing samples will go with them? Only the last few? Selected samples to show cumulative growth? These are local decisions and will vary, unlike federal laws and court decisions that have national application.

Be Fair and Impartial

Probably no issues related to assessment are more emotionally and educationally charged than those related to "bias" and "fairness." One of the harshest criticisms of standardized tests is that they may be biased against children who are not of the dominant culture and language or are from families with low income and educational levels. This concern for fairness extends to all assessment procedures. Indeed, informal appraisals that rely on an individual to gather information and determine its meaning increase the potential for bias (Smith, 1990).

Bias usually refers to a test, procedure, result, or use that unfairly discriminates against one group in favor of another. It is a complex concept, not easily simplified, and involves not only tests and assessment procedures but also use of the results (Berk, 1982; Cronbach, 1990; Jones, 1988; Shepard, 1982). The overplacement of young minority group children in special education classes on the basis of test results is a frequently cited example of test bias (Mercer, 1972). The term *bias* has such changeable meaning and so many negative connotations that some scholars attempt to avoid it altogether (Cronbach, 1990).

To be fair to all children in our socially, economically, and culturally diverse society, be as objective as possible and be knowledgeable about and sensitive to the ways in which diversity may influence assessment.

Be as Objective as Possible

To be objective, try to obtain and use facts, information, or data without distortion by personal feelings or prejudice. Lack of objectivity results when personal experiences or characteristics strongly influence perceptions of events, facts, or behavior. For example, if we believe that boys are "better at" mathematical and mechanical tasks, we may perceive children through those beliefs unless we take great care to look at what individual children know and can do. If we believe that girls are "better at" language and reading, those beliefs may influence our assessment and instruction in many subtle ways.

No one is totally objective. The information we choose to collect is influenced by our personal experience, beliefs, and interests. One teacher observing children at play may focus on their social interactions; another may note the cognitive and language aspects of what they are doing; still another may zero in on their physical development. We may judge children on whether or not their hair is clean and neatly combed; the appropriateness of their clothing; dialect variations in their speech; the match of their personality and interests to ours; and deeply embedded cultural values—often so much a part of us and so subtle that we do not realize they are there. Although we usually think of prejudging in connection with low-income or minority families, it extends to all children: those of single parents; those whose mothers work outside the home; children who are intellectually, socially, or economically privileged; or those who are "different" in any way.

In addition to personal experiences and beliefs that may color what we see and hear, we become accustomed to observing certain things or getting certain results, and thus take them for granted, failing to notice their importance or significance. Or we may assume that other people think, feel, and act as we do (Irwin & Bushnell, 1980).

Objectivity in collecting, recording, understanding, and using information about children can increase the fairness, accuracy, and usefulness of assessment. By no means should personal insights, feelings, and intuition be excluded, but most of us need the discipline of objectivity to achieve impartiality (Bentzen, 1992).

Avoid Categories and Labels.   It is easy to place a "halo" on some children and see everything they do in the best possible light. We may consistently interpret the actions of other children less favorably. Others may always be seen as just average, regardless of their performance (Almy & Genishi, 1979). This lack of objectivity may mask the needs of the "halos" and substantive progress of the others.

Labels—often in current jargon—slip out so easily: "ADHD" (Attention Deficit Hyperactivity Disorder), "shy," "withdrawn," "acting out," "overachiever," "underachiever," "gifted," "troublemaker." Once a child is labeled, we may cease to see the child except in terms of that label. A label may give the false impression that a real and unchanging characteristic has been identified and can stick to a child for years, regardless of its accuracy. Labels usually have connotations, often negative, that may set up inappropriate expectations about individual children. Concentrate on describing and understanding individual children instead of labeling them (Goodwin & Driscoll, 1980).

Sometimes children have to be diagnosed as being in a certain group to receive appropriate services, but such diagnoses are beyond the authority of the classroom teacher. Educators and funding agencies are trying to move away from the requirement that children be placed in labeled categories to receive services.

Be Objective in Collecting Information.   An objective description focuses on the facts and details of what is occurring with as little interpretation and filtering of information as possible (Boehm & Weinberg, 1987). The observer captures what he sees and hears without analyzing the information. An inference is an interpretation of a child's behavior and may include speculation about the child's possible feelings, intentions, motivations, thinking processes, attitudes, or dispositions. Inferences may also include evaluations and judgments about the significance of a behavior for future development or comparisons of behavior with past actions. Distinguish between the description of what happened and the interpretation or analysis of what happened. Both are important but are different.

Almost everyone has trouble separating facts and details about an experience from inferences based on those facts and details. Teachers usually interpret the intentions and motivations of a child simultaneously as behaviors are experienced. This skill is essential to respond appropriately to children. Ms. Dupont sees Marcia rush at Julia with her arms raised, yelling. If Ms. Dupont thinks that Marcia is just "pretending to be King Kong" and is not intending to hurt the other children, she will react one way. Her reaction will be different if Ms. Dupont thinks that Marcia intends to hurt Julia. To make assessment objective, a teacher must step out of the role of responding to a child (Almy, 1969; Jagger, 1985). Momentarily suspend interpretation and analysis, and concentrate on what you see and hear: "Marcia rushes at Julia with her arms raised and yells."

Be Objective in Recording Information.   A record should be an objective, accurate recounting of what occurred. Record information in precise terms in the sequence in which it happened (Bentzen, 1992). In some cases, the context or setting is important, including the people involved, where the child is sitting, time of day, and activity. As much as possible, capture what children actually say, rather than paraphrasing it. Sometimes this requires inventing spellings for sounds such as "suspusketti" (spaghetti) or "asseptable" (acceptable).

In initial recording, avoid words that convey emotional tone, feelings, motives, or thinking processes. Such conclusions cannot be directly observed, but are inferred from what took place. For instance, record "Jerrod paused, looked around the room, then moved the block into place," rather than "Jerrod thought about all the things he might want to do with the block, then moved it into place." To describe what Jerrod is thinking requires making an inference. Another person might observe the same behavior and conclude that Jerrod was nervous, uncertain, slow, or something else altogether.

Record inferences so they can be identified and distinguished from the factual recounting of what took place. Write the inference in a special place on the record labeled "interpretation," with a different colored pen or on a separate piece of paper attached to the record.

Inferences should be separated from the record of behavior for several reasons. Isolating what was seen or heard from inference decreases recording errors (Cronbach, 1990). Inferences made immediately may or may not prove useful later. For example, a teacher may have a different interpretation of "Marta grabs the toy and hits June" after one incident than after several observations over a period of time. Keeping inferences separate allows a teacher to go back and examine the pattern of behavior from a different perspective.

Inferences or conclusions help summarize and interpret information so it can guide future classroom activities. Appropriate inferences are those that evaluate the developmental and learning significance of a behavior or identify a behavior that should be monitored in the future. Examples of acceptable inferences are "Needs more practice"; "Should be monitored"; "Progressing satisfactorily." Avoid inferences that label children: "She's always out to hurt other people" or "Another example of gifted behavior."

Be Objective in Evaluating Classroom Procedures and Instructional Practices.   Being objective involves more than objectivity in collecting information on children. Teachers should observe and evaluate not only children, but also how classroom procedures, instructional practices, and teachers influence children's behavior and learning. Not everything can be attributed to child characteristics or learning needs. A child who is "distractible" in a noisy, chaotic classroom may be task-oriented in a different setting. In a study of "circle time" in early childhood classrooms, teachers blamed children's restlessness and lack of attention on the children or their poor home background rather than considering whether the circle time was too long, uninteresting, or held in a place with competing activities (McAfee, 1985). A teacher who has worked hard to help a group of children master something may find it difficult to believe evidence showing that children still have much to learn. Even more difficult to achieve is the insight that instructional practices may need to be changed.

Be Knowledgeable about and Sensitive to the Ways Diversity May Influence Assessment

Young children in the United States vary in race and ethnicity; language dominance and fluency; socioeconomic and educational level; rural, urban, suburban, inner city, or rural-isolated home location; family structure; prior school experience; culture; and degree of acculturation. Any of these variations may influence assessment. Chapter 11 gives guidelines for sensitivity to diversity during appraisal.

Ensure the Accuracy and Trustworthiness of Assessment Information

The freedom that teachers have in alternative, informal assessment is accompanied by professional responsibility to make sure the information is accurate, trustworthy, and dependable (Cambourne & Turbill, 1990). Reliability and validity, concepts most often associated with test construction and development, also apply to classroom assessment. Standardized achievement and screening tests meet rigorous standards before they are deemed reliable and valid, and statistical information relating to reliability and validity is published so that potential users can evaluate it. Such rigor is not necessary for information used for ongoing, *continuous assessment* (Shepard, 1991a), yet there must be some check on reliability and validity to make sure the results represent what a child can do.

Evaluation of the trustworthiness of assessment information is a part of the overall process of assessment and should be done continuously—as information is being collected and recorded, as it is summarized, analyzed, and used to make decisions or reports. It is easy to assume that because you are directly measuring something, the appraisal is valid and reliable. This is not the case. Although there are no statistical tests that apply to informal, in-class assessments, some general guides will help increase reliability and validity.

Reliability. The results of assessment should be reliable, consistent, and dependable. They should be reproducible—you should be able to obtain a similar performance at another time or place. The way information is collected, the assessment situation, the child's mental or physical state, and lucky or unlucky guesses can influence reliability.

The assessment method can cause incorrect answers. Vague or confusing questions and requests yield unreliable results because they can be interpreted in different ways at different times. Direct and persistent questioning can make children uneasy, resulting in a performance that does not reflect their true abilities. The situation in which the assessment takes place influences reliability. Environmental distractions such as a noisy group discussion in another part of the room, interruptions by other children, or a strange situation can cause unreliable results (Maeroff, 1991). Unexpected events such as a loose hamster, unplanned assembly, or fire drill can affect a child's responses and, therefore, the reliability. When Ms. Olsen's math appraisal was interrupted by a fire drill, she noticed that children assessed after the fire drill missed more questions than those assessed before. The interruption—the fire drill—is the probable reason for the pattern of poor performances, not mathematics skills. How the child is feeling, including mental state, illness, fatigue, lack of interest, anxiety, or a "bad day," also impacts reliability. An argument at home, on the school bus, or on the playground can make appraisal done that day unreliable.

An assessment can also be unreliable if a child's performance is influenced by a number of lucky or unlucky guesses. Check to make sure differences between performances are related to learning or growth and not luck.

Be alert for uncharacteristic behavior or inconsistencies. The information obtained on one occasion should be comparable to information obtained on other occasions and consistent with other information collected at other times from other sources and methods (Sattler, 1992). Ms. Maclaren is measuring social interaction of a group. As she reviews her record of the interaction, she finds that José stayed alone most of the morning. Ms. Maclaren thinks, "This is so unlike José, he is usually right in there making suggestions." Ms. Maclaren concludes that this is not a reliable sample of José's social interaction because it does not capture his normal behavior. On another day, he would probably interact freely. The wide differences in performance suggest unreliability of the assessment.

To increase reliability, make more than one measurement of the same behavior. If you decide information from an assessment is unreliable, do not use it. If you suspect information may be unreliable, mark it, and then have the child repeat the activity or demonstrate the behavior in a different situation. One of the big advantages of informal assessment is that youngsters can have more than one chance to demonstrate what they know, think, feel, or can do.

Validity.   Validity has to do with both the assessment and the interpretations, conclusions, or inferences that can be made based on the information gathered (Cronbach, 1990). Valid assessments appraise what they were designed to; that is, they provide accurate information about the item under consideration. The interpretations or conclusions are also reasonable and fair given the information that has been collected (Gage & Berliner, 1992).

In addition, teachers need to think of validity in terms of what is being assessed (Herman, Aschbacher, & Winters, 1992). Is it significant and important? Is it aligned with curriculum—what children have had or will have an opportunity to learn? Will it be meaningful to you, the child, and others who are concerned with the child's learning and development?

Validity can be increased by (1) having enough samples to cover or adequately represent a behavior, (2) having "balance" in the samples—that is, not overemphasizing one type of information or one context, (3) by checking to see if information obtained in different ways converges, and (4) by ensuring that the objective of the assessment is being met.

All assessments are samples because it is physically impossible to assess every possible incidence of a behavior (Sattler, 1992). A valid assessment must have enough samples to be representative of the entire behavior. There are no hard and fast rules about how much information is needed to cover or adequately represent a behavior (Cronbach, 1990). This depends partly on the behavior being assessed. It takes only a few items to yield valid results on a specific behavior such as using a ruler or equal-arm balance. Much information will be necessary to make valid statements about development in a large and complex domain such as cognitive or social development.

To be valid, the representative sample must be balanced (Hopkins, Stanley, & Hopkins, 1990). The assessment should not overemphasize one type of information or oversample one context. An assessment of a child's ability to identify letters should not rely solely on information gathered from written work. To obtain a valid measure of a child's sharing behavior, a teacher must observe in several contexts: outdoor play, snack, cooperative learning groups, and others. Evidence from a variety of sources, methods, and contexts measuring the same thing should converge, or "triangulate" (Cronbach, 1990).

To be valid, assessment must provide evidence about what it is supposed to assess and not something else. Suppose a teacher is interested in the number of roles children will assume during a dramatic play activity. He sets up a bus and invites several children to play. During the assessment, one child makes herself bus driver and insists that all the other children act as the children on the bus. When any of the other children suggest roles other than being children, the "bus driver" shouts them down. The total number of roles played in the session is one per child, although different children attempted but were not allowed to change roles. The appraisal is not measuring the number of roles children take but the social interaction when one child dominates the group. The teacher must make another to measure role-taking and role-changing behavior.

One way to check validity is to compare children who do well with those who do not and to identify reasons for those differences. If the reason for the differences is the behavior you are trying to measure, then the assessment is probably valid. If differences are due to something else, then the assessment is not valid. For example, Ms. Aptos designed an art activity using small seeds glued to paper to measure patterning abilities in children. Comparing the group who produced a pattern with those who did not, she found that there were no differences in the ability to make a pattern with blocks and beans—objects larger than the small seeds she used. But results from the seed project were similar to those of her appraisal of fine motor skills. Children who did well in the fine motor assessment did this patterning activity well also. This was not a valid assessment of patterning because fine motor skills were assessed, not the ability to produce patterns.

Do not use invalid data. Repeat the assessment, modifying the way information is gathered for that particular individual or group. If information was not representative or too few indicators were included, use assessment to obtain the missing data.

Use Assessment Results in Appropriate Ways

Know the Limitations of Each Method of Assessment, and Guard against Overreliance on Any Single One

Each way of getting and recording information about children has strengths and limitations. Checklists, for example, are a good way to record the presence or absence of knowledge or skills but give little information about the precision and subtlety of children's thinking processes. Interviews, discussions, or children's reflections are needed to tap thinking processes. One type of information complements the other. For important, "high-stakes" decisions, use multiple assessment windows—several sources, methods, and contexts—to get the best information you can (American Psychological Association, et al., 1985). Results of standardized tests or inventories should be weighed against the outcomes of other types of assessment. Appropriate tests, clinical assessment, or in-depth diagnosis by a specialist can validate or cast doubt on the results of informal appraisals. Human behavior is complex, and our instruments for assessing it are relatively crude. Assessment results are estimates, at best. Teachers must regard them as tentative, subject to error, and subject to revision on the basis of additional information.

Use Assessment Results for the Intended Purposes

The primary purposes of assessment are to help teachers "support children's learning and development, to plan for individuals and groups, and to communicate with parents" (National Association for the Education of Young Children & National Association of Early Childhood Specialists of State Departments of Education, 1991, p. 32). Other purposes include reporting to and communicating with other professionals, administrators, funding and regulatory agencies, and citizen groups, and helping us know and understand the children we work with. Inappropriate uses are to delay children's entrance to school, retain children in grade, place or retain children in special programs without proper safeguards, threaten or humiliate children, or place them in rigid, unvarying groups or "tracks."

Legal and ethical responsibilities demand that teachers know the limitations of each type of assessment, guard against overreliance on any one method, and use the results for appropriate purposes.

Summary

As early childhood teachers assume additional assessment responsibilities, they also assume professional responsibilities specific to assessment. Legal and ethical responsibility relates to giving children equal opportunity to learn. Teachers should know and abide by laws and court rulings pertaining to assessment information and its use; abide by school and center policies; be fair, objective, and impartial; and guard the trustworthiness of classroom assessment data and use it in appropriate ways.

Children and parents have the basic rights of equal protection under the law, due process, and privacy. These are safeguarded by laws and court interpretations that apply to all children, families, and schools. Policies relating to assessment vary but influence how and what teachers assess and how that information is reported. Fairness, impartiality, and objectivity will help teachers avoid discrimination against children because of race, ethnicity, language, culture, gender, economic or educational level—or any other bias. Teachers should be as objective as possible in assessment and be knowledgeable about and sensitive to the ways in which diversity in children and families may influence assessment.

Teachers can increase the trustworthiness of the information they collect. The concepts of validity and reliability apply to all assessment information, not just to standardized tests. Although validity and reliability in classroom assessment cannot meet statistical standards, professional teachers work to increase trustworthiness.

Reliable information is consistent, reproducible, and dependable. Teachers can increase reliability by being aware of the ways in which information is collected, the situation in which assessment takes place, the child's mental and physical state, and the fact that guessing can influence reliability. They should be alert for uncharacteristic behavior and inconsistencies and make more than one measurement of items they assess.

Valid assessments appraise what they were designed to and result in reasonable interpretations or conclusions. Teachers can increase the validity of classroom assessment by having enough samples to adequately represent whatever they are assessing, having "balance" in the samples, checking to see if information obtained in different ways converges, and making sure they are assessing what they intended to. One of the big advantages of classroom assessment is that children can have more than one chance to demonstrate what they know and can do.

For Further Study, Discussion, and Reflection

1. Objectivity is essential in assessment, yet no one is totally objective. Reflect on your thoughts, feelings, and attitudes in your interactions with young children. What do you detect that might interfere with your objectivity? What do you detect that could aid your objectivity? Identify some possible reasons for these tendencies.
2. The school you are teaching in plans to use paraprofessional classroom assistants to help observe and make records of children's performance. Identify what classroom assistants and teachers need to know and do to safeguard the ethical and legal responsibilities of the school.
3. Underline the portions of the following observation record that are inferences and not a description of what was actually observed. Justify your decisions.

Tina and Norm are playing a game of tag outside. Tina accidentally trips Norm. He lashes out at her, pushing her to the ground. Her feelings hurt, Tina begins to cry and runs to the teacher. The teacher is more sympathetic toward Tina than Norm because he is usually a discipline problem in the classroom. She says, "What happened to you, Tina?" Tina replies, "Norm pushed me down and I hurt myself." The teacher takes her hand and walks over to Norm, who by now is quite angry and feeling sorry for himself. "Norm," says the teacher, "did you push Tina down? Why did this happen?" Norm says, "She tripped me first." Tina says, "Well, I didn't mean to." Tina and the teacher realize that there is a misunderstanding. Norm is an aggressive child and always responds aggressively.

4. Mr. Hiller is assessing Matthew's reading comprehension and recall by evaluating an oral book report given in front of the class. Matthew says very little when giving his book report orally to the class. Mr. Hiller suspects that Matthew's anxiety level is very high, so he talks to Matthew informally and confirms his suspicions: Matthew was too nervous to talk! Using the concepts of reliability and validity, discuss how Mr. Hiller should understand this assessment and in what other ways he could check Matthew's reading comprehension and recall.

Suggested Readings

Almy, M., & Genishi, C. (1979). *Ways of studying children.* New York: Teachers College Press.

American Federation of Teachers, National Council on Measurement in Education, & National Education Association. (1990). *Standards for teacher competence in educational assessment of students.* Washington, DC: Author. (Call your local or state AFT or NEA office.)

American Psychological Association, American Educational Research Association, & National Council on Measurement in Education. (1985). *Standards for educational and psychological testing.* Washington, DC: Author.

Bentzen, W. R. (1992). *Seeing young children: A guide to observing and recording behavior* (2nd ed.). New York: Delmar Publishers.

Feuer, M. J., Fulton, K., & Morison, P. (1993). Better tests and testing practices: Options for policy makers. *Phi Delta Kappan 74*(7), 530–533.

Sandoval, J., & Irvin, M. G. (1990). Legal and ethical issues in assessment of children. In C. R. Reynolds & R. W. Kamphaus (Eds.), *Handbook of psychological and educational assessment of children: Intelligence and achievement* (pp. 239–252). New York: Guilford Press.

Wolery, M., & Wilbers, J. S. (1994). *Including children with special needs in early childhood programs.* Washington, DC: National Association for the Education of Young Children.

CHAPTER THREE

Why, What, and When to Assess?

Imagine yourself with a new job in a school or center that emphasizes developmentally appropriate practices for young children, including developmentally appropriate assessment. The case study you spent a semester on in college can't possibly be done with a room full of children. Expectations are for something more than checklists of skill mastery. There is even a whole new vocabulary: "portfolio assessment," "continuous assessment," "keeping track," "performance assessment," and "authentic assessment," with many procedures, rating scales, observation records, participation charts, and checklists from which to choose.

Where do you start? How do you approach this task without having it detract from teaching? Like many things teachers do, there is no one way or even a "best" way. Teachers put their personal stamp on what and how they assess, how they organize files, and how they use information.

If you are beginning, or want to modify and improve what you are already doing, making key decisions consciously and explicitly can help organize the assessment process.

Assessment Decisions

Decisions have to be made before the process even starts: Why is assessment being done? What will be assessed? When? Deciding how to assess requires decisions about collecting and recording information (see Chapters 4 and 5). Compiling, summarizing, and interpreting information help us understand what it means so we can use it for the intended purposes (see Chapters 6, 7, and 8). Looking at assessment as a decision-making task is a way to simplify the process. Figure 3–1 highlights major decisions in the assessment cycle.

Some decisions may be made by other people. A group of teachers, building committees, parent councils, administrators, or funding or regulatory agencies may already have decided some of the why, what, and when to assess. They may require that certain records and summaries be made on standard forms so that information can be easily transferred and put with other records. Within those requirements, teachers still have to exercise much professional judgment. In addition, information that is required for official purposes is seldom sufficient for classroom instruction purposes.

Figure 3–1   *Major Decisions in the Assessment Cycle*

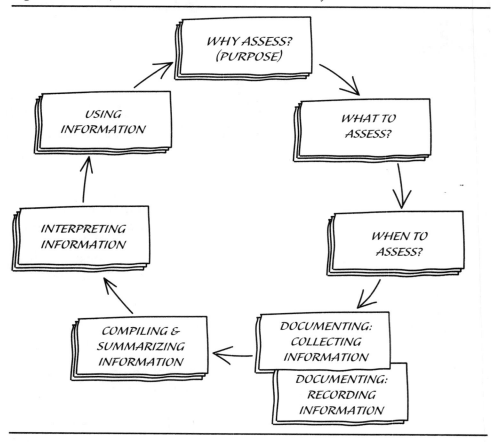

Why Assess?

"Assessment is more than just the collection of information; it is collection with a purpose" (Salvia & Yesseldyke, 1995, p. 3). The purposes of assessment—why do it at all?—guide everything that follows. The basic and most fundamental reason to assess is to determine individual children's developmental status at a given time and their progress and change over time. *Status* refers to children's current condition or situation with respect to any particular aspect of growth, development, or learning. What do they know? What are they able to do? What are their feelings, interests, attitudes, and dispositions as well as their physical health and well-being? Status is concerned with "where children are" in their development.

This basic information is then used for other purposes. The primary one is for classroom planning and decision making, to make classroom procedures and activities more responsive to and appropriate for individual children and the group. Assessment information is also used for other purposes: to identify children who might benefit from special help or challenge and to document that need, for reporting and communication with others, and to help solve individual and classroom problems and concerns (Hills, 1992; Stiggins & Conklin, 1992). These purposes are not entirely separate, of course. The same information that guides classroom planning for children will also be used for reporting; ongoing informal assessment during daily activities may spot concerns about individual children that other measures might miss.

Let's look at each of these purposes separately.

To Determine Children's Status and Progress

A Child's Developmental Status at a Given Time.   David Elkind cautions that "we cannot take anything for granted insofar as the child's knowledge or understanding is concerned" (1979, p. 147). Such a caution is particularly needed in contemporary classrooms where diversity of every kind is increasing (Lewis, 1991). Teachers can't assume that any given child or group fits their expectations of what children that age are like. All 4-year-olds or 6-year-olds are not the same weight and height, nor do they all know and do the same things. We assess to determine what this child and this group know and are able to do; their attitudes, habits, and dispositions; their physical strengths and needs. Such information gives perspective on the development and learning of an individual child (Sulzby, 1990).

A Child's Progress and Change over Time.   Teachers keep track of children's progress for several reasons: to assure themselves that learning and development are taking place; to provide evidence of learning to parents and children; to guard against the assumption that since "we've worked on that" the children have learned; and to make needed changes in response to what the children have or have not learned.

Because teachers and aides work daily with children, they may not realize how much children are developing and learning. Progress often comes gradually, in small increments. Only when a child's or group's performance is compared with what they did on the same task a month or several months ago is progress evident.

Solid evidence of progress motivates adults and children alike. Most teachers are elated when a child who has been having trouble with something "gets it." They are delighted when the experiences they have planned and implemented result in desired outcomes—and are motivated to continue. Hearing about or seeing examples of what they have learned motivates and reinforces children. Parents should receive regular reports on children's progress.

Assess to guard against the assumption that if children are given an opportunity to learn—whether through experiences, materials, "working on" something, explicit instruction, or just general support and expectation—they will automatically grow, develop, and progress. All teachers are inclined to think that if something is "taught," learners will "learn." This can't be assumed, either with a preschooler trying to learn how to enter and become a part of a play group or with a primary youngster trying to master regrouping in addition and subtraction. Periodically, a focused look and comparison with earlier information are needed.

To Provide Information Useful for Classroom Planning and Decision Making

Assessment information "is essential for planning and implementing developmentally appropriate programs" (Bredekamp, 1987, p. 4). Assessment "in the service of instruction" helps decide where and how to begin, how long to work on a given goal or objective, when to review, and when to make changes to help children learn. Initial assessment and periodic assessment of progress, placed against program goals and expectations, can help teachers make long- and short-range plans. Assessment also helps teachers in day-to-day classroom planning, as what children do one day prompts changes in plans for the ensuing days. If a new art activity captures the children's interest and leaves them wanting more, a teacher has definite guidance in shifting tomorrow's or the next day's plans to take advantage of that interest.

Teachers use information gained from ongoing, continuous assessment "to understand specific children and to gain information on which to base immediate decisions on how to direct, guide, teach, or respond" (Phinney, 1982, p. 16). Teachers seek to understand children's thinking and learning processes, not just what they know and can do. During interactive teaching and instructional conversations, they adjust what they say and do to recognize children's current level of understanding and try out words and strategies to increase that understanding. As children respond, teachers revise and modify their approach in a continuing interplay. They also use assessment information to help them choose materials and strategies, select one activity and reject another, allocate more or less time to a given portion of the day, decide what to do about the continuing squabbles in work groups, and decide how to rearrange learning centers to increase interest. Effective, developmentally appropriate programs depend on some kind of assessment, no matter how formal or informal the program or how old or young the learners.

Suppose a teacher in a program that values sociodramatic play assessed children's level of play using The Smilanski Scale for Evaluation of Dramatic and Sociodramatic Play (Smilanski & Shefatya, 1990). She found that 7 of the 19 children in the prekindergarten class did not stay in the play situation for more than two or three minutes at a time and did very little make-believe with regard to actions and situations. Informal observation and counts of participation in activities confirmed the findings on the Smilanski Scale. Since the sociodramatic play centers were well supplied with materials to enhance and support play, and children had ample time and encouragement to play, the teacher planned direct adult intervention to enhance these 7 children's play skills (Bodrova & Leong, 1996; Rogoff, 1990; Smilanski & Shefatya, 1990).

To Identify Children Who Might Benefit from Special Help

Assessment may help identify children who need special help. A few may need to be referred to specialists. Some may need more challenge; others may be falling behind and need more help in class.

Systematic assessment also keeps teachers from "losing" individual children. In any group of children, certain ones get lots of adult attention. Some demand it by their spirited behavior; others get it because they are so cooperative or responsive or because they have great need. Others may get lost along the way unless teachers take care to know them and meet their needs.

To Collect and Document Information for Reporting and Communication

Teachers, schools, and centers may report selected information about children to parents, other professionals, funding or regulatory agencies, boards of directors, school boards, or citizen groups (see Chapter 10). Reporting expectations vary with the age of the children, sponsorship and funding sources, purposes of the program, and tradition. Regardless of the reasons for sharing information, or the person or group with whom it is shared, such information must be accurate and grounded in solid evidence, not based on wishful thinking, broad conclusions, or general impressions. It must be appropriate for the audience and the way they will use it.

What to Assess?

Human development is so complex that teachers cannot assess everything of interest. They must focus, select, and sample (Stiggins & Conklin, 1992). Teachers make decisions about what to assess in four categories:

1. Major child growth and development domains
2. Expected outcomes of the program for individual children
3. Children's unique patterns of development, knowledge, attitudes, and interests
4. Problems or concerns about a child or group

Major Child Growth and Development Domains

Plan to gather at least some information on major aspects of children's development. These major developmental domains may be called different things: cognitive, affective, and psychomotor; or intellectual, social, emotional, and physical. Some people add language as a separate category. Others add aesthetic, moral, and spiritual development. Schools working with older children may think in terms of curriculum areas or subjects, such as literacy development, physical education, social studies, health and nutrition, and others. Even if a school or center emphasizes one or two developmental areas more than others, children cannot be divided up and part of them set aside. A youngster's lagging social development will plague him in all he does; poor muscle development and motor coordination will hold her back in the classroom as surely as on the playground. If reporting on children's progress in certain areas is not required, the information is useful for classroom planning; it is invaluable in getting a sense of and planning for a child as a whole.

Items to be assessed should be those that centers, teachers, and parents can and are willing to do something about, that are sensitive to appropriate instruction or amelioration, or that aid in understanding the child or the group. Sometimes there is little teachers can do with information except use it for understanding and social guidance. For instance, a very tall or short youngster may encounter difficulty, but nothing the school can do will change the child's height.

Expected Outcomes of the Program for Individual Children

Assessment should focus on the program's expected outcomes for children. These outcomes are stated as purposes, aims, standards, goals, or objectives, depending on how specific they are. Purposes or aims are quite broad and general, such as "to enhance the child's total development" or "to prepare children to participate fully in society." Standards, goals, and objectives are more specific.

Standards.   The term *standard* as used to refer to outcomes is relatively new and is employed in varying ways (Cohen, 1995; Eisner, 1995). Sometimes the terms "essential learnings" or "essential knowledge and skills" are used instead of "standard." In general, standards identify what learners should know and be able to do, and what dispositions and habits of mind they should develop.

Content standards state what should be learned in various subject areas, including critical thinking, problem solving, reasoning, information-gathering strategies, and learning processes appropriate to that discipline.

Performance standards define the levels of learning that are considered satisfactory and suggest ways of gauging the degree to which content standards have been attained (Lewis, 1995; Ravitch, 1995). They sometimes identify *benchmarks* as points of reference for measurement, assessment, and instruction. These benchmarks are statements of expected or anticipated skill or understanding at different developmental, age, or grade levels. Most standards identify benchmarks for a few key levels, such as grades 4,

8, and 12, and K–2 or K–3. The physical education standards have benchmarks for kindergarten, second grade, and every second year thereafter. Although there is inconsistency in how standards and benchmarks are stated, some examples will illustrate their nature.

A sample benchmark relating to the science standard "the structure of matter" reads that by the end of second grade, "students should know that objects can be described in terms of the materials they are made of (clay, cloth, paper, etc.) and their physical properties (color, size, shape, weight, texture, flexibility, etc.)" (American Association for the Advancement of Science (AAAS), 1993, p. 76).

Sample K–2 benchmarks for the K–12 science standard "understands energy types, sources, and conversions, and their relationship to heat and temperature" read

Knows that the Sun applies heat and light to Earth

Knows that heat can be produced in many ways (e.g., burning, rubbing, mixing chemicals)

Knows that electricity in circuits can produce light, heat, sound, and magnetic effects (AAAS, 1993, p. 83)

Such benchmarks are both educational targets and points of reference to determine whether or not a youngster has reached the expected level.

One of the physical education standards developed by the National Association for Sport and Physical Education (1995) states that children should achieve and maintain a health-enhancing level of physical fitness. Sample benchmarks to guide assessment of kindergarten children suggest that they should be able to:

- sustain moderate to vigorous physical activity for short periods of time
- identify the physiological signs of moderate physical activity, such as heavy breathing and fast heart rate

Rubrics identify different levels of attainment of each benchmark or standard. See Chapter 7 for examples of ways to use standards, benchmarks, and rubrics for evaluating children's learning.

States and local school districts have also developed standards. Many are more specific in what they want children to learn, whether stated as standards, essential learnings, goals, or objectives. For example, Colorado's model content standards for K–12 reading and writing have six broad standards, such as "Students read and understand a variety of materials, . . . write and speak for a variety of purposes and audiences, . . . apply thinking skills to their reading, writing, speaking, listening, and viewing." Each standard further specifies the content and skills to be learned (Colorado Department of Education, 1995, p. 4).

How national and state standards will work in the real world of schools and centers is still untested (Bredekamp & Rosegrant, 1995; Education Week/Special Report, 1995; Kane & Khattri, 1995). Their origins are in the school reform and improvement efforts spearheaded by the

National Governors' Association and the U.S. Department of Education (Ravitch, 1995). Their use by state or local education agencies is voluntary. National professional organizations and associations developed, reviewed, and published suggested standards in mathematics, science, geography, civics, the arts, physical education, health education, history, social studies, economics, English language arts, foreign languages, and "workplace skills." In most cases the standards represent a broad-based consensus. However, some of the standards have been controversial, and organizations have even issued competing standards. In addition, the standards are inconsistent in scope and format, are often quite abstract, and taken as a group are overwhelming in the amount of content pupils are expected to learn. Efforts are underway to integrate and reconcile the varying standards to make them more accessible to and usable by educators (Kendall & Marzano, 1994). In spite of their drawbacks, they do provide guidance by the leading educational organizations.

Goals and Objectives. Most early childhood programs state expected outcomes for children as goals and objectives. These may vary in specificity from "understanding and respecting social and cultural diversity" to long lists of discrete skills. No stated or agreed-upon national standards or goals exist for preschool and primary children. The current tendency is to state broad and flexible goals appropriate for a wide age span and to encourage appropriate local adaptation. Teachers have to synthesize information from several sources and select goals appropriate for their specific situation (Herman, Aschbacher, & Winters, 1992; Geography Education Standards Project, 1994).

The National Educational Goals Panel (Kagan, Moore, & Bredekamp, 1995) identified and defined five dimensions of early childhood school readiness: physical well-being and motor development, social and emotional development, approaches toward learning, language development, and cognition and general knowledge. Professional organizations (National Association for the Education of Young Children & National Association of Early Childhood Specialists of State Department of Education, 1991, p. 18) suggest sample program goals for children ages 3 through 8: "develop a positive self-concept and attitude toward learning, self-control, and a sense of belonging"; "construct understanding of relationships among objects, people, and events, such as classifying, ordering, number, space, and time"; "develop relationships of mutual respect with adults and peers, understand perspectives of other people, and negotiate and apply rules of group living"; and "use language to communicate effectively and to facilitate thinking and learning." Others exist in all major developmental domains.

From the General to the Specific. If standards, goals, or objectives are general, teachers have to make them more specific in order to assess and teach effectively. For example, references to helping children develop concepts of relative location or space are usually found or implied in most goal statements. If curriculum guides, frameworks, benchmarks, or suggested assessment tasks do not identify the experience, action, or behavior children will do to show their experience and learning, teachers need to. Which of the many concepts of location and space should they learn? Which do they already know, and at what level of understanding? What is involved in understanding and using location and space concepts such as "above/below," "over/under," "left/right," "top/bottom"? What can teachers watch and listen for that will show that children understand and can use these complex spatial concepts?

Developing a specific objective that can be taught and assessed involves breaking down general statements of intent into appropriate objectives, then identifying *indicators* of progress toward or achievement of those objectives. Then authentic assessment tasks and activities can be identified or devised. Figure 3–2 shows how a desired outcome ("understands concepts of location and space") can be translated into specific items for assessment and teaching.

One of the advantages of authentic assessment is that it is flexible and comprehensive enough to assess progress toward achievement of almost any goal or standard, not just knowledge and skills.

Figure 3–2 *Example of Specification of Items to Assess and Teach, and Indicators of Attainment Within a Given Developmental/Curriculum Area*

Area of Development/ Curriculum	Cognitive development; language; science (Preschool–Primary)
Relational Concepts	Position/location in space; time; size; weight; quantity; volume of sound; speed; texture; temperature
Specific Focus Concept	Relative location or position in space
Specific Learnings	*Concepts to be developed:* in front of/behind (in back of); beside/next to/between/in the middle; under/over; above/ below; front/back; in/out, into/out of, inside/outside; top/bottom; up/down/upside down; on/off; near/far; first/last; left/right—own body, then projective; others

Ways and levels of knowing:
- Experience
- Experience linked with words (Look, you put this block on the top.)
  - Comprehension (place; point to; hand me . . .)
  - Recognition (Is Tran behind you or in front of you?)
  - States location (Tell us where you're going to sit.)
  - States and uses concepts in new situations
- Uses words and concepts spontaneously and functionally
  - Understands relational aspects of position in space
  - Understands that position in space is sometimes relative, sometimes not (top of head is always top of head; top of a blank sheet of paper is determined by position)
  - Is able to shift perspective and viewpoint physically and mentally
  - Understands and states concept of overlapping position (e.g., playground equipment is outside school, but inside fence)

Unique Patterns of Development, Knowledge, Attitudes, and Interests

Children and groups often have their own unique "approaches to learning"—attitudes, values, habits, and learning styles that influence what and how they learn. Approaches to learning include "(1) openness to and curiosity about new tasks and challenges; (2) initiative, task persistence and attentiveness; (3) a tendency for reflection and interpretation; (4) imagination and invention; and (5) cognitive styles" (Kagan, Moore, & Bredekamp, 1995, p. 25). Project Spectrum, based on Howard Gardner's theory of multiple intelligences (1985), deliberately identifies children's "distinctive cognitive and stylistic profiles" in language, mathematics, and mechanical, scientific, spatial, physical, musical, and social abilities (Krechevsky, 1991, p. 43). Knowing these individual approaches to learning enables us to use that uniqueness to help children develop and learn.

Interesting topics, themes, and projects motivate children to learn and to integrate and consolidate their learning. Teachers planning a project or theme should assess "this group's" level of knowledge and interest as well as their attitudes, prior experience, and understanding of the topic. Maybe they already know more about the Pilgrims, dinosaurs, or dragons than they ever wanted to.

Assess children's strengths as well as needs. Too often we focus on what children can't do, rather than on the many things they do well.

Problems or Concerns about a Particular Child or Group

Teachers often need information on a problem or concern—about a particular child, a small group, or the total group—to give clues for its solution. "Allie is interested in everything but completes nothing." "What is going on in the dramatic play area? Almost everyone used to participate over the course of a few days. Now Danielle, Monica, and Latasha seem to have taken over." "Jordan talks all the time, but never seems to read or write anything." "I don't like what's happening in our opening class meeting. Instead of thoughtfully planning what they are going to do, the children just say the first thing they think of."

If the problem is clearly an individual one, there is no need to assess the whole class. Focus on the child. However, remember that many things influence what a child does. Often we have to look beyond an individual or group to the physical environment, scheduling, materials available, and other children and adults to find the sources of a problem.

Indications of a developmental "red flag"—is something wrong?—call for gathering more information. Be alert for and document concerns so children who need help can receive it as soon as possible (see Chapter 11).

Practical Considerations

In addition to developmental, teaching, and learning considerations, practical ones help determine assessment priorities, such as achieving a balance between recorded and unrecorded information, teaching load, age of children, years of teaching experience, and selection of relevant items to assess.

Given the situation in this classroom, this school, this program, what is possible?

Balance of Recorded and Unrecorded Information.   It is neither possible nor desirable for teachers to record everything. Teachers use much information immediately to adjust interactive teaching, shorten or lengthen the time spent in an activity, or guide a child's social interaction. Other information helps them develop a sense of the child's personality and style over a longer period of time. Much of this is never written, nor is there any need for it to be. However, if information collected in the classroom is to be the primary source of information about children's development and learning, there needs to be documentation. Most teachers could keep better track of children's learning if they recorded more. Throughout this book are suggestions for ways to achieve a balance that enhances both assessment and teaching.

Teaching Load.   Class size, adult:child ratio, available classroom and clerical assistance, hours per day and week teachers are with children, number of classes a teacher has, number of hours and quality of aide and volunteer assistance, length and placement in the day of planning time, availability of assistance for special needs children, and other factors over which teachers have little control influence the teaching load and the amount and quality of assessment it is possible to do. However, a lighter teaching load does not necessarily mean better assessment. One kindergarten teacher described a comprehensive system of record keeping and explained the reason for it: "I teach two classes of over 25 children each, every day. I have to have good records to keep track of 50-plus children."

Age and Development of Children.   Although teachers always have final responsibility for assessment, children's abilities to record what they have done, to select and file their own papers and materials, and to do self-assessment and self-reflection vary with age, development, and prior experience.

Teaching Experience.   A teacher who is still learning how to teach cannot be expected to incorporate systematic assessment into the classroom as easily as one who has taught for several years, has gained confidence and proficiency, and is ready to take on a new challenge.

Too Many Goals and Objectives.   If statements of standards, goals, and objectives resemble either idealistic wishes or a shopping list of all possible items, try to determine more realistic expectations. Check with experienced teachers and the administrator. Review reporting instruments—progress letters, report cards, sample portfolios, or other progress reports—to find indications that some objectives are emphasized more than others. They may show items that are not mentioned in objectives, such as the ability to get along with other children, attention span, self-regulation, or work habits. Start with priority expectations: items that are simple, developmentally on target, and related to immediate teaching decisions.

If program objectives are overwhelmingly specific and discrete—perhaps listing all the names of body parts, animals, means of transportation, or nursery rhymes that children might know—try grouping them into logical categories that can be assessed and taught together. Use an integrated curriculum to reach many goals simultaneously. Another approach is to assess and teach the items to reach other goals, such as classifying, comparing, seeing relationships, or solving problems.

Representativeness, Significance, and Authenticity of Items.   There is no end to items that could be assessed. Select items that are significant and worthwhile in and of themselves or because they stand for a group of other items. For example, many items on readiness inventories bear little relationship to the skills and understandings required in reading. They may or may not be important, but new knowledge and new conceptions of how children learn to read and write have made them obsolete (Sulzby, 1990).

One of the advantages of classroom assessment is that we can often find out what we need to know directly, not through a test or performance task that stands for a whole class of other items. To find out if a child can use classroom tools—crayons, scissors, chalk, paintbrushes and pencils—assess those skills directly and authentically.

Astute sampling is often appropriate. Children don't have to perform every large muscle task of strength, coordination, and endurance, only representative ones.

When to Assess?

Ideally, a plan for when to do different types of appraisal will be in place before the school year begins. The plan may be modified by the realities of classroom life, lack of time, or unexpected external requirements, but it will provide a time frame for assessment (see Chapter 9).

Do as much as possible before school starts. Determine school and center expectations. If tests or other information-gathering procedures are required, find out what they are and when they are scheduled. Mark the dates on a master planning calendar. Learn about reporting expectations. If parent conferences are at set times, schedule those times, since they will require you to summarize information, review portfolios, and prepare for reporting. Organize filing and record-keeping systems (see Chapters 6 and 9). Study existing records, information from parents, and transition materials from previous programs. If tradition, time, and resources permit, visit children's homes.

Make tentative plans for the different times you will be gathering information: ongoing, continuous appraisals integrated with teaching and learning; periodic ones, including initial, interim, and final summaries and assessments; assessments before and after major units of study, themes, projects, or investigations; and "as needed" to address specific problems or concerns. Teachers collect different information, using different procedures, at these times. They also make assessment serve two purposes, such as when a major project or unit of study coincides with the end of a reporting period.

When assessment is done influences the type of information gathering and recording you will do. Initial "sizing up" (Airasian, 1994; Gage & Berliner, 1992) calls for efficient procedures, such as sensitive group observation, checklists, written parent reports, and child-generated performance samples. Ongoing assessment allows greater depth, using procedures that may take more time, such as recording observations through short narrative records or participation charts. Figure 3–3 summarizes when teachers carry out three types of assessment. The section that follows concentrates on assessment that goes on in the classroom while children are there.

Assess Day by Day

Good teachers continuously appraise children and revise their procedures and interactions accordingly. A teacher does not have to stop being a teacher to gather and record data. In fact, some of the best and most useful information is obtained while a teacher is taking dictation from a child; listening to a child read a story he has written; assisting with paints, papers, or modeling clay; helping with math story problems; conversing during snacks; participating in a board game; leading a discussion; guiding playground activities; or working with manipulatives. Assessment is embedded in the interactive processes of teaching. Mr. Sena lays out the beginning of a pattern of rods of differing lengths for Tui, to see if she can discern and continue the pattern. She does not perceive the pattern he started, but does continue the line of rods across the table. When Tui has finished, he lays out another, much simpler pattern for her, bringing the task closer to her level. For Cecile, sitting beside Tui, he may increase the difficulty of the pattern, since she so clearly enjoys studying and mastering the complex and varied patterns Mr. Sena starts for her. Sketches and notes about the children's work will go in the files. Just as important, Mr. Sena immediately integrates the information into his interactions with the children. He

Figure 3–3   *Schedule for Three Major Types of Assessment*

Before the School Year Starts	Determine expectations
	Organize filing and record-keeping systems
	Study existing records
	Study information from parents
	Study materials from previous years
	Review assessment measures you have used in previous years
During the School Year, While Teaching	Initial ("sizing-up") assessments
	Continuous appraisals
	Periodic assessment
	Before-and-after themes of study
	As needed to address specific concerns
	Portfolios (Chapter 6)
During the School Year, Outside of Class Time	Summaries (Chapter 6)
	Profiles (Chapter 6)
	Portfolios (Chapter 6)

may also make written or mental notes about future ways to help children grasp the concept of pattern based on today's appraisal.

Some teachers use cooperative learning groups to keep tabs on social skills. Miss Gardner is helping her primary pupils with cooperative learning processes. Today she'll be surveying "sharing ideas and materials" and moves among the groups with a recording sheet. Such an approach tells little about the children's disposition to use that skill in other settings, but it tells Miss Gardner a lot about whether children have the skill and can use it or whether she needs to reteach and review. Such an approach to ongoing observation may increase children's motivation to practice and master the skill, since knowing that something is important enough to observe and document may enhance its value to the learner. Miss Gardner also has the groups briefly evaluate their own cooperative work, naming and documenting two things they did well and one thing they need to do better (Johnson, Johnson, Holubec, & Roy, 1984). These two ongoing procedures integrate assessment and daily learning experiences.

Assess Periodically

If continuous assessment is done conscientiously, there may be little need for additional data gathering; summarizing what has already been documented may be sufficient. However, focused initial, interim, and final assessments on one or more goals in development or curriculum areas sometimes are required. This does not imply the need for testing or for stopping other activities to "assess." Rather, the focused information gathering takes place as part of classroom activities. Over the period of a week, children might demonstrate their abilities to solve measurement problems in mathematics and science or represent ideas through art and construction.

Initial assessment occurs when a new group, part of a group, or a new child begins. It yields information on a child's or a group's initial status—what they can do, their attitudes and dispositions, their prior knowledge and understanding, and their skills and habits in relation to what the school or center emphasizes—to provide basic information for planning classroom activities and experiences. This initial reading or sizing up (Airasian, 1994; Gage & Berliner, 1992) should be done as soon as possible, but held tentatively, as all first impressions should be. Interim assessments are usually done halfway, or one-third and two-thirds of the way through the time the children are in the classroom. If children begin in September, a January or February "How are we doing?" allows for midcourse correction. Final assessment is done toward the end of a group's time with a particular teacher or teachers. It is a summing up before a youngster moves on to another teacher, unit, or school.

Centers and schools with nontraditional yearly schedules—year-round schools or child care centers, and child development centers or preschools that operate for a relatively short time—modify times to fit their schedule. Sometimes schools or centers require information at specified periods, such as each six or nine weeks or once per quarter or semester. This data collection or summary can serve the purposes of interim assessment. If it is done only for reporting, expand it to provide a basis for improving the quality of the educational experiences as well.

Assess before and after a Concentrated Emphasis

Assess before making final plans for any sustained unit, project, or topic, and again at its conclusion. Determine what children already know and can do, and consider their thinking and reasoning in relation to whatever is being planned. At the conclusion, summarize assessment information collected during the project, and if necessary look again to determine what children have learned, in what ways they have developed, and what continuation activities are needed.

Appraise children's interests, attitudes, and level of understanding of the essential elements of the topic, which may be quite different from recall knowledge. Consider what concepts the children hold about the topic and how it relates to other learnings. Look at the pattern of errors and the size of the gap between "where they are" and "where they are to go."

Let's look at one way to appraise before beginning a unit of study, theme, or project. "Webbing" or "mapping" is often recommended as a way for teachers to organize the concepts and relationships in a topic (Katz & Chard, 1989). It can also be used to assess how children organize their thinking, which is equally important for teachers to know. It is, after all, the children who need to learn the content and relationships.

Mr. Waner is planning an integrated unit on insects to work toward district objectives in science, reading, writing, mathematics, cognitive processes, and social development in his combined first and second grade class. He brings to class insects in a terrarium and colorful insect posters and books. He and the assistant observe and note what the children do: who approaches; who avoids; who asks what questions; which children say, "Yuck, I hate bugs"; which display considerable prior knowledge; and other indicators of interest, attitude, and knowledge. Such an approach allows him to do a preliminary appraisal of how suitable the topic is for this group. After several days of informal observation and recording, Mr. Waner plans a class discussion to find out what the children can say about insects and what they would like to learn. In preparation, he has developed some key questions, boned up on his own knowledge of insects, and slipped a new tape into the classroom tape recorder. He has posted several large, heavy sheets of paper to "map" or "web" the children's current knowledge, attitudes, and interests concerning insects. As he and the children talk, he places key words and phrases in groupings on the chart, ranging from many "Icky," "Scary," "Nasty," "Don't touch," and "I hate bugs" to an assured, "Moths have shorter and fatter antennae, and butterflies have longer and thinner antennae."

As the discussion proceeds and the chart develops, Mr. Waner begins to have a good idea of the current knowledge, attitudes, and interests of this group and its individual members, including a wealth of misconceptions and negative attitudes. He may or may not note names beside children's contributions on the chart. He'll play the tape after class to fill in contributions and nuances of expression he may have missed.

Only after Mr. Waner has studied his previous notes and information from the class discussion will he make a decision about how to approach a project on insects. He may decide to proceed with the full group, paying special attention to children's feelings and attitudes. He may decide to scale back, letting those children with a special interest conduct their own investigation, and plan to desensitize and give positive experiences to the fearful ones. He may do something else with the insect topic. What he will *not* do is proceed with the plans laid out in the "suggested unit" or the topic of study he developed in science methods class. He will adjust, modify, and shape his planning based on assessment of children's knowledge about and attitudes toward insects.

Assess to Get Information about a Specific Problem or Concern

Concerns about specific children, a subgroup, or the total group don't always correspond to units of study or reporting periods, nor is continuous assessment always adequate for problem solving. Whether or not it fits the "assessment schedule," take a closer look as needed. Suppose a usually attentive, interested second grader becomes restless, inattentive, and aggressive or anxious and clingy. If illness is not the cause, turn to other sources for information to shed light on this unusual behavior and ways to help the youngster. Problems outside the classroom, such as parental separation, death, divorce, job loss, moving, a birth in the family, and innumerable others may influence children's behavior. Observing the child won't give you the necessary information.

Children who move frequently from one school or center to another present a special problem. If adequate records are sent with them, continue from there. More often, children come with minimum enrollment information. Integrating them into the life of the classroom is top priority. What you can assess depends on when children enter and how long they stay. At the least, try to send a file with something of worth in it to inform the next teacher.

Some Final Thoughts

Although we have teased apart aspects of classroom assessment and curriculum for study and discussion, in the classroom there is no such distinction. They are merged. Questions of why, what, when, and how to assess are also closely related. Assessment is not an invariant linear or time-bound sequence, in that you do the first step at the beginning of the year and the last one at the end of the year. On the contrary, information collected early in the year may result in immediate program modifications. Ongoing continuous assessment keeps teachers and the program sensitive and responsive to children. A teacher may quickly "size up" (collect data on) a particular situation, understand its meaning, and use the information on the spot. For example, a sensitive teacher leading a group discussion may see and hear the children whispering, nudging each other, yawning, playing with a neighbor's hair, or making faces at someone across the circle. She collects this information (actually, it forces itself on her), understands its meaning to be "this group discussion is off-target," and uses that interpretation as a signal to switch to something more appropriate. Another teacher reading a counting book to a small group of children finds that when he asks, "How many balloons does the clown have?" the children either just sit or say,

"Blue and red." He collects enough information to confirm his suspicions that they either don't know what "how many" means or don't know how to count, and switches his request to one that helps them learn both things: "Let's count together to see how many balloons the clown has." This is "assessment in the service of instruction" at its best.

Summary

Thinking about assessment as a series of decisions helps simplify a complicated process. Basic decisions pertain to why, what, and when to assess. Teachers also decide how to collect and record information and how to organize, summarize, interpret, and use it. This chapter focused on basic decisions—why, what, and when.

Assessment helps determine children's status and progress in growth, development, and learning. This information is used to guide classroom program planning and decision making, to identify children who might benefit from special help, and to collect and document information for reporting and communicating to parents and children, other professionals, and funding, regulatory, and advisory groups. Decisions about what to assess may be influenced by the need for information from major developmental domains, the goals and objectives of the program, the need to know something about the uniqueness of each child, classroom or individual problems or concerns, and practical considerations.

The timing of assessment determines much of its utility, so a tentative plan should be in place and preliminary tasks done before school starts. Different types of appraisal take place at different times. Continuous assessment is integrated with ongoing classroom activities. Periodic assessment or summarizing existing information takes place initially, midway, and for a final "summing up." Focused appraisals take place before and after a concentrated curriculum emphasis or when need for specific information exists. Assess as needed to focus on a problem or concern.

For Further Study, Discussion, and Reflection

1. Teaching experience is a practical consideration in making assessment decisions. Appraise your own teaching experience. In what ways might the amount and type of your experience influence the assessment decisions you make?
2. Secure samples of the report cards or progress reports for parents that local school districts use. Analyze these for (1) likenesses and differences in type of reporting, (2) guidance they might give a teacher about what should be assessed, and (3) balance and comprehensiveness of the curriculum.
3. Interview the teacher of a neighborhood school or center to find out what assessment of children is done (1) in his or her classroom and (2) throughout the school. (If you are already teaching, interview a teacher from another type of school.) In what ways is the information used? When does the teacher assess? Combine what you find

out with that of other students to see if there are any likenesses, differences, or general conclusions you might draw.

4. The kindergarten teacher at Hillside Elementary, a 25-year veteran teacher, organizes the reading portion of the kindergarten curriculum around a simple approach—letters of the alphabet. The first full week is "A" week, and so on. Evaluate this approach from the standpoint of assessment.

Suggested Readings

Almy, M., & Genishi, C. (1979). *Ways of studying children.* New York: Teachers College Press.

Herman, J. L., Aschbacher, P. R., & Winters, L. (1992). *A practical guide to alternative assessment.* Alexandria, VA: Association for Supervision and Curriculum Development.

Morrow, L. M., & Smith, J. K. (Eds.). (1990). *Assessment for instruction in early literacy.* Englewood Cliffs, NJ: Prentice Hall.

National Association for the Education of Young Children & National Association of Early Childhood Specialists of State Departments of Education. (1991). Guidelines for appropriate curriculum content and assessment in programs serving children ages 3 through 8. *Young Children, 46,* 21–38.

Schickedanz, J. A., Hansen, K., & Forsyth, P. D. (1990). *Understanding children.* Mountain View, CA: Mayfield Publishing.

CHAPTER FOUR

Documenting: Collecting Information

Finding out what children know and can do and discovering their interests, unique characteristics, attitudes, and dispositions is called data collection, gathering information, appraisal, or obtaining evidence. Recording is a separate process.

The two processes—collecting and recording—are often thought of as the same. Ask teachers how they find out about children's progress, and you may get an answer such as "We have a checklist," or "Anecdotal records." Checklists and anecdotal records record and preserve information. They are records, not ways of collecting information. Information was collected using systematic observation or watching what children did. Keep these two steps separate to open up options both for learning about children and for recording what you find out.

There are many ways of obtaining information about children and as many ways of recording that information. Teachers are free to mix and match

these methods as appropriate. The same information can be recorded using several different procedures. An observation of Stacy's problem-solving strategies can be recorded either on an anecdotal record or checklist. Information collected in different ways can be documented with the same recording technique. A checklist could record reasoning strategies observed in a cooperative science project, elicited by teacher questions or reported by a child after building with blocks.

This chapter focuses only on collecting information, not recording it. Consult Chapter 5 for the recording process.

Multiple Windows

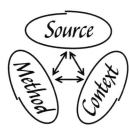

Teachers can gather information about children through many "windows"—combinations of sources, methods, and contexts (Bailey & Simeonsson, 1988). Multiple perspectives collect and capture, as completely as possible, the development and learning of a rapidly changing child. Think of a house with many windows looking out on a panoramic view. To see the entire panorama, you must look through each window because each includes and excludes part of the view. From one window you see the mountains, but miss the lake. From another, you see only part of the lake but get a good view of the meadow. It is the same with assessment. Different ways of "finding out" yield distinct "pictures" or pieces of information. No one source of information tells everything. One method reveals aspects of a child's behavior that another does not. One context facilitates certain behaviors while another does not. Brian's journals, dictation, stories, conversations with other children, responses to questions from adults, and wordplay showcase particular aspects of his language development. If his journal is the only source of information, the picture of Brian's language capabilities would be incomplete.

In addition, one window or approach "is likely to provide a less valid estimate of a student's achievement than is some combination" (Gage & Berliner, 1992, p. 654). Any single assessment is an estimate of a child's or group's status and is not an exact indication of performance (Airasian, 1994). Using multiple windows results in better and more complete information about children (Bailey & Simeonsson, 1988) and increases reliability and representativeness (Cronbach, 1990). Multiple windows free teachers from the rigidity imposed by overreliance on one approach and decrease the possibility for errors.

Three aspects of classroom assessment can be varied to provide multiple windows or perspectives:

1. The source of information—the child, other children, parents, specialists, other adults, or written records about children
2. The method of obtaining information—systematically observing, eliciting responses from children, collecting products from classroom activities, or eliciting information from parents and other adults
3. The context, setting, or situation for the appraisal—outdoors or indoors, at a desk or on the floor, in the classroom or a testing room,

using paper and pencil or manipulative materials, alone or in groups, or with familiar classroom staff or strangers

Sources of Information

The source of information refers to "who" or "what" provides information about children. These are the primary sources:

1. The child
2. Parents, specialists, classroom assistants and volunteers, and other adults
3. Written records from other teachers, specialists, or any other source

Sources provide information directly from children or indirectly through the eyes of other people. Both types serve important purposes and, together, give a diverse, well-rounded picture of a child. Assess the variety of Jeremy's fine motor skills by asking him to fold napkins at snack time; by listening to his gleeful report of tying his shoe; by watching him build with Mary and Tony; by noting when his dad says, "Jeremy helped string snow peas for dinner"; and by reviewing written records in which Jeremy's previous teacher recorded that he can use scissors. Each source presents distinct, valuable information about Jeremy.

The Child as a Source of Information

The child is the best source of authentic assessment data. The most obvious and direct way of obtaining information is by watching, analyzing the work of, talking with, and listening to *that child.*

Opportunities for obtaining information from children occur as a natural outcome of day-to-day classroom interaction. After reading a story about friendships, a teacher discusses it with a small group of children and later records their conception of what a friend is. A child's construction with math manipulatives reflects sense of number and pattern. Explaining the reasoning behind a graph, a child gives you a glimpse into her thinking processes as well as a work product.

Children volunteer information about their own activities, making comments about what they like and dislike and what they understand. Sometimes these self-reports are unprompted and unsolicited: "I've done this before," or "I have one like this at home," or "I know how to do this." At other times children respond to questions: "What would you like to learn about tornadoes?" "What is the most interesting thing you have done this week?" "What do you know about George Washington Carver?"

Advantages of the Child as a Source of Information

1. The child is the most direct, authentic source of information.
2. Directly observing or interacting with a child builds rapport and communication.

3. Self-reports reveal information difficult to obtain in another way, such as what a child is thinking and feeling, or attitudes and dispositions.

Disadvantages of the Child as a Source of Information

1. Young children may have trouble articulating or demonstrating some behaviors, such as internal mental processes.
2. Some behaviors cannot be observed at school, such as a child's relationship with neighborhood friends or grandparents who live in another city. Parents may be a better source of information.

Recommended Procedures for Using the Child as a Source

- *Make sure the child feels at ease.* A child's level of comfort and familiarity with a situation influences the response you receive. For example, one child will show more persistence working on a weaving project than trying to jump rope.
- *Provide opportunities for self-reporting.* Set aside a time of day to talk with children. Solicit child opinion by saying, "I'm interested in what you think."

Parents and Other Adults as a Source of Information

Other people—parents, specialists, teachers, aides, and other school personnel—are an indirect source of information about child behavior.

Insights from other people, particularly parents, improve and deepen a teacher's understanding of a child. Meimei seldom talks in school and never participates in singing or fingerplays during group time. The teacher learns something important when parents report, "When Meimei comes home from school she tells us everything she did. She sings the songs and chants the words to all of the fingerplays." Children may not display their most mature behavior at school, or they may reveal a different side of their personality to a particular teacher.

Parents provide a special perspective. They have known their children better and longer than anyone else. They have information about events occurring at home that might affect a child's behavior in the classroom. They may see a side of the child that is not revealed at school. Parents provide insights about home culture and home/school differences that are essential for teachers in today's multiethnic, multicultural classroom.

Other teachers or aides may observe a "different" child because they supervise other activities or have a unique relationship with a child. For instance, Martina is quiet and subdued during any reading activities or journal writing. The teacher has to struggle to get her to write or to talk. On the playground during free playtime, Martina is a full participant, leading other children in rough-and-tumble games. The playground supervisor has a different picture of Martina than does the reading teacher.

Teachers obtain information from other professionals, including speech and language specialists, nurses, and psychologists. By working together, participating in formal meetings and staffings, and reading written records, teachers gain important additional insights. A shadow study (Hills, 1992) is an example of how other adults can help a teacher understand an individual child. It consists of a series of observations of one child made by different staff members in different contexts and at different times. It provides a rich multidisciplinary perspective on a specific child.

Advantages of Using Parents and Other Adults as a Source

1. Information from parents will give insights about child behavior outside the classroom.
2. Parents can provide information about home/school and cultural differences.
3. Other people's insights and descriptions add to knowledge about a child. Parents can provide a long-range perspective of child behavior from birth to the present. Specialists with a deeper knowledge in an area of expertise and different professional skills can augment a teacher's understanding of a child.

Disadvantages of Using Parents and Other Adults as a Source

1. Other people's biases can color your perceptions of a child.
2. If parents are not familiar with the purpose of the assessment, they may misunderstand and place pressure on the child to perform in a specific way.
3. Shadow studies are time consuming and should be used only when other ways of assessing specific cases have been exhausted.

Recommended Procedures for Using Parents and Other Adults as a Source

- *Make a distinction between prying into family affairs and knowing enough about the family to help a child learn.* Keep all family information strictly confidential.
- *Make a sincere and professional effort to determine other people's knowledge and perceptions of children in varied situations.* Be sure this information is not gossip, "talking about" or labeling a child, or the sometimes unprofessional exchange of opinions occurring in a teachers' lounge.
- *Make sharing of information between teachers and other professionals as formal as possible.* Designate a specific time to talk, and select the subject of discussion beforehand.

Written Records as a Source of Information

Written records include attendance records, intake records, health and school history records, progress reports, report cards, narrative reports from previous teachers, inventories, checklists, parent questionnaires, and results of standardized tests. Some programs are experimenting with passing on a cumulative portfolio that documents growth year after year. The type, quality, and quantity of information in written records will depend on the program's policies and procedures.

Some teachers choose *not* to look at records until they know a child and have made their own assessment. Others regard records as important background in knowing children's prior experiences. The "don't look at the records" approach has several drawbacks. The transfer of written records is one way to help children make a smooth transition from one setting or grade to another (Love & Yelton, 1989). A professional teacher should be able to weigh such information against other evidence, regard it as tentative, and combine it with other information and perceptions to assess a child more quickly and accurately. Other people's insights and knowledge can augment a teacher's, if only because there is disagreement. Previous accomplishments are not forgotten and the continuity of learning is reinforced. Children frequently move from one school to the next and one community to another. It is not fair to children or parents to have to start totally anew in each setting. Finally, time, money, and energy are invested in screening, diagnostic, achievement, and health tests and in other written records. They should be used.

Advantages of Written Records as a Source of Information

1. They give teachers an additional vantage point from which to understand children.
2. They can help teachers get to know a child quickly.
3. Passing on portfolios ensures that accomplishments are not forgotten and gives a long-range perspective to child growth and learning.
4. Previous screening, diagnosis, achievement, and health tests will not be repeated.

Disadvantages of Written Records as a Source of Information

1. Information can be old and inaccurate—children change.
2. Information may vary in quality, amount, and usefulness.
3. Teachers unfamiliar with testing terms and statistics will need help to interpret test results.

Recommended Procedures for Using Written Records as a Source

- *Find out program guidelines for looking at written records.*
- *Check the date and source of all written material.* The older the information, the more likely the child has changed.
- *Weigh written information with your knowledge, experience, and current assessments.* Consider what you know about this child along with information in written records.
- *Evaluate test results in light of current knowledge about tests and testing results, including reliability and validity.* If you are unfamiliar with testing terms or the test itself, seek help from a professional psychologist or a tests and measurement specialist before interpreting scores.
- *Use test information appropriately.* Do not label, group, or categorize children based on test results.

Methods of Collecting Information

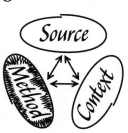

The method of assessment is the "how" or way information is gathered; it can be formal or informal (Goodwin & Driscoll, 1980). Formal methods are usually research instruments, clinical techniques, or standardized tests such as screening or achievement tests with limited uses in classrooms. Although they may yield some useful information, formal methods require that the teacher have special knowledge and expertise, to ensure correct interpretation. Informal methods involve normal classroom activities and are directly relevant to classroom decision making and keeping track of progress toward developmental goals.

There are many informal methods to obtain information about children. This section covers four major ones:

1. Systematically observing children
2. Eliciting responses from children
3. Collecting products from classroom activities
4. Eliciting information from parents.

Systematically Observing Children

The most common way of gathering information about children is watching and listening to them. All teachers, of course, observe the children with whom they work. Some observation is routine and informal—Eseme got a haircut; Kevin spent most of the time playing with blocks. Some is intuitive or "sensed"—the children are losing interest; Brad is tired. But there is a type of observation that is systematic, focused, and used for collecting information. Teachers cannot take in everything happening with a group of 15 to 20 children. Just looking does not guarantee *seeing*. Attention must be directed to a child, a particular pattern of behavior, a situation or problem, or progress toward an identified goal. This kind of observation is called "systematic observation."

Valuable information is collected through focused watching and listening. Teachers listen for verbal behavior, including the actual words said and the way they are said—voice intonation, enunciation, and pronunciation. Simultaneously, teachers watch nonverbal behavior, such as body movements, motor or nonverbal responses, gestures, and facial expressions.

Advantages of Systematic Observation

1. A child does not have to read or write an answer to be assessed.
2. Children can be minimally aware that their behavior is observed.
3. It does not require changing classroom routines or activities.
4. It is the most direct and valid way to obtain information about some behaviors. For example, a teacher must watch and listen to children interacting to find out how they negotiate taking turns.
5. It is accepted as an appropriate method by most early childhood educators.

Disadvantages of Systematic Observation

1. Some important aspects of development, such as feelings, attitudes, values, and other mental processes, cannot be assessed by observing overt behavior.
2. Systematic observation requires focused attention and is difficult to do while interacting with children.

Recommended Procedures for Systematic Observation

- *Focus observation on a specific child, behavior, situation or problem, or identified goal.*
- *Observe verbal and nonverbal behavior.*

Eliciting Responses from Children

Conversing, asking questions, or requesting children to do something are part of normal daily classroom interaction and a flexible, useful way of collecting information about children. When teachers elicit a response, attention is focused on the information needed. Instead of waiting for a response to appear spontaneously, teachers save time by requesting it. Eliciting a response through instructional conversations or dialogues is a way of finding out about internal thinking processes that cannot be observed (Berliner, 1987).

Dynamic assessment is a specific way of eliciting information from children, using Lev S. Vygotsky's concept of the Zone of Proximal Development (ZPD). Instead of seeing a child's performance as only what the child can do independently, dynamic assessment probes skills that are on the verge of emergence; they can be tapped as teacher and child interact. Teachers try to identify learning strategies a child already uses as well as instructional processes most likely to promote future learning (Berk & Winsler, 1995). The hints, prompts, cues, and questions the teacher uses are recorded along with the child's responses. Examining the assistance that makes a difference in the child's ability to perform a task tells about the child's current level of understanding and skill and gives direction for future teaching. Dynamic assessment provides information at both levels of the ZPD: the lower, or unassisted, level and the upper, or maximally assisted, level. It integrates assessment with responsive teaching.

Melissa is at the beginning stages of learning about sound–symbol relationship. Ms. Mansfield and Melissa look at a picture of a horse in a meadow with "horse" written underneath. Ms. Mansfield points to the word. Melissa looks at her expectantly. "I wonder what this word is," Ms. Mansfield says. "Sun," replies Melissa, looking at the sun in the picture. "This word starts with an . . . ," prompts the teacher. "H . . . is it tree? Pony?" asks Melissa. "H. . . .," prompts the teacher. "Oh, horse," says Melissa. Ms. Mansfield notes that Melissa uses picture cues to try to read, doesn't connect the sound of *H* to the word without prompting, but once prompted, thinks of a word that both makes sense and has that beginning sound. By prompting with *H*, Ms. Mansfield exposed more knowledge about sound–symbol relationship than she would have if she had just stopped at the child's response to "I wonder what this word says," or "This word starts with an . . ."

To use this method successfully, teachers plan prompts and hints to provide more and more assistance as the child needs it. Assistance can be with specific skills and knowledge, or with broader strategies such as problem solving and seeing relationships. Dynamic assessment has been used to assess literacy (Clay, 1985; Smith-Burke, 1985), math skills (Campione, Brown, Reeve, Ferrara, & Palinscar, 1991), and different levels of cognitive reasoning (Tharp & Gallimore, 1988). Several studies have found that dynamic assessment predicts child achievement as well as—and sometimes better than—standardized tests (Spector, 1992). Dynamic assessment may also be a way to address cultural differences found in assessment and instruction (Stanley, 1996).

Performance samples elicit a response to a specific task to see if a child can "translate his knowledge and understandings into action" (Gage & Berliner, 1992, p. 628) by demonstrating learning. Performance samples mirror the goal or objective being assessed. To see if children can solve a problem, the teacher has them solve one. Children count the number of raisins on a plate or count to play a game (Kamii, 1990). They read books to demonstrate literacy. Performance samples assess observable, definable behaviors. Properly designed performance tasks are tools for learning as well as tools for measuring children's progress (Arter, 1994).

Interviewing and conferencing are other ways of eliciting information. An interview usually involves a planned sequence of questions; a conference implies discussion, with teacher and pupil sharing ideas. Interviews can be conducted on almost any subject and at any level of complexity, but lend themselves to open-ended and varied questions: "What are some things that are easy for you to do?" "What did you like about our field trip?" or "Explain your thinking" are queries that reveal unique approaches to learning and insight into the individual. They also help children learn how to give extended responses to an adult.

Conferences are usually conducted in relation to work a child has done, such as writing, science, or mathematics. Teacher and child discuss the work, each one contributing insights and suggestions. Conferences can reveal pupils' level of understanding and confidence (Stenmark, 1991).

Types of Questions and Statements Used to Elicit a Response.   Asking questions; making requests, statements, and suggestions; giving directions, hints, and clues; nonverbal cues; and presenting a task or problem are examples of ways to elicit a response. To decide which is most appropriate, consider what information is needed at what level of performance. Several frameworks are helpful in these decisions:

1. Convergent versus divergent questions or statements
2. Receptive versus expressive levels
3. Recognition versus recall levels
4. Levels of cognitive complexity (Bloom's Taxonomy) (Bloom, Englehart, Furst, Hill, & Krathwhol, 1956)

Convergent questions or statements request a specific verbal or nonverbal response and have correct answers: "What color is this?" "If I had two apples and I gave you one, how many would be left?" "Put this animal next to his home." "Mavis, show me you can climb this ladder!" "Point to the *L*." "Write your name right here."

Divergent questions or statements are appropriate when eliciting a child's opinion, thoughts, reasoning, or feelings; they do not have specific correct answers. "As you read, think of some reasons the animals in this story try to solve their problem in different ways. We'll discuss these reasons when you finish." "What did you like about our trip to the zoo?" "Help me think—what are some ideas we could have in a story about a bear?" Divergent questions or statements are phrased to indicate that several answers or responses are appropriate.

Requests at the *receptive level* call for a motor response, such as "Point to a circle" or "Go around the tree, and then up the ladder." *Expressive-level* questions and statements direct children to express, produce, or state ideas in words, such as "Tell me the name of this shape." Generally, receptive-level questions are easier to answer than expressive-level questions.

Asking the child to choose the correct answer from an array taps *recognition*: "Is this one bigger or smaller than this one?" "What do we call the animal we saw on our walk—a squirrel or a chipmunk?" At the *recall* level, children must give the correct answer without the benefit of alternatives to choose from, as in "What is two plus two?" or "Who is this book about?" Children, like adults, are usually able to recognize information before they can recall it (Berk, 1994; Bukatko & Daehler, 1992; Steinberg & Belsky, 1991).

Bloom's Taxonomy (Bloom et al., 1956) suggests levels of cognitive complexity that are helpful in selecting questions and statements. The taxonomy lists cognitive processes in order of increasing complexity:

Knowledge. The ability to recall, remember, or recognize an idea or fact. "What is the name of this shape?" "Point to the letter *B*."

Comprehension. The ability to translate or explain in your own words. "Explain in your own words what a mammal is." "Tell me the names of some things having a *circle* shape."

Application. The ability to use information, applying it to new situations and real-life circumstances. "Use your math skills to divide up this pizza." "Use your reading skills to figure out which of these words rhymes with *look*."

Analysis. The ability to break information into parts. "Compare a tiger to a pet cat." "What is the difference between a triangle and a square?" "What information do you need to solve this problem?"

Synthesis. The ability to assemble separate parts into a new whole and recombine information from various sources into a new form. "Let's make our own poem using words starting with *B*." "Make your own pattern from these cubes."

Evaluation. The ability to make judgments about information using a standard or a set of criteria. "Could this really have happened?" "Explain why you think the ending of this story was a good one." (Bloom et al., 1956)

Alternative assessment should tap complex thinking skills (Herman, Aschbacher, & Winters, 1992).

Type of Performance Requested.   Consider how the child will respond and the type of performance requested. Teachers can request an individual response—one child at a time—or a group response—all children together. Responses can be verbal, nonverbal, or written. A verbal response would be saying the answer aloud. Nonverbal responses are any motor action or physical response, such as pointing to, nodding, holding up a hand, or performing the behavior or skill. A written response entails drawing, circling, checking, or writing an answer. For example, a child could be asked to say the name of the animal, point to the animal, or circle a picture of the animal.

In many performance samples, children are told exactly what to do and how to do it. For example, "Jump on your left foot five times without touching the floor with your right foot." The criteria are transparent (Gage & Berliner, 1992). As children become proficient at reading and writing, written responses are used to appraise knowledge in reading, writing, spelling, and math. These include written performance samples, activities, practice papers, and informal tests made by teachers or taken from teacher resource books. Informal tests for beginning writers usually ask children to identify the correct answer from an array by checking, circling, underlining, drawing a line to it, or making an *X*. These tests have fewer items and more picture cues. Questions are read aloud or are printed on the test. As children get older, they are required to read directions and questions and write answers.

The younger the child, the less valid and appropriate are written tests. Young children's fine motor skills may interfere with writing. Weak reading and writing skills cause poor performances even when children know the answers. For suggestions about choosing and designing informal tests, consult an educational psychology textbook, such as those written by Gage and Berliner (1992) or Beihler and Snowman (1991); or books on tests and measurement, such as those by Airasian (1994) or Hopkins, Stanley, and Hopkins (1990).

Figure 4–1 shows a teacher-designed test for a second grade classroom. Teacher resource books or manuals often include children's tests.

Advantages of Eliciting Responses from Children

1. It focuses both the teacher's and child's attention on a specific behavior. Instead of waiting until a child spontaneously says, "That is the letter *J*," teachers save time by asking.
2. It can probe the level of a child's understanding or clarify answers. For example, a teacher can say, "Explain this to me in your own words," or "I didn't understand what you meant. Please explain it again."
3. It is a more effective and reliable means of checking if a child understands than using incidental, nonverbal cues (Berliner, 1987).
4. Performance samples assess whether children can apply and demonstrate what they know.

Figure 4–1 *Teacher-Made Informal Classroom Test*

4. How does Grandpa read books?

_____

_____

_____

5. In the story, Grandpa smells hot bread. What foods can you name by smelling them?

_____

_____

_____

_____

6. Grandpa does not have the sense of sight but he can use four of his other senses. What are they?

_____

7. Describe how these things would feel in your hand.

honey _____

clay _____

a cello _____

a squirrel _____

Grandpa's Book _____

5. Interviews and conferences give insights into children's thoughts, understandings, and feelings.
6. Informal classroom tests give valuable information about children who are able to read and write, they are easy to administer, and they can be designed to assess specific knowledge and skills taught.

Disadvantages of Eliciting Responses from Children

1. A child's response can reflect social factors, not "knowledge." Children who have difficulty answering may lose self-confidence and fail to respond although they know the answer. Cultural differences in adult–child interaction in the home and at school may influence children's responses. A child may guess or answer what he or she thinks the teacher wants to hear.
2. The way a question is framed will influence responses. If questions are confusing or misleading, a child may not understand what the teacher wants him or her to do.
3. Written tests taken by young children may be invalid and unreliable.
4. Tests from textbooks may be invalid because they are inappropriate for children in that particular classroom or cover material the teacher has omitted.

Recommended Procedures for Eliciting Responses from Children

- *Frame questions and statements clearly, directly, and explicitly.* If a specific response is required, include it in the directions. Say "Jump up and down" or "Tell me which one you like best." Avoid being indirect ("Would you like to show me the red one?") or vague ("How many times can you jump up and down?").
- *Have more than one way to ask the same question.* If one way does not work, you will be prepared with another.
- *Decide how children will be directed to respond or the type of performance requested—as individuals or in a group, verbally, nonverbally, or by writing answers.*
- *Make sure children understand your question or request.* Use a few practice items to confirm that children understand what you want them to do.
- *Allow enough time to think and respond.* When appropriate, encourage a calculated guess, give hints, or model the response you want.
- *Develop a series of questions, statements, and hints on different levels or aspects of a problem.* For dynamic assessment, list the levels of information you expect; arrange questions from easy to difficult, or list the aspects of a problem. Create questions to probe each level or aspect. You do not have to begin with the easiest questions first. Starting with more difficult questions and dropping back to easier ones is effective. Keep track of the hints and how a child uses them.
- *Use performance samples that directly elicit behaviors, skills, strategies, and information.*
- *Combine information gathered from informal classroom tests with information from other appraisals.*

- *Keep in mind children's level of reading and writing when choosing or developing informal classroom tests.* Paper-and-pencil tests must be appropriate to a child's reading level and should include visual and pictorial clues.
- *Teach children how to take informal classroom tests.* Read directions, identify questions, model what children are supposed to do, and answer practice items together.
- *Analyze tests from textbooks to make sure they cover the knowledge and skills taught.*

Collecting Products from Classroom Activities

Many classroom activities result in a product or object that provides valuable evidence of a child's status and progress. So although the clay snake Josefa made will not be saved, the fact that she can make snakes shows small muscle development. Jacob and Mara have built an elaborate town using interlocking plastic blocks. The town is evidence of task persistence and social skills—cooperation and negotiation used in building a joint structure. A comparison of Van's self-portraits at the beginning and end of the year reveals growth in cognitive representation. These items are important assessment windows that are often lost in the rush of cleanup or sent home without a second glance (Kuschner, 1989).

Advantages of Collecting Work Products

1. Classroom products capture information that would be time consuming and difficult to put into words.
2. A child's use of materials reveals information about several aspects of development, steps in learning, and progress toward a goal.
3. Products or artifacts are easy to collect because they are the outcome of many classroom activities.
4. They can be collected for groups and individuals.
5. They can be collected and compared over a period of time.

Disadvantages of Collecting Work Products

1. Children will have unique products, making it difficult to get a sense of classroom needs.
2. Overemphasis on assessment of products may shift the classroom focus away from "process" to "product."
3. It is difficult to know which and how many examples to save.
4. Much important development and learning does not result in a product. For example, a child who has learned to take another child's perspective will not have a product to show for it.

Recommended Procedures for Collecting Work Products

- *Develop a plan for selecting products.* For example, plan periodic sampling for those items meant to show progress. Collect a variety of products in different media to document all developmental and content areas. Choose products based on how well they show what a child has learned or experienced. Look for "breakthrough" samples—products that show particular growth and development. Do not worry if products are not neat or pretty. Choose products because of the process they show. Figures 4–2 and 4–3 show two children's abilities to represent events and objects. Jennifer's picture of the swimming race shows a purposeful and successful use of paper strips to represent objects in the event, and her dictation captures the whole story. Troy constructed seemingly unrelated objects, some of which require a label to be recognized. His dictation consists of one or two word names for the objects. There are also differences in fine motor skills, as evidenced by the use of glue and paper.

Choose products because they demonstrate a child's unique approach to a problem or conceptualization of something. Marta, for example, makes intricate patterns with whatever materials she has. Tyler, using the same materials, will create something about favorite

Figure 4–2   *Example of Product*

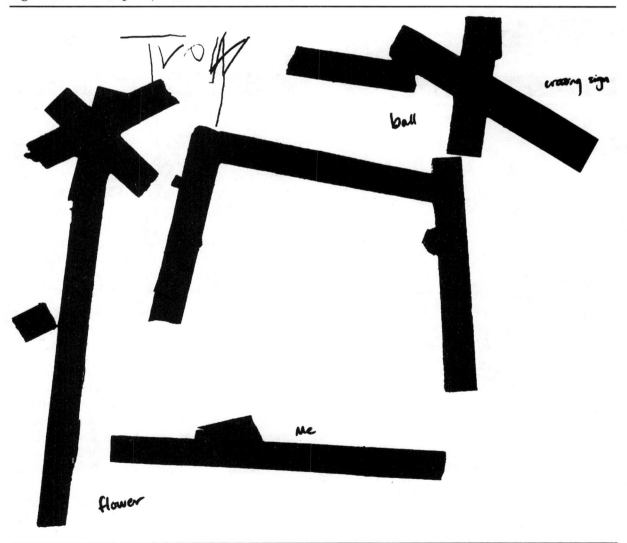

Figure 4–3   *Example of Product*

There was a swimming race and my sister won!

TV shows. See the section on portfolios in Chapter 6 for more ideas on how to choose and organize work products.

- *Set up a system for storing and summarizing products.* Record a child's name, the date, and reason for saving directly on a product or on an entry slip attached to it. Store pieces in chronological order. Cross-reference group products.
- *Avoid making "projective" interpretations of children's artwork.* A "projective" interpretation reads psychological meaning into things such as choice of color or figure drawn. Choice of a particular color may have more to do with the paint available than emotional state.

Eliciting Information from Parents

Information about children from parents usually comes in an information exchange: informal conversations and communications, interviews, conferences, home visits, forms and questionnaires, and involving parents in assessing their own children. All involve one-to-one communication—asking questions, attentive and active listening or reading, and responding. One experienced primary teacher asks parents to come in for interviews early each fall. Parents are pleased to have the opportunity to describe their children, and the teacher learns "parents' views of the child's strengths, any concerns they have, the child's relationships with siblings," and other information. The early interviews also allow her to establish positive relationships with parents. She tape-records the interviews and listens to them before parent–teacher conferences to remind her of parent concerns and views (Evans, 1991, p. 12). Many parents do not realize that family events may influence a child's behavior at school and that a teacher can be more understanding and helpful if he knows what is going on. Let parents know that you would like to know, and why, giving some examples: being up late the night before for a special event, not sleeping well, still recovering from the flu, as well as significant events such as the birth of a baby, moving, illness in the family, divorce, marriage, death, death of a pet, and others. If schools have voice mail or voice messaging, parents can leave a message at any time.

Informal exchanges take many forms and are frequent in a small community or a school where parents bring and pick up their children. In many settings, those brief interludes are the major vehicle for information exchange (Powell, 1989). Have a specified place for exchanging messages to take full advantage of the opportunity. Some schools and centers provide a place for comments on or near the daily sign-in/sign-out notebook or forms. In others, teachers plan the day so they are available to exchange information with parents. Telephone calls help overcome distances when children ride a bus, walk to school, or are dropped off outside. Don't wait until there is a problem. Call one family every day or a given number of families every week, at times that are best for the parent. Communication folders or envelopes carried between home and school by the child can solicit information from parents as well as keep them up to date (see Chapter 10).

A short set of questions calling for written responses can be attached to the school enrollment form and then relayed back to the appropriate classroom. Send questions home in communication folders, newsletters, or as a special request. They can be filled out at kindergarten roundups, back-to-school nights, or parent meetings. Because you want thoughtful responses, allow several days for response. Send forms home ahead of time when parents are to respond during a meeting. Have more available at the meeting. Many teachers send out questions in preparation for parent–teacher conferences. If some parents do not read and write English, questions should be in the home language. If parents are not comfortable writing, discuss the questions face to face.

Some teachers simply ask parents, "What would you like for me to know about your child?" Similar open questions are listed in Figure 4–4.

Many programs have joint teacher–parent goal setting. Parents list what they expect of themselves and the teacher, then respond to prompts such as those shown in Figure 4–5. Parents and teachers keep a copy. At the end of the year, both give their perspectives on how the child has progressed.

Background information on enrollment forms may be helpful or essential, providing details such as previous schools, family composition, custody arrangements, health concerns, and allergies. Such questions are usually "check one," "check all that apply," or short answer.

During parent conferences, telephone calls, and home visits, teachers usually use open and informal interview techniques to obtain general information about children and their families. Sometimes, however, there is a

Figure 4–4   *Examples of Open-Ended Requests to Solicit Information about a Child from Parents*

"What do you hope your child will get out of being in this program?"
"Current play (reading, learning) interests."
"Child's strengths."
"Special needs for us to be aware of."
"Things you do as a family."
"We would like to know about your child's friends and friendships at home and in the neighborhood—ages, what they play, how they get along."
"Other things you would like us to know."

Figure 4–5   *Examples of Items Used for Joint Parent–Teacher Goal Setting*

"I would like to see my child doing more of the following:"
"I would like to see my child doing less of the following:"
"At school, I would like the teacher to help my child with the following:"
"At home I would like to help my child do the following:"
"Ways in which we can work as partners in the child's total education:"
"I would like to know more about my child's . . ."

need for specific information related to a problem or concern. Some teachers describe what they see at school, and then solicit parents' insights, similar experiences at home, and any other information that will help them understand and determine a course of action. Be honest about concerns, but open to parent perceptions and viewpoints.

A different approach to getting information from parents is to have parents do some assessment. The tasks have to be nonthreatening ones that parents and children can do in the home, with clear directions. Include suggestions about sensing when to stop, keeping the tasks casual, and picking appropriate times. Some ideas: Have parents or older children write the names of a child's favorite books as he names them, noting how many were recalled immediately and how many were described by the cover or gist of the contents or looked up. Children who write can do their own. The child can then tell why one or two were his favorites. Figure 4–6 gives examples of ways in which parents can help with assessment.

Figure 4–7 is an example of a reading log that parents and children can keep at home. Parents keep the log for children who are not yet writing. Children dictate their comments. Children who write keep their own log, noting whether parents read the book to them or they read it themselves. Explain and give examples of what goes in the "comments" section. When the page is full, place it in the child's school portfolio with the log kept at school.

Not all parents will cooperate in supplying information about their child, but many will, benefiting everyone. Continued efforts by teachers result in increased parent involvement (Epstein, 1987). The ideas presented here are used with families of all types, income levels, and backgrounds.

Figure 4–6 *Examples of Ways That Parents Can Participate in Assessment*

The teacher can send home a request with directions, any necessary materials, guides that might be helpful, and directions for what and how to return information to school or center. Ideas for parent participation follow.

Interview the child about information to be used in planning for a unit.
"What are your favorite things to do at school? Least favorite?"
"What are your favorite things to do at home? Least favorite?"
"What are your favorite television shows (books, computer games, sports, and so forth)? Why?"
"What is your favorite thing to eat? Tell me how to make it and I will write it down."
"What are some things you are learning (have learned) at school?" (Use only if the school is making an effort to help children become aware of and remember what they are learning. Use for both short-term and long-term memory.)

Tape-record the youngster reading to them at home, to get reading samples for portfolios.

Help child keep a log of books read to the child and books the child reads independently.

Answer teacher-prepared questions about homework, noting type of help the parent gave the child:
"How long did the assignment take?"
"How difficult was the assignment? Easy? About right? Difficult?"

Note study habits the child needs help with.

Advantages of Eliciting Information from Parents

1. It sets up a way for parents to share their insights, and lets them know you want their perspective.
2. Parents involved in helping with assessment will also learn about their children and goals for the classroom.

Disadvantages of Eliciting Information from Parents

1. Reactions to parents who don't respond or respond negatively may bias your attitude toward the child.
2. Some parents may be uncomfortable assessing their own child and sharing that information.

Recommended Procedures for Eliciting Information from Parents

- *Have several ways for parents to get information to you.*
- *Help parents know what information would be helpful.*
- *Use sensitive and respectful discussion, interview, and question-asking techniques.*
- *Make communication with parents a two-way process.*
- *Let parents know how information will be used.*

Figure 4-7 *Example of a Reading Log to be Kept at Home*

Name _____ Date _____

READING LOG

| Name of Book | Dates | | Comments* |
	Start	Finish	

Home or School
(Circle One)

* Comments can be impressions, opinions, reactions to the book or writing; relating events in the book to prior knowledge or experience; reflections on the meaning of the book, or other personal reactions. Use as many lines as you need.

Contexts for Assessment

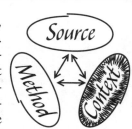

The context or setting is defined by tangible factors in the environment, such as physical space or people (Bentzen, 1992; Boehm & Weinberg, 1987). It has a powerful effect on children and adults; any variations affect the outcome of assessment and influence the type of behavior and interaction that occurs (Barker, 1968). The context can increase child motivation and personal involvement, which, in turn, affect the complexity and maturity of responses (Cazden, 1972). Behavior in an interesting, involving activity will be different from behavior in an uninteresting activity. Likewise, if a child feels at ease in a setting, he will do better. Anxiety in an unfamiliar, strange situation may cause uncooperative behavior, such as acting silly or refusing to respond. Context is a key factor in determining how a child will act (Bodrova & Leong, 1996). Systematically change contexts to get authentic assessment.

Consider the following factors when choosing a context for assessment: physical space, materials, activities, people, and amount of teacher structure.

Characteristics of the Context

Physical Space.   The arrangement of physical space can increase the frequency of certain behavior and minimize distractions. For instance, put climbing equipment in a line to increase the likelihood that children will use the pieces in sequence and will climb, swing, and balance. Also, children are less apt to interrupt each other's progress if there is an implied order.

Materials.   Adding new materials or changing the ones normally present will affect assessment. A new book in the reading area, new mystery rocks at the science table, or other subtle variations often produce changes in behavior. Adding one or two props in the dramatic play area may encourage a child to join in who would not ordinarily do so.

Activities.   Activities have a direct impact on behavior. More large muscle skills are observed in certain activities, such as outdoor play, a game of tag, or a movement activity, whereas artistic behavior occurs more in others. Pick activities that are sufficiently involving and interesting. Activities that are a usual part of the classroom may be too familiar to elicit interest and involvement. To attain the level of involvement and interest necessary for a good assessment, modify familiar activities. Sometimes activities not commonly associated with a specific behavior are novel enough to increase child interest. For example, counting jumps in an outdoor activity may be more involving and interesting than the usual counting tasks with manipulatives.

For children younger than age 7, the activity most likely to elicit complex and mature behavior is play (Bodrova & Leong, 1996). Watch the child when she is playing or pretending. Perhaps a child cannot sit and listen while the teacher reads a story to the group. However, when she is playing school with a friend who pretends to read, she can listen attentively for ten minutes.

People.   Child behavior is also influenced by the number of people present and who they are—friends, peers, adults. Group behavior is more than the sum of individual behavior—a complicated dynamic exists within the group, influencing social interaction. The personality, interests, and behavior of each individual influence the functioning of the whole. For example, a child's academic ability and social status may influence participation in cooperative groups. At the same time, group interaction affects individual behavior. Stacy's strong desire to have other children do what she want influences group interaction. She makes constant efforts to get children to play her way, dominates conversations, and tries to keep other children from talking. Stacy's behavior in turn is influenced by Jason, who follows her lead, and Marta, who resists. Subgroups within a larger group also have an effect on interaction, such as when two best friends dominate a cooperative learning group by constantly rejecting other children's suggestions.

Amount of Teacher Structure.   Contexts range from those with little teacher intervention to structured settings where teachers directly modify and control the environment. In most assessments, teachers provide some sort of structure, ranging from putting out new materials, to organizing an activity, to participating in activities. For informal classroom assessments, it is helpful to think of distinctions in terms of the amount of teacher structure—materials introduced or activities planned. Structured activities flow with normal classroom interaction patterns and are not noticeably different from them. To observe cooperative behavior, set up a cooperative game. During the game, you will see more examples of cooperation than usual, yet children view the game as a normal part of classroom life.

Examples of Contexts for Assessment

Many contexts lend themselves to assessment. Some are obvious, such as using the manipulatives area to assess small motor development or the book area for literacy skills. Others are overlooked, although they are excellent contexts for appraisal. Consider the following:

1. *Daily routines.* Assess during snack, cleanup, lunchtime, transitions, and other daily routines.
2. *Outdoors.* Watch children as they play in organized games or alone. Many aspects of development can be observed, including large muscle, social, and cognitive problem solving.
3. *Dramatic play.* Dramatic play can be a context for assessing social, language, and cognitive development, as well as fine motor skills.
4. *Learning centers.* Children can be assessed or assess themselves as they work in learning centers. By collecting learning center products, the teacher has a record of what the children have done. Children who read and write can be taught to assess themselves by filling out charts and rating scales, or by tape-recording comments.
5. *Classroom meetings or large groups.* An often overlooked context for assessment occurs when the class gathers together. Teachers can

assess group functioning and individual participation as well as specific knowledge and skills.

6. *Cooperative group activities.* Cooperative groups are the ideal context for assessing the social and content goals for those groups.

Recommended Procedures for Selecting Contexts

- *Make sure children feel at ease.*
- *Think about each factor in the setting separately: physical space, materials, activities, people, and amount of teacher structure.*
- *Use physical space to increase desired behaviors and minimize distractions.*
- *Do not use distracting materials.*
- *Make the context interesting enough to engage children.*
- *Remember that the size and composition of the group influence interaction.*
- *Remember that the addition or subtraction of one member of a group will change interaction.*

Choosing the Appropriate Assessment Window

Because so many possible combinations of sources, methods, and settings exist in an early childhood classroom, a teacher can vary the assessment window often. As you decide which combination to use, consider the following:

1. Identify the behavior to be assessed.
2. Use authentic assessment windows.
3. Maximize the frequency or chance of seeing behavior.
4. Use multiple sources, methods, and settings.

Identify the Behavior to Be Assessed

The focus behavior guides the choice of a source, method, and setting, so describe, as explicitly as possible, the behavior you have decided to assess (see Chapter 3) and what you want to learn about it.

Two illustrations clarify this: If a teacher is interested in how children function in small groups during dramatic play, he should choose the group as the source of information. Systematic observation is a good method for assessing social interaction because it can be done without interfering with group dynamics. To pick the best context, the teacher must consider the number of children, materials, and composition of the group, such as ages and friendships of members.

Next, if "using inches, feet, and yards to measure" is the focus behavior, the most authentic source of information is the child. The best method of assessment is eliciting information in a performance task so the teacher can focus attention on specific facts and behaviors. Any context where children can demonstrate these skills would be good, such as measuring the sidewalk, crackers at snack, or objects to be used in a cooperative construction.

Use Authentic Assessment Windows

Consider whether the source, method, and setting will produce an authentic assessment. The assessment window must be a direct measure of responses to real, practical challenges. Use direct sources of information, except when you cannot obtain information from the child or group or when the attitudes and opinions of parents and other adults are your focus. If you are assessing a behavior that usually occurs in a specific context, use that context. Obviously, an authentic assessment of cooperative learning is a cooperative learning activity. Although cooperation also occurs in dramatic play, it is not the same kind that takes place in cooperative learning. Appraisals should tap the identified behavior as directly as possible.

Maximize the Chances of Seeing a Behavior

Assessment windows should maximize the chance of seeing focus behaviors. To determine how many children can classify objects by one attribute, choose activities in which children sort and classify objects. One person or source may see behavior more frequently than another source; for instance, the playground supervisor sees more gross motor behavior than the reading specialist. Certain settings tend to restrict interaction and limit the type of behavior. Spontaneous play happens more often during dramatic play than in a teacher-directed activity. Certain activities are more engaging and elicit better, more reliable samples of behavior. Contexts can affect motivation—children might be more motivated to add during a toss–catch and answer session than during a paper-and-pencil test.

Use Multiple Assessment Windows

Multiple assessment windows ensure a richer, more balanced picture of a child. Using multiple assessment windows to gather information improves reliability and validity for the entire process (Airasian, 1994; Sattler, 1992). Any weaknesses of a particular source and method will be offset by the strengths of others.

No formula exists for deciding how many different assessment windows are necessary. Teachers must use their own judgment. Consider the following general guidelines:

- To assess progress validly, at least two assessment windows must be similar. A drawing collected at the beginning of the year should be compared with a drawing collected later, not with a painting. Compare the same skills or behaviors in a similar context.
- Whether or not a window is overused depends partly on the total number of appraisals being made. If five samples of problem solving will be collected, make sure no more than two or three of them come from the same source, method, or setting. If ten assessments will be made, then three or four of the same method are acceptable.

As a guide, look at the total number of times data will be collected; the more data collected, the more assessments can be from similar windows.

Summary

Implementation of assessment begins with the choice of an assessment window—the source, method, and context used to gather information. In early childhood classrooms, sources of information are the child, parents, other adults, and written records. Methods of gathering information include systematic observation, eliciting responses from children, and collecting and analyzing products of classroom activities. Contexts are defined by physical space, materials, activities, and people present during assessment.

Assessment windows are created by combining sources, methods, and settings. Several criteria are useful in choosing the most appropriate combination. Windows must be chosen to fit the purpose of assessment and should be authentic. The source, method, and context should maximize the chances of seeing the behavior. Finally, use a variety of windows and avoid overdependence on one source, method, or context.

For Further Study, Discussion, and Reflection

1. Teachers often have strong opinions about studying written records made by other people as a source of information about children. Examine your own beliefs about written records. What are some of the reasons for those beliefs?
2. Mr. Lee is interested in finding out how many of his children can count by 1s, 2s, and 5s. Identify three different assessment windows to gather the information. Explain your choice of sources, methods, and settings.
3. Mr. Bonatti wants to know if Marcia exhibits the same amount of physical and verbal aggression in other settings as she does in the classroom. Identify three possible sources, methods, and settings for obtaining this information. Explain your choices.
4. Write convergent and divergent questions or statements calling for a response about a book a child has just read. Write a question or statement at the receptive and expressive levels about a concept. Write a question or statement at the recall and recognition levels about the concept of an insect. Use Bloom's Taxonomy to develop questions and statements about the concept of food.

Suggested Readings

Airasian, P. W. (1994). *Classroom assessment.* New York: McGraw-Hill.
Bentzen, W. R. (1992). *Seeing young children: A guide to observing and recording behavior* (2nd ed.). New York: Delmar Publishers.

Boehm, A. E., & Weinberg, R. A. (1987). *The classroom observer: A guide for developing observation skills.* New York: Teachers College Press.

Cartwright, C. A., & Cartwright, G. P. (1984). *Developing observation skills.* (2nd ed.). New York: McGraw-Hill.

Irwin, D. M., & Bushnell, M. M. (1980). *Observational strategies for child study.* New York: Holt, Rinehart and Winston.

Stenmark, J. K. (1991). *Mathematics assessment: Myths, models, good questions, and practical suggestions.* Reston, VA: National Council of Teachers of Mathematics.

CHAPTER FIVE

Documenting: Recording Information

Information collected and recorded during an appraisal is the original assessment record or primary data record (Engel, 1990). Accurate and complete primary data records are essential to ensure the trustworthiness of information. Such records preserve information so it can be consulted, studied, and combined with other data to show progress, reveal patterns, and provide perspective that may be lacking in daily interactions with children. Records of what children have done and learned are the basis for communicating with other people. Teachers depend on records to help them remember what children know and can do (Leong, McAfee, & Swedlow, 1992). During an average school day, teachers have 1,500 interactions with children (Billups & Rauth, 1987); they cannot rely on memory.

Recording information in a systematic way helps focus attention on each child's development, on important educational targets, and on the way authentic assessment and good instruction are linked. The discipline of documenting—collecting and recording information—makes us better observers and teachers.

Figure 5–1 *Comparison of Information Recorded as a Description, Count, and Record of Inferences*

Description	Count or Tally	Record of Inferences
Standing in front of class, C says with a loud voice as she points to each word in her journal, "My Friend Jana."	3/12/9— reads dictated story 3/12/9— points to words while reading 3/12/9— speaks with confidence	Shows confidence 1 3 ⑤ Enjoys writing 1 ③ 5 Enjoys reading 1 ③ 5

Teachers and researchers have developed a bewildering array of recording techniques that we can group into three basic types:

1. Those that describe
2. Those that count, time, or tally
3. Those that record inferences, judgments, and reflections

Combining these techniques expands the options. Use these groupings to help you sort through the choices and weigh which one is most appropriate.

Any behavior can be recorded in several ways: as a description of what occurred, as a count or tally of behavior, or as an inference about what occurred. Descriptive records are "pictures" of a behavior that are written, drawn, photographed, or tape-recorded, such as anecdotal records, jottings, or sketches. Counts or tallies save information by noting the number of times a behavior or item occurs, usually on a checklist of some type. Inferences record the teacher's impression, judgment, or evaluation of events, work products, or behavior on a rating scale or rubric, or with comments. Figure 5–1 compares the information from one incident, recorded using the three procedures: describing, counting, and recording inferences.

We include only basic recording tools that are feasible for teachers to use and encourage you to vary them and use others to meet your own recording needs. Current word-processing programs make it easy to develop forms tailored to a specific need.

This chapter is divided into two sections: (1) guidelines for selecting a recording procedure and (2) survey, description, and examples of recording procedures.

Guidelines for Selecting a Recording Procedure

The appropriateness of a recording procedure depends on the following:

1. Purpose of the assessment
2. What is being assessed?
3. Amount of detail
4. Practical considerations

Purpose of the Assessment

Whether teachers describe, count, or record inferences depends on how a record will be used. Descriptive records may be best if the purpose is to share information with parents. For a teacher's use, a count or tally may suffice. A program or school may mandate the type of records needed for certain uses, such as referral.

What is Being Assessed?

Certain behaviors and products are best captured by a description, others by counts or records of inferences. The most appropriate way to preserve what a child says is to record the actual words. A count is a good way to keep track of the number of times a child participates in group discussion or the presence or absence of skills and subskills. Attitudes and dispositions may be documented in a record of inferences or can be inferred from descriptions and tallies.

Amount of Detail

Records capture varying levels of detail or amounts of raw information. Writing down exactly "who said what" and "who did what" preserves more detail than "had an argument." Tallying discrete units of behavior, such as appropriate and inappropriate initiations and responses to other children, preserves more detail than a tally of "social interaction" as one broad category.

The amount and type of detail needed depend on how a record will be used and the area of development or curriculum assessed. Records that document problems and concerns, or for determining program placement, should contain as many specific details as possible about important behaviors. Detail may be less significant for everyday planning. Focus description on those aspects of performance that are relevant. For example, knowing a child pronounced "Robert" as "Wobert" is significant when appraising language development, but less so when examining motor development.

More detail is not always better. Detail usually increases the time needed to prepare the recording form, to make the record, or to analyze it later. Superfluous, unnecessary detail is distracting and makes recording more laborious and time consuming. In documenting if a child understands how to measure time, the way she is standing and whom she is talking with are not important. On the other hand, too little detail makes a record inaccurate, so to note only the child's understanding of minutes would leave out important information about hours and other time concepts.

Teachers can adjust recording procedures to fit the level of detail needed. Descriptive records are easiest to adjust—write or draw more or fewer details or take more or fewer pictures. Since they require little preparation, these adjustments can be made during recording. Increase the detail of tallies by counting smaller subcategories, components of skills, or units of behavior. Instead of counting "prosocial" behavior, count the number of appropriate and inappropriate initiations to others, number of responses to other children, and number of social conflicts resolved successfully. Because tallied behaviors are identified before assessment starts, adjustments to procedures will be difficult to make while recording.

Practical Considerations

Teachers must weigh practical considerations when selecting a recording procedure. These include preparation time, amount of attention needed to record data, and whether to use group or individual records.

Preparation Time versus Recording Time. Some procedures require much preparation time before assessment starts, but take less time to record. Rating scales and rubrics take lots of time to prepare, especially those designed to be used by people other than the teacher. Items must be carefully phrased, and the scale must be developed. Counting and tallying procedures also require preparation to identify behaviors, determine the level of detail, develop descriptions of what will be observed, and prepare recording forms. Recording on rating scales, counts, and tallies is quick—a circle, a check, or a tick mark.

Procedures that require little preparation, such as jottings, anecdotal records, and narrative descriptions, take more time to record. The recorder must have enough time to write the information, not just check or circle an item.

There are trade-offs either way. Think through the time available for recording during class. If you have sufficient time to make detailed recordings in the classroom, then those procedures may be best. On the other hand, when classroom time is limited, invest the time in preparation so that you keep recording during class at a minimum.

Amount of Attention Needed to Record Data. Procedures that require a teacher's total focus for recording information are difficult if not impossible without the presence of other adults helping in the classroom. For example, to write an accurate descriptive narrative of group interaction in a complicated project, one person must do nothing but record. Procedures requiring moderate amounts of teacher attention can be done without the aid of other adults if teachers are interacting intermittently with children. During an art activity, the teacher interacts with children, steps back to make short notes describing fine motor coordination, and then returns. Making a record becomes part of the flow of interaction. Since some procedures require only making a mark or pushing a clicker, a teacher can record as he talks and works with children. For instance, as a teacher leads a group discussion, he can check names of children who participate.

Procedures recorded outside of classroom time do not take time away from teaching but rely on teacher memory, which may or may not be accurate. An example is an anecdotal record written at the end of the day about a dispute that happened just before lunch. The many events between lunch and three o'clock will make remembering the details of that incident difficult. Do not depend on these procedures to record important classroom information, but use them as a supplement to normal recording procedures.

Consider classroom resources when choosing a procedure. If an aide or another adult is present, attention-intensive techniques will be feasible. Teachers who don't have extra help may opt for procedures that can be used while teaching or interacting intermittently (see Figure 5–2).

Group versus Individual Records.   Information for all the children in a group can be recorded so that the whole group's achievements can be seen quickly; usually one sheet of paper suffices, or each child can have a separate record. Although both types are used in most classrooms, practical considerations limit the number of separate individual records a teacher can make.

Concisely recorded and displayed information about each child in the class is called a *group matrix record* (see Figure 5–3, and Figure 5–11 on page 87). Group matrices are the most efficient way to document appraisals of all the children in a classroom. One group record can display data collected during one or several appraisals, done at one time or spread over a period of time. It can also serve several purposes: primary data record, a list of who has and has not been assessed on that item, and a group profile or summary (see Chapter 6).

Individual records document one child's performance or behavior. They usually are used for unique or in-depth information about a child or small group (see Figure 5–4, and Figures 5–5 and 5–8 on pages 78 and 81). To get a picture of the group as a whole, the information has to be transferred to a group profile or summary, which requires another step.

Practical considerations suggest that when the knowledge or behavior under consideration lends itself to a group record, that might be a wise choice.

Figure 5–2   *When Recording Procedures Can Be Used*

Procedures Difficult to Use While Interacting	Descriptive narratives Anecdotal records made while behavior is occurring
Procedures Easy to Use When Interacting Intermittently	Jottings Diagrams, sketches, pictures Rating scales Duration counts Time samples
Procedures Easy to Use When Interacting	Checklists Participation charts Frequency counts Audiotapes Videotapes Collecting work products
Procedures Recorded Outside of Classroom Time	Anecdotes recorded after behavior has occurred Teacher journals and logs Computer tracking systems

Figure 5–3   *Example of a Form for a Group Matrix Record*

Item(s) *Emergent Reading*   Date 4/ 12 / 9

Group *Entire Class*

Observer *Thomas*

	Ashamet, J	Bianco, A	Bonilla, C	Chang, K	Cisan, P	Cloos, C	Feren, D				
Identifies a Rhyme											
Gives a rhyming word											
Knows initial sounds											
Ball Bat Big											
Sell Sat Said											
Toy Top Tim											
Uses picture cues											
Self corrects word											
Comprehends word											
Can recount information											

Figure 5–4 *Example of an Individual Record*

Items: Cognitive Development

Child: M. Harvey   Date: 1/27/9- — 8/2/9-

Memory:

Said "I put it in my memory bank," as he touched his
forehead. 2/2/9_

Observed M repeating the words of the song to himself after
the song was over. 2/25/9_ (Good example of practice)

During classification activity, M repeats the "big and small"
in a sing-song voice over and over as he puts the objects in
the groups. Was able to group 15 objects into big and small
red circles and big and small green circles. 2/26/9_

Survey, Description, and Examples of Recording Procedures

This section presents selected recording procedures useful in early child-hood settings:

1. Procedures that describe
2. Procedures that count
3. Procedures that record inferences, judgments, and reflections

Recording Procedures That Describe

Procedures that describe preserve raw data in a form that is closest to what actually happened, in the following ways:

1. Narrative records
2. Jottings
3. Diagrams, sketches, and photographs
4. Audiotapes and videotapes

Narrative Records: Descriptive Narratives and Anecdotal Records.
Narrative records are detailed, storylike descriptions of what occurred. The two types of narrative records are descriptive narratives and anecdotal records.

Sometimes called *running records, specimen descriptions,* or *specimen records,* descriptive narratives are more detailed than anecdotal records. They include the same amount of information as a videotape—a continuous written record of everything said or done during the assessment. They are written as the behavior is observed. When used to document systematic observation, they may include many types of behavior and activities, as well as many children and adults. They may be used to document verbatim responses in interviews (see Figure 5–5).

Anecdotal records are focused narrative accounts of a specific event (Bentzen, 1992; Goodwin & Driscoll, 1980; Irwin & Bushnell, 1980). They are used to document unique behaviors and skills of a child or a small group of children. Anecdotal records may be written as behavior occurs or at a later time (see Figure 5–6).

Advantages of Narrative Records

1. They preserve the detail and sequence of events.
2. They require a minimum of equipment and preparation.

Disadvantages of Narrative Records

1. They take more time and attention to record than other methods and can inhibit interaction with children.
2. Anecdotal records recorded several hours after the assessment may be unreliable.

Specific Recommendations for Narrative Records

- *Describe exactly what you see and hear; don't summarize behavior.* Use words conveying exactly what a child says and does. Record what a child did when playing firefighter or solving the problem: "He put on a firefighter's hat and said, 'Let's save someone!' " or "F

Figure 5–5   *A Descriptive Narrative Record*

Items: <u>Socio-dramatic play</u>

Child <u>M. Pierce & D. Smits</u>   Date <u>5/12/9</u> – Time <u>10:00 am</u>

Observer <u>Franklin</u>   Setting <u>dramatic play area</u>

Marica and Dolores are standing next to the sink. Dolores
hands Marica an apron. They both tie the aprons around their
necks like capes. Dolores grabs the yellow mop and Marica
takes a purse. Dolores begins to march around the room.
"Follow me everybody," she says, pushing the broom up and down
like a majorette. Marica, still in the dramatic play area,
starts addressing an empty chair. "You have been sooooooo bad.
I'm going to make you eat mushy mushy mush mush. Here." She
walks back to the sink, turns several pots over, rummages
around. Dolores returns--holding Kathy's hand, and says to
Kathy, "You come play with us, O.K.? We need a baby. Want to
be it?" Kathy looks away toward the sink, and lets go of
Dolores' hand, and says "What is this?" . . . .

Notes/Interpretation:

Few roles. Talk is primarily statements. Beginning to assign
roles.

Figure 5–6   *An Anecdotal Record*

Items: <u>Social Interaction</u>

Child <u>**Martinez, L & Wong, B**</u>   Date <u>9/15/9–</u> Time <u>2:30 pm</u>

Observer <u>Montoya</u>   Setting <u>Child selected</u>

Leslie and Brian are playing in the science area. Leslie says, "Let's see what happens when we mix yellow with blue." Brian says, "Let's dress up first. Can I be the Daddy?" Leslie puts a drop of the yellow water on the dish and adds a drop of blue. She says, "O.K. I would do that." They leave the science area and go on to housekeeping. Leslie puts on a big hat and Brian puts on a firefighter's hat and grabs a purse. They both sit down in the rocking chair. Brian says, "I know, I will drop you off on my way to work. Then you call me from your office."

Notes/Interpretation:

This is the first time Leslie has allowed Brian to take the lead in the interaction. Until now, she has dominated the play.

Looks at PP (puzzle piece) & looks at P (puzzle). Puts PP on & slides with one hand. PP drops in."

- *Interpret anecdotal records written after the event with caution because the recorder's memory may not be reliable.* When possible, record anecdotal records as information is collected.

Jottings.   Jottings are condensed accounts or short notes about significant aspects or characteristics of a behavior. They take less time to write than descriptive narratives and anecdotal records but contain the same important details.

Jottings are a flexible, popular recording technique. They can be made quickly between direct interactions with children. They preserve detailed information in a small space and can be used in a group matrix. Jottings are often added to products from the classroom to provide supplemental information.

Document relevant aspects of a behavior and skill by writing in phrases, leaving out unimportant words, and using abbreviations. An example of a jotting is: "Runs around obj. easily, arms balanced, jumps rope, attempts jumping jacks." Figure 5–7 shows a typical way of recording jottings for groups of children. A teacher must be familiar with the behavior or skill being assessed so that significant elements are identified.

Advantages of Jottings

1. Jottings are quick and simple.
2. They can be used to add supplemental information on products.
3. They can be recorded on a group matrix, preserving the details of information but allowing more than one child's behavior and a number of different goals or developmental areas to be recorded on one sheet of paper.

Figure 5–7 *A Record Using Jottings*

Items: <u>Counting skills</u>

Group <u>PM Kindergarten</u>   Date <u>1/5/9–</u> to <u>4/10/9–</u>

Observer <u>Wong</u>

Name	Rote	Meaningful	Notes:
Beck, A.	1/22/9_ To 5 no errors 5–10 w/ prompt	3/25/9_ To 3 Prompts not used	
Benny, D.	1/22/9_ To 20 no errors To 50 w/prompts	2/22/9_ To 20 no errors To 50 w/prompts	Has number conservation for 3, 4, & 5

Disadvantages of Jottings

1. Jottings that are too brief can be unreliable.
2. When teachers are unfamiliar with a behavior, significant elements may be missed.

Specific Recommendations for Jottings

- *When jottings are used to supplement other information, place them in a specific place on the record.* For example, place jottings describing how children constructed a block design on a separate sheet of paper attached to the sketch of the design, or write them directly on the product in a consistent place.
- *Keep jottings in chronological order.* Write the jottings so that you can distinguish the order of events.

Diagrams, Sketches, and Photographs. Not all records have to be in written form. Diagrams, sketches, and photographs preserve important details of products and processes otherwise requiring lengthy written descriptions. Older children can sketch and take pictures of their own work. Figure 5–8 is a teacher's sketch of a child's block construction. Figure 5–9 on page 82 is a sketch a kindergarten child did of his own block construction.

A special type of diagram used to record children's knowledge and learning about a concept or process is called a *web, semantic map,* or an *idea map.* Webs and semantic maps document one child's thinking or the ideas of a group. Children are asked to state what they know about a specific topic or idea. As ideas emerge, the teacher asks questions to find out what a child means by an idea and to find out the relationship between ideas. For example, when a child says, "Insects are alive," the teacher may ask, "What does alive mean?" or "How do you know they are alive?" Correct information and misconceptions are both recorded. Like ideas are placed in relationship to each other in a diagram, forming a web of ideas

Figure 5–8 *An Example of a Diagram/Sketch Made by the Teacher of a Child's Block Construction*

Items(s): <u>Small block Construction</u>

Child <u>Morgan, T</u>   Date <u>5/14/9–</u> Time <u>9:00</u>

Observer <u>Schulhammer</u>   Setting <u>Manipulatives</u>

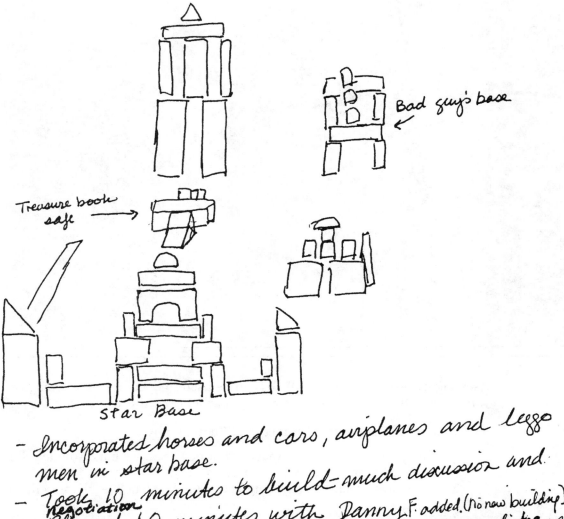

- Incorporated horses and cars, airplanes and lego men in star base.
- Took 10 minutes to build—much discussion and negotiation.
- Played 10 minutes with Danny F. added. (no new building)
  Discussed play in detail. "Star base to save the great treasure book." All three boys played both "good" and "bad" guys. In the end, the good guys saved the treasure book and punished the bad guys who went to prison.

Figure 5–9   *An Example of a Diagram/Sketch Made by a Kindergarten Child of His Own Block Construction*

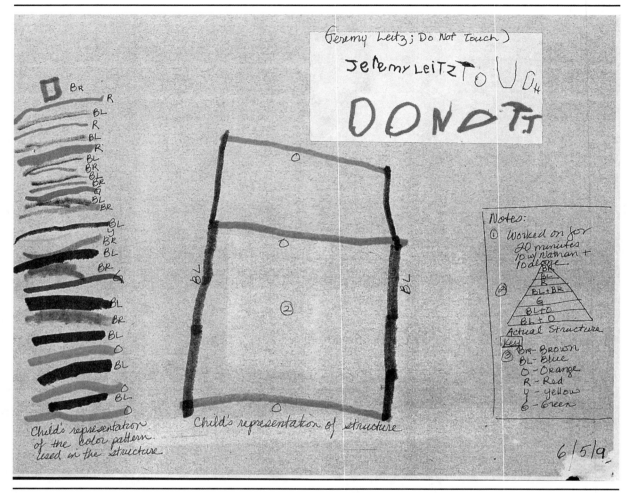

(see Figure 5–10 on page 83). Webs can be used to document knowledge or processes, and they can be recorded by teachers or children.

Advantages of Diagrams, Sketches, and Photographs

1. They capture a product that cannot be saved, such as a model, diorama, display, or block construction.
2. They preserve important details of a process, such as changes made to a design.
3. Sketches and diagrams are quick and easy to complete. Instead of a lengthy description in words, the teacher quickly sketches what she saw. Artistry is less important than accuracy.
4. Webs or idea maps record a child's knowledge base and the relationship between the elements in it.
5. Webs or idea maps are flexible and adaptable and can be used for individual children or groups.

Figure 5–10   *Example of a Web*

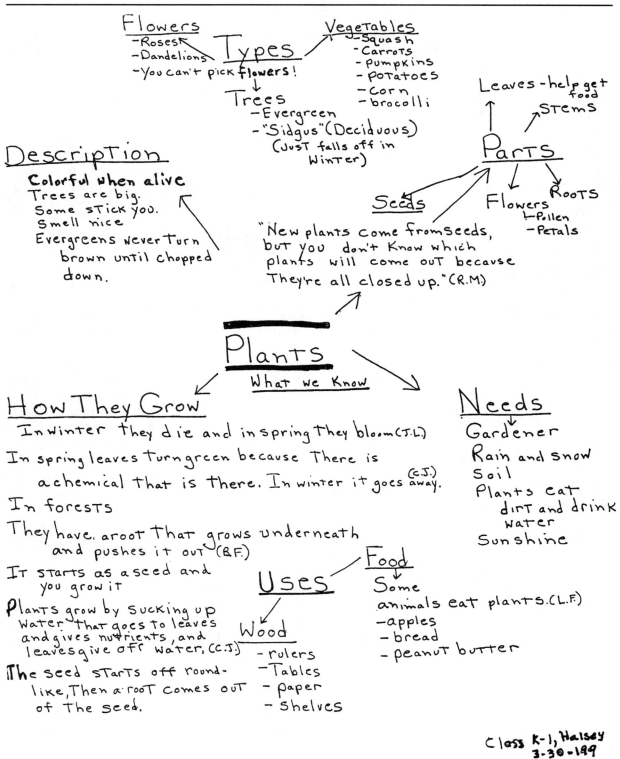

Flowers
- Roses
- Dandelions
- You can't pick flowers!

Types

Vegetables
- Squash
- Carrots
- Pumpkins
- Potatoes
- Corn
- brocolli

Trees
- Evergreen
- "Sidgus" (Deciduous)
  (Just falls off in Winter)

Leaves - help get food
Stems

Parts

Seeds

Flowers
- Pollen
- Petals

Roots

"New plants come from seeds, but you don't know which plants will come out because they're all closed up." (R.M.)

Description

Colorful when alive
Trees are big.
Some stick you.
Smell nice
Evergreens never turn brown until chopped down.

Plants
What we Know

How They Grow
In winter they die and in spring they bloom. (J.L.)
In spring leaves turn green because there is a chemical that is there. In winter it goes away. (C.J.)
In forests
They have a root that grows underneath and pushes it out (B.F.)
It starts as a seed and you grow it
Plants grow by sucking up water that goes to leaves and gives nutrients, and leaves give off water. (C.J.)
The seed starts off round-like, then a root comes out of the seed.

Needs
Gardener
Rain and snow
Soil
Plants eat dirt and drink water
Sunshine

Uses

Food
Some animals eat plants. (L.F.)
- apples
- bread
- peanut butter

Wood
- rulers
- Tables
- paper
- Shelves

Class K-1, Halsey
3-30-199

Disadvantages of Diagrams, Sketches, and Photographs

1. Photographs can be expensive.
2. Young children may have difficulty describing the relationship between different ideas and will require teacher coaching and support to produce a web.

Specific Recommendations for Diagrams, Sketches, and Photographs

- *Use diagrams, sketches, and photographs for classroom products you cannot save.*
- *Use two or three diagrams, sketches, and photographs to record a process.* For example, sketch a child's first attempt to equalize the weights on two sides of a balance, the second attempt, and the final "product."
- *Attach a short note or write directly on the item, explaining why the sketch, diagram, or photograph was made, the date, and other pertinent information.*
- *Develop a set of probing questions to help children generate a web or map of ideas.*
- *Accept correct ideas and misconceptions when generating a web.* If you correct children at this time, they will be less likely to contribute their ideas.

Audiotapes and Videotapes.   Audiotapes and videotapes can capture complex performances that give authentic evidence of the integration and application of learning. Presentations, exhibits, demonstrations, displays, dramatizations, reading aloud, explaining and summarizing a project or investigation, and other integrating activities are candidates for taping. Assessment of needs and progress in oral language and literacy is easier when speech is captured on an audiotape for later analysis (Rhodes & Shanklin, 1992). Use videocassette cameras to preserve both speech and action. A taped record serves as a backup and supplement to other methods of recording. Both methods allow teachers to be included and are a useful, sometimes jolting, record for teacher self-evaluation. Audiotapes are useful for recording parent comments, especially if parents are not comfortable writing information.

Children, teachers, aides, parents, or other adults can audiotape activities in a center, during individual or small group activities, or with the entire class. Adults or older children can run video cameras. In fact, at many school exhibits or class demonstrations, the number of video cameras may almost equal the number of families present.

Advantages of Audiotapes and Videotapes

1. Audiotapes and videotapes are exact recordings of what occurred.
2. They can be listened to or viewed repeatedly by different people.
3. They easily record behaviors that occur too quickly for teachers to make notes (Irwin & Bushnell, 1980), or are too complex to capture in words.

4. They are a backup to other methods of recording information. For example, take notes and at a later time use an audiotape to fill in important details or check the accuracy of a written record.
5. Young children can make and evaluate their own performance on audiotape.
6. Teachers can involve parents in assessment by sending a cassette recorder and audiotape home.
7. Videotape captures the context of a situation, allowing detailed analysis of the setting, interactions, and other variables. It is especially helpful in analyzing problems.

Disadvantages of Audiotapes and Videotapes

1. Audiotapes and videotapes preserve an overwhelming amount of information that teachers must review to find relevant events.
2. Videotaping can disrupt normal interaction until children get used to it.

Specific Recommendations for Audiotapes and Videotapes

*   *Focus audiotapes and videotapes on specific assessment situations.* It is tempting to record "everything" and later sort through information for important kernels of behavior. It may be difficult to locate the exact 15 minutes you intended to capture, and it is time consuming to review tapes.
*   *Set up the video recorder so it is not obtrusive.* Allow enough time for children to become accustomed to having the recorder in the room.
*   *Use other adults—parents, aides, older children—to help you make videotape recordings.*

Recording Procedures That Count or Tally

Counts or tallies preserve information about the presence or absence, frequency or number of occurrences, or duration of a behavior. Good behaviors to tally have an identifiable beginning and end (Cartwright & Cartwright, 1984), such as building a structure or talking. Counts or tallies document expected, anticipated behaviors or products. Behaviors and products are identified before the assessment begins, and a recording form is developed that contains only selected items. For example, during a math assessment, counting and making patterns, both expected behaviors, are placed on the tally record. Unexpected events—those not identified beforehand—would not be recorded. Although a wonderful example of cooperation occurs spontaneously during the math assessment, it would not be recorded on the math tally.

Behaviors must be mutually exclusive or non-overlapping. For example, aggression and hitting overlap since hitting could be counted both as aggression and as hitting. It would be better to use hitting and biting, two mutually exclusive behaviors.

Behavior tallies use either sign systems or category systems (Boehm & Weinberg, 1987; Irwin & Bushnell, 1980). Sign systems are representative of a larger set; a few behaviors that are indicators or *signs* of a skill are appraised instead of every behavior. Being able to hold a pencil is a sign that a child is probably able to hold a crayon, marker, or a watercolor paintbrush.

A category system is exhaustive—all possible behaviors are categorized and recorded. Parten's breakdown of play (Parten, 1933) is a category system that records play behaviors in four categories: solitary, parallel, associative, or cooperative. Time samples and duration samples are used primarily in research or when a specialist is assessing a child. These are the procedures most commonly used in the classroom:

1. Checklists
2. Participation charts
3. Frequency counts

Checklists.   Checklists record the presence or occurrence of behavior and are a practical, flexible way of documenting many types of behaviors, skills, attitudes and dispositions, and even products. They can record inferences or teacher judgments, such as a child's confidence when speaking in front of the group. They preserve information from any area of development—physical, cognitive, and social—or curriculum, such as social studies, science, or art. Because they are so adaptable, they are widely used, especially to record literacy and mathematics skills.

Checklists can originate from instructional objectives or developmental sequences. Items may record specific skills or different levels of performance. For example, a checklist might record a child's ability to recognize, point to, say, or use a concept. Checklists can be used to note a child's attitudes and dispositions.

Once set up, checklists can be modified to fit specific classroom needs and to collect information from an individual or groups. Checklists can be filled out gradually; not all children have to be assessed at the same time. Also, checklists can document appraisals made at different times and thus create a progress record.

Figure 5–11 is an example of a group checklist using a grid system adapted from Golden & Kutner (1986). Figure 5–12 is an example of a published developmental checklist.

The way a checklist is marked can increase its value in the classroom. Some teachers mark only presence of a behavior. Others develop detailed coding schemes to record different types of information simultaneously, such as:

- *Items attained or mastered.* Mark checklists used only once with a check, X, or yes/no. Ongoing checklists completed over several days should be marked with the date the child performed the item.
- *Items performed partially or at different levels of performance.* Some teachers use a slash for beginning level and make the / into an X when the child masters the item. Others use B for beginning or P for partial. Still others highlight the blank with a special color indicating partial achievement and write over the highlighting the date the child achieves mastery.

Figure 5–11   *Checklist for Recording Individual Performance on a Group Record*

Item _Relative Size_   Date _4/20/9–_
Observer _M. Sena_   Group _King Prekindergarten_

Key:
U in upper left of cell = understands ("Point to," "Pick up....")
S in lower right = says ("What size," length, etc.)

Name	Big	Little	Large	Small	Tall	Short	Long	Short	Wide	Narrow	Broad		
Askamit, Jay													
Bianco, Angie													
Bonilla, Carly													
Chang, Kanji													
Cison, Paige													
Cloos, Cory													
Ferem, David													
Ganse, Amber													
Govene, Kelley													
Jaramillo, Jo													
Juel, Noah													
King, Taylor													
Kostiuk, B.J.													
Larson, Megan													
Lee, Jana													
Martinez, Carlos													
Medina, Luan													
Yamashita, Steve													

Figure 5–12   *Example of a Published Developmental Checklist*

SOCIAL-EMOTIONAL

Social-Emotional Expressing feelings and interacting with others. This includes, among other characteristics, expressing and controlling feelings, cooperating with others, showing social awareness, self-concept development, relationship to parents and relationship to adults in general.

Social-Emotional		Date: _____ Occurs Occasionally	Occurs Consistently	Date: _____ Occurs Occasionally	Occurs Consistently	Date: _____ Occurs Occasionally	Occurs Consistently	Date: _____ Occurs Occasionally	Occurs Consistently
1. Identifies Body Parts	Points on request to face, arm, leg or foot.								
2. Shows Feelings	Smiles and shows other appropriate emotional responses.								
3. Separates from Parents	Separates from parent without reluctance.								
4. Relates to Adults	Calls by name two adults on staff; relates positively to adults but is not overly dependent.								
5. Interacts with Children	Talks comfortably with other children.								
6. Seeks New Experiences	Eager for and seeks out new activities and experiences; exhibits curiosity.								
7. Maintains Interest	Maintains interest in play activity without encouragement from an adult.								
8. Plays Cooperatively	Plays cooperatively in groups of three or four children.								
9. Modulates Voice	Controls volume of speech when directed and when participating in singing and language games.								

- *Items a child attempted but could not perform appropriately.* Many teachers use a special code, such as a circle, or highlight the blank with a specific color. If the child performs the behavior or skill later, they write the date over the code or highlighted blank.
- *Items not assessed because a child was absent or the target behavior was not observed.* Use a blank (no mark) or a special code, such as *A* for absent or *N/O* for not observed.
- *The quality of a child's performance.* Incorporate the use of codes that characterize a child's behavior. For example, *R* for the use of representation in a drawing and *L* for when letters or "writing" was included. You can also make a separate column for comments.

Advantages of Checklists

1. Large amounts of information are recorded quickly.
2. Checklists are flexible and versatile. They are easily analyzed, interpreted, and quantified.
3. Other people, such as aides, can be trained to use checklists.
4. Checklists do not have to be completed in the day or week they are begun; they are ongoing.
5. Checklists keep track of a child's progress as well as achievement at a specific time.

Disadvantages of Checklists

1. Checklists that contain only a limited number of representative items must be interpreted cautiously.
2. They may oversimplify complex behavior and learning.

Specific Recommendations for Using Checklists

- *Group like items and put them in sequence if appropriate.* Leave spaces between groups.
- *When possible, break behaviors into subskills, levels, or steps. List each separately.* Such a breakdown will give more information about the child's behavior. Do not use "knows numerals" as an item. Break it down into:
  _____ points to or places fingers around a numeral when asked
  _____ says name of numeral when asked
  _____ volunteers name of numeral
- *State items in the positive to avoid confusion.* For example, use:
  _____ Jumps on right foot and _____ jumps on left foot. Do not use _____ doesn't jump on left foot.
- *Choose representative items that are important indicators.* When using developmental sequences to select items, choose a few below and above what would be expected for children in your classroom.
- *Decide on and use a consistent marking system.* Changing systems from assessment to assessment is confusing.

Participation Charts.   Participation charts can record both the quantity and quality of participation. They can document that a child joins in, the number of times and activities involved, and the quality of a child's contributions. Participation charts can be recorded by the teacher, other adults, or the children.

A participation chart highlights different participation rates and provides insight into children's preferences, dispositions, and patterns of participation. A chart filled in over several days will show a child's preferred activity pattern. For example, over one week, Leigh worked exclusively in the manipulatives or science areas during free choice time and did not engage in any art activities. Participation charts can document the degree and quality of engagement in group discussions or cooperative learning activities, such as whether a child's contributions are relevant, irrelevant, or disruptive. Participation charts also identify activities or areas of the room that are overutilized or underutilized. They clearly document the teacher's pattern of communication, such as a tendency to solicit or favor comments and contributions from a few children rather than all. Participation charts called *room scans* record which areas children are involved in at different times of the day (see Figure 5–13).

Mark or place the child's name or initials next to the area or activity. When participation can occur several times, as in group discussions, use multiple tally marks to record the number of times a child participates. Codes document the quality of participation, such as *R* for relevant, *I* for irrelevant, and *D* for disruptive. Figure 5–14 shows a child-recorded participation chart, and Figure 5–15 shows a chart recorded by a teacher.

Advantages of Participation Charts

1. They are a simple, quick, flexible way of recording quantity and quality of participation.
2. Children can report on their own participation.

Disadvantages of Participation Charts

1. The rate of participation may not necessarily reflect how much a child is learning. A child who is observing and listening might be absorbing as much as the children who are talking or doing.
2. They may give the impression that participation is the child's responsibility, when it is a complex performance influenced by many factors.

Specific Recommendations for Participation Charts

- *Put the participation chart in the area being observed.*
- *For child-recorded participation charts, teach children how to make the record.* Leave plenty of space, or put extra lines on the chart.
- *For teacher-recorded participation charts, develop a coding system for recording the quality of participation, if appropriate.*

Frequency Counts.   A frequency count or event sample tallies *each* time a behavior occurs and documents the number of times or rate of occurrence. Frequency counts are a practical way to record behaviors such as social initiations and responses to others, aggressive and disruptive behavior, and a

Figure 5–13 *A Room Scan Participation Chart*

Date___/___/___

Observer_____   Group_____

Make one tally mark /
for each 15 minute
scan.

	Art Area	Books/Listening	Science Center	Manipulative	Dramatic Play	Blocks	Table Games	Computers	Not involved
Arndt, Jaral									
Beamer, Megan									
Curtis, Larissa									
Carone, Louis									
Gaburo, Kevin									
Galena, Mona									
Hardin, Ramon									
Kubiac, Dimitri									
Kwan, Ellis									
Lane, Loren									
Osborn, Jessica									
Shaw, Lesley									
Shaw, Wesley									
Showalter, Tina									
Slobovka, Elena									
Yazzie, Ben									

Figure 5–14   *A Participation Chart Recorded by Children*

Items(s): <u>Participation Chart</u>

Group <u>Entire class</u>   Date <u>3/12/9–</u> Time <u>9–10:00 am</u>

Observer <u>Child Recorded</u>   Setting <u>Outdoor hunt & study</u>

Figure 5–15   *A Participation Chart Recorded by a Teacher*

Items(s) <u>Participation in Cooperative Learning Task</u>

Group <u>Albie, Baker, Thomas, Zuchers</u>   Date <u>3/23/9–</u> Time <u>10:25</u>

Observer <u>Wickelgren</u>   Setting <u>Science project</u>

Name	Collects & contributes materials	Participates in discussion	Participates in final project
Albie, T	IIOOIII	TНН OI	I
Baker, J	IIIO	OOIIIII	I
Thomas, F	OOIIOI	OOOIOO	I
Zucher, A	OIIIOI	OIOO	I

Code: I   relevant contribution
         O   irrelevant contribution
     Blank   no contribution

child's requests for help from teachers or peers. If Marcia raises her hand three times, the record would read "I I I." Frequency counts may document behavior during a specified period, such as ten minutes, during group time, or for an entire day. Focus on a limited number of children and behaviors.

Define the behaviors to be tallied on the record. Counts of the same behavior conducted at different times can be recorded on the same form. Divide the space used for the tally into three columns as shown in Figure 5–16. List the dates of the assessment in the left column, and record a tick mark for each occurrence in the center column. A column for totaling each tally is on the right.

To record information unobtrusively make the tally on a wide piece of masking tape taped to the inner side of your wrist or a 3 × 5 inch index card held in one hand. A wrist clicker is also useful but limits the frequency count to one behavior and one child. The disadvantage of using masking tape or a clicker is that the teacher must transfer the information to a conventional form to save it.

Advantages of Frequency Counts

1. Frequency counts are useful for examining the rate or changes in the rate of frequently occurring behaviors.
2. Behaviors can be recorded unobtrusively during classroom activities.

Disadvantages of Frequency Counts

1. Infrequent behaviors are time consuming to track and cannot be adequately captured.
2. It is difficult to do frequency counts on more than one person at a time or on more than three behaviors, especially if behaviors occur frequently.
3. Frequency counts do not record information about the sequence of events or antecedent and consequent events.

Figure 5–16 *Example of a Frequency Count*

Items(s) **Aggressive Behavior**　　　Dates **3/5/9–** to **3/8/9–**

Child **Munja, K.**　　　Time **12:45** to **1:00 pm**

Observer **Delos**　　　Setting **Outdoor play**

Frequency count: **Number of times child deliberately hurt another child, including: hitting, biting, pushing, shoving, kicking, slapping.**

Date	Frequency	Day Total
3/5	THN	5
3/6	II	2
3/7	THN III	8
3/8	THN	5

4 DAY TOTAL: 20

Specific Recommendations for Frequency Counts

- *Count frequently occurring behaviors.*
- *If you are making a frequency count while interacting with children, limit the number of children and behaviors to be observed.*

Procedures That Record Inferences, Judgments, and Reflections

Rating scales, rubrics, and narrative writing attempt to capture complex performances and thoughts.

Rating Scales and Rubrics.   Rating scales record inferences or judgments about the quality of a behavior. They can document "global" impressions or an evaluation of characteristics, such as a child's level of confidence or motivation. They are often used to capture the quality of classroom products or performance.

Rating scales can record information from teachers, parents, and other adults. Children who write and read can use a rating scale to document their own attitudes and opinions. Figure 5–17 is an example of a rating scale.

Rubrics are a form of rating scale used to evaluate children's progress toward a "benchmark" or "standard." Because rubrics have a list of specific characteristics describing performance for each point on the scale, they are more descriptive than global rating scales. Figure 5–18 is an example of a rubric to help evaluate one aspect of a child's ability to collaborate and cooperate in groups. See Chapter 7 and Figures 7–5 and 7–6 for further explanation and examples.

Rating scales and rubrics are sometimes used to summarize several observations or work products in a portfolio. These summary ratings require a global judgment based on examples collected over a period of time and are difficult to do reliably. If they are based on information collected at previous times, make sure the substantiating information contains enough detail. The points on the scale must be specific enough that items are rated in the same way for each child.

It is easy to read too much into summary ratings. A child may receive a different rating because the quality of her work is different, not necessarily because it is better or more mature than another child's. One of the dangers of rating scales is that they convert complex performances into a numerical

Figure 5–17 *Example of a Rating Scale*

Child O'Neil _____   Date 10/22/9–

Rated by Johnson _____

Behavior	Rating				
Stays on task	Never	Sometimes	(Usually)	Always	N/A
Participates in activities	Never	Sometimes	(Usually)	Always	N/A
Volunteers Ideas	(Never)	Sometimes	Usually	Always	N/A

Figure 5–18   *Example of a Rubric*

Works toward the achievement of group goals.

---

4   Actively helps identify group goals and works hard to meet them.

3   Communicates commitment to the group goals and effectively carries out assigned roles.

2   Communicates a commitment to the group goals but does not carry out assigned roles.

1   Does not work toward group goals or actively works against them.

---

rating, which can then easily mean that a five is superior to a one. For example, Susan and Luray are using invented spellings in their writing. On the rating scale being used to summarize their work, children who have more invented spellings are given a higher numerical rating. Susan is using many invented spellings of simple words such as "there" and "were." Luray has fewer invented spellings, but they are of words such as "atmosphere" and "triangle." Susan would receive a higher rating, even though the number of invented spellings may have less significance than the difficulty of the words attempted.

Developing a rating scale is an art. First, give a brief description of the behavior, followed by a scale arranged from low frequency or quality to high frequency or quality. Words or numbers define levels of the scale (never, usually, always; 1, 2, 3, 4, 5; top 10%, top 25%, top 50%, lower 50%, lower 25%). Always include "does not apply" (N/A) as a rating option.

Rating scales should not be used when the actual frequency or number of times a behavior occurs is important. For instance, a frequency count would be a better way of recording disruptive behavior than a rating scale. The frequency count gives the actual number of times a child was disruptive. The rating scale documents one person's impression of the level of disruptive behavior. The rating is less precise and can even be inaccurate. If you are interested in learning to construct rating scales or rubrics, study one of the books listed in the suggested readings.

Advantages of Rating Scales and Rubrics

1. Rating scales record inferences, evaluations, and judgments about behavior.
2. Rating scales are a quick way to solicit opinions from others.
3. Rating scales can be used to record summary evaluations and qualitative aspects of complex performances.

Disadvantages of Rating Scales and Rubrics

1. Rating scales record judgments, *not* descriptions of behavior. Rater biases may color or slant responses.
2. People tend to rate toward the center of a scale or differ in their definition of a scale.

Specific Recommendations for Rating Scales and Rubrics

- *Avoid terms that imply a value judgment about whether a behavior is good or bad* (Irwin & Bushnell, 1980). Avoid *excellent, average,* or *extremely bad.*
- *Terms used to identify points on the scale should not overlap.* Do not use *sometimes* with *part of the time* and *infrequently.*
- *If you can count, time, or directly measure a behavior, do not use rating scales.*
- *Interpret rating scales cautiously.* They are less reliable than direct methods of recording. Assigning numerical values to qualitative differences may be misleading. Numerals and the intervals between them may suggest greater precision than actually exists.
- Rubrics should clearly identify the characteristics under consideration.

Narrative Writing.   Teachers and children record inferences, conclusions, judgments, and reflections in their own words in journals, logs, reports, summaries, reviews, and other work products. Children dictate or write their reflections and judgments.

Some teachers keep a daily or weekly chronological journal of their reflections about their teaching practice, concerns, and impressions. They record notes about children, plans for the future, or achievements, or they reflect on past and present experiences. Journals may help teachers improve their own teaching by encouraging self-reflection (Lay-Dopyera & Dopyera, 1987). Reflection on events may result in insights that would never occur in a busy classroom.

Other Procedures

Some means of preserving information cut across all the categories and can be used for any of them. These include children's work products and a computer record system. Preserving children's performances through their work products is treated in the section on portfolios in Chapter 6.

Computers can record any type of information, including flat work products, which can be optically scanned and stored. There is much experimentation with computer technology as a way of recording assessment information. Information management programs allow teachers to fill out forms, write and print progress reports, and store recorded information on a computer disk. Some teachers enter and store anecdotal records and jottings made during the day.

Some computer teaching programs keep track of a child's errors and progress on skills taught in that program. Computer tracking systems or "grade book programs" compile information from many different assessments. To use them, teachers must enter the class list and all student scores and observations. These programs are useful when cumulative scores, such as grades, are calculated using projects and tests with different weighted values. The computer can generate the child's cumulative score as well as scores on individual assessments. It can also produce graphs showing the child's performance relative to that of other classmates. However, they are time consuming to learn and use.

Summary

Accurate and complete primary data records are essential to ensure the trustworthiness of authentic assessment. Records preserve information for future use, serve as the basis for communicating with other people, and help teachers remember what children know and can do, helping them become better observers and teachers.

Recording procedures can be grouped into (1) those that describe, (2) those that count, time, or tally, and (3) those that record inferences, judgments, and reflections. To select a recording procedure, teachers consider the purpose of the assessment, what is being assessed, the amount of detail needed, and practical classroom considerations—such as the amount of preparation time, attention required to record, and whether information is recorded by groups or individuals.

Examples of practical classroom recording procedures include descriptive narratives, anecdotal records, jottings, diagrams, sketches and photographs, audiotapes and videotapes, checklists, participation charts, frequency counts, rating scales and rubrics, and narratives. Work products and computer systems will be discussed more fully in Chapter 6.

For Further Study, Discussion, and Reflection

1. Much current writing on assessment suggests that teachers keep a journal or log documenting their own experiences with child assessment, and then evaluate and reflect on those experiences. Thoughtfully consider that suggestion, weigh its advantages and disadvantages, and then write your opinion concerning it.
2. You are planning an assessment of social interaction during a cooperative learning activity. You are particularly interested in whether children can organize themselves into a group, follow directions, help each other, and resolve disputes. Give two recording procedures that would be appropriate for the situation. Justify your choices.
3. You are planning an assessment of math skills—understanding "more than/fewer than." Give two alternative recording procedures appropriate for this situation. Explain why you chose these two procedures. Talk about the disadvantages and advantages of one of the procedures.
4. Watch a videotape of several children interacting. The first time you watch, write a descriptive narrative of what you see. The second time you watch, count the social initiations that children make to each other, such as invitations to play or bids for attention. Compare the two methods. Which would be most useful to a teacher interested in social development? Why? Which was easiest to record?

Suggested Readings

Almy, M., & Genishi, C. (1979). *Ways of studying children.* New York: Teachers College Press.

Bell, D. R., & Low, R. M. (1977). *Observing and recording children's behavior.* Spokane, WA: Performance Associates.

Bentzen, W. R. (1992). *Seeing young children: A guide to observing and recording behavior* (2nd ed.). New York: Delmar Publishers.

Boehm, A. E., & Weinberg, R. A. (1987). *The classroom observer: A guide for developing observation skills.* New York: Teachers College Press.

Cartwright, C. A., & Cartwright, G. P. (1984). *Developing observation skills* (2nd ed). New York: McGraw-Hill.

Irwin, D. M., & Bushnell, M. M. (1980). *Observational strategies for child study.* New York: Holt, Rinehart and Winston.

Marzano, R. J., Pickering, D., & McTighe, J. (1993). *Assessing student outcomes: Performance assessment using the dimensions of learning model.* Alexandria, VA: Association for Supervision and Curriculum Development.

Workman, S., & Anziano, M. C. (1993). Curriculum webs: Weaving connections from children to teachers. *Young Children 48*(2), 4–9.

CHAPTER SIX

Compiling and Summarizing Information

Teachers compile and summarize classroom data to integrate and distill information from different sources, contexts, and methods, reduce it to a manageable size, and keep past assessments accessible for continued analysis and interpretation. Similarities and patterns in behavior across different contexts emerge only when several appraisals are integrated. Knowing and understanding a specific child or group of children involves distilling information from many sources, methods, and contexts. For instance, Mrs. Ting, a kindergarten teacher, compiles information from a work product, several anecdotal records, a performance sample, and a child participation chart to understand Nancy's literacy skills. Planning new activities to support the development of classification skills, Mrs. Ting compiles and summarizes for the whole class information related to classification: observations, performance samples, and products.

COMPILING & SUMMARIZING INFORMATION

As the year progresses, the number of records increases—more than anyone could possibly commit to memory. "The wealth of data provided by continuous assessment of student behaviors . . . can be overwhelming, even if systematically recorded. . . . Only through [checklists, profiles, and other means of summarizing] can the vast amount of information on each child be reduced to manageable proportions" (Athey, 1990, p. 180).

Summaries keep past appraisals accessible so they can be analyzed and interpreted in light of the new information that is gathered. Instead of looking through all previous appraisals, the teacher looks at distilled data, saving time and effort.

Three complementary ways of compiling and summarizing information are discussed in this chapter:

1. Portfolios
2. Individual profiles
3. Group profiles

Portfolios

Description and Definition

"All schools should incorporate observations by teachers and performance portfolios in the assessment and evaluation of young children" (National Educational Goals Panel, 1991, p. 10). What is a *portfolio,* and where does it fit in assessment? A portfolio is an organized, purposeful compilation of evidence documenting a child's development and learning over time. It is not a "method" of appraisal or assessment, but a way of keeping together and compiling information from many methods. It exhibits to the child and others the experiences, efforts, progress, and accomplishments of that child, showing a person's unique capabilities as well as accomplishments they share with others. In the process, portfolios provide a basis for evaluation and a guide for further learning and development.

Portfolios are part of almost every alternative assessment system and are popular with teachers, children, and parents at all levels of education. They have generated widespread and intense interest, development, and use.

Physically, a portfolio is a folder, file, box, computer disk, or other container that stores evidence of a pupil's learning (see Chapter 9).

Conceptually, a portfolio is an evolving concept rather than a term with agreed-upon, precise definition. Valencia and Place (1994) identify four major types of portfolios:

- The showcase portfolio, which shows a pupil's best or favorite work
- The evaluation portfolio, in which most of the contents are specified and scored
- The documentation portfolio, which holds evidence of children's work and progress selected to build a comprehensive description of each child
- The process portfolio, which contains ongoing work for a larger project, usually chronicled and commented on by the pupil

People select different types depending on their purposes and what will best serve a particular group of teachers and children (Murphy & Smith, 1990).

Portfolios are well suited to organizing, storing, and preserving informal, authentic primary and summary data about all aspects of young children's development. Portfolios

- Are flexible and adaptable. They can be varied to suit the age and development of children, the developmental or curriculum domain, school or center goals, or other considerations.
- Capture many dimensions of children's development and learning.
- Focus on children's strengths—what they can do.
- Help children assume responsibility for their own learning.
- Lend themselves to samplings over time from a variety of assessment windows.
- Involve children in selection of and reflection on items as appropriate to their development and the item under consideration.
- Can contain information that is common to every child in the group, as well as that which is unique to each child.
- Provide for ongoing, dynamic assessment, not static reports, grades, or scores.
- Are a rich source of information for communicating with and about children and their learning.

Purposes

Portfolios fulfill most of the basic purposes of assessment: determining children's status and progress, informing instruction, providing information for reporting and communication, and preliminary identification of children who might benefit from special help. Portfolios often serve additional purposes, which influence what is included and how the portfolio is organized (Arter, 1990; Arter & Spandel, 1992). If children are to be graded on the basis of work in the portfolio, the child or teacher probably include the best or final work. If the purpose is to show growth over time, representative or best work is included at several points in time. If the portfolio is meant to show how children plan and carry out a project, a record of all activities, assignments, field trips, meetings, drafts and revisions, displays, and reflection on the processes and products might be kept. Other purposes include motivating children and promoting learning through reflection and self-assessment (Murphy & Smith, 1990). "Composite" portfolios tell the story of a group's efforts, progress, or achievements, such as those of a kindergarten or second grade (Arter & Paulson, 1991). Several states and school districts are experimenting with portfolios for large-scale assessment and accountability purposes.

Portfolios serve teachers as well as children. The reflection, discussion, and interaction generated among teachers as they examine, compare, and interpret children's portfolios are as important as the content (Murphy & Smith, 1990). Portfolios remind teachers that assessment is ongoing and can enhance children's learning (Valencia, 1990; Wolf, 1989). Portfolio development and conferencing can increase communication among child, teacher, and parent. Many teachers develop their own portfolios, complete with reflection and self-assessment, to guide and document their personal and professional growth.

Basic Approaches to Portfolio Building

There are four basic approaches to portfolio building: requiring specific items; requiring evidence in given developmental or curriculum areas but not specifying the items; collecting individual, often spontaneous samples from ongoing classroom activities; and combinations of the above.

Required Items. Required items, "core" items (Meisels & Steele, 1991), or "common tools" (Valencia & Place, 1994) specify certain items to be collected for all children in a given class or at a given level. Teachers assess the same thing in the same way within designated time intervals or collection periods, such as crayon self-portraits done at the beginning and end of the year or child responses to a uniform drawing or writing prompt. The Kamehameha Elementary Education Program specified the measures used in six aspects of literacy in kindergarten through third grade (Au, 1993). These included samples of responses to literature to document reading comprehension, teacher observations and logs of voluntary reading, and running records to identify word-reading strategies. The first grade Integrated Language Arts Portfolio in Juneau, Alaska, required a teacher checklist on reading and oral language development; a student reading attitude survey; one sample per quarter of text that a child can read; two writing samples per quarter; open-ended tests of reading comprehension; the number of books read; a checklist of language arts skills; and scores on a year-end standardized test (Arter, 1990). Specific requirements such as these ensure appropriate documentation for all children on important goals, and they guide portfolio development.

Required Evidence. Required evidence portfolios specify certain types of things, such as a sample of creative art; a sample of the child's ability to represent events, objects, or actions; a language sample; or evidence of fine motor development, but leave exactly what is collected up to the teacher and child (Valencia, 1989).

Individualized Sampling. Individualized sampling relies on selection from ongoing classroom work or activities. These systems are more open, allowing the teacher, child, or both to select work and other documentation (interviews, observations, children's interactions, participation in given activities) that exemplify how children feel, act, or think. They show each child's unique approach, progress, and understandings (Chittenden & Courtney, 1989). They may show a child's "favorite," "best," or "most-improved" work. There is no requirement to collect similar items for each child except as the items reflect progress toward important goals. Some schools using this approach include only items selected by children.

These portfolios identify and document an individual child's unique interests, knowledge, skills, dispositions, and "style" of development and learning—their "personal signature" (Eisner, 1991, p. 17) or "approach to learning" (Kagan, Moore, & Bredekamp, 1995). Such insight can be extracted from other documentation, but is more likely to be identified, recognized, and valued in a portfolio.

Combinations.   Required core items or indicators plus optional individualized items selected by the teacher and child seem most appropriate for young children. They combine systematic documentation pertaining to important goals with the opportunity to capture evidence that occurs spontaneously and may be unique to that child or that situation.

Selection of Content

A portfolio is not just a folder of student work or a catch-all file of checklists, notes, test results, and other information and records. It must be thoughtfully planned and organized.

Appropriate Types of Items.   Portfolio items vary with the age and development of children, goals of the program, the curriculum or developmental domain under consideration, the type and purpose of the portfolio, and teacher preferences. Figure 6–1 suggests the possibilities. No school or center would use all these, but would select a combination to provide "multiple windows"—different sources, methods, and contexts—on a child's accomplishments.

Item Selection.   Unless they are involved in large-scale assessment, teachers in a given school or center usually have much latitude in identifying portfolio items. When they discuss and agree upon what they are going to put in a portfolio, they are more likely to know what to collect and to actually do it. Teachers can decide how many and which items are sufficient. Indiscriminate additions to a portfolio quickly become overwhelming, but a too-scanty portfolio will not have enough information to be useful, and certainly will not provide multidimensional evidence of a child's progress over time.

Items should be *informative, easy to collect,* and representative of *meaningful* classroom activities (Meisels, Jablon, Marsden, Dichtelmiller, Dorfman, & Steele, 1994). *Informative* items reveal several aspects of a child's learning and development. Work included in the portfolio should occur regularly in the classroom, so it is *easy to collect.* Classroom activities that result in high-quality portfolio items are *meaningful* and interesting to the children.

Who chooses items to go in the portfolio—teacher, child, or both? In what proportions? Much depends on the age, developmental level, and previous experience of the children. Preschool and primary children cannot assume major responsibility for their own portfolios, even though they may play an active role. Three- and 4-year-old children are unlikely to be discriminating in what they want to include, and the portfolio could be full or empty at the end of a month; second-graders may be able to make many choices. Teachers must judge how much choice and access young children have, and monitor them to ensure that important information is not missing (Maeroff, 1991).

Figure 6–1   *Types of Items Appropriate for Portfolios*

Work will be done in different ways at different ages and levels, and for different developmental and curriculum areas. Teachers and children may develop many imaginative variations on these basic types. For more ideas, see Figure 9–2 in Chapter 9.

- Work products done on paper—samples of cutting, drawing, any art medium, printing, practice papers, pasting, writings—initial drafts, editing, final drafts. Dictations by nonwriters.
- "Journals"—math, science, writing; children's drawings, scribbles, collages reflecting their experiences and growth.
- Records of data collection and presentation in math, science, social studies, health.
- Sketches of a child's work, made by the child or an adult (block structure, pattern blocks, sand, any 3-D work). Sketches of the plan for that work.
- Photographs of a child engaged in significant work or play.
- Photographs of exhibits and displays prepared by child or group.
- Audiotapes and videotapes.
- Printouts of work done on computer—draw/paint, math, writing programs, games.
- Participation chart—what a child did on a given day or during a given period. Include qualitative information.
- Logs of activities and results (books read to or by child; parents can help).
- Time sample or count of what a child did on a given day or period.
- Interviews—audio/video/written. Elicit reports or descriptions of a process—how to make a favorite food, getting to school, making friends, playing a game, or "favorite" activities, books, things to do. Child can draw it and then dictate explanation to an adult.
- Structured observation, performance assessment, or dynamic assessment results. Do one or two children a day.
- Anecdotal records or jottings grouped according to the portfolio categories, and/or affixed in chronological order. Use Post-its, gummed labels, or quarter sheets of recycled office paper (tape them on).
- Awards, certificates, citations.
- Parents comments and goals, notes from parent–teacher and child–teacher conferences; drawings and dictated or written messages to parents from children.

Age and Developmental Level of the Children.   The portfolio concept must be adapted to the developmental level and prior experience of each group, and in some cases, each child. Children who read and write proficiently will have different portfolio items than those who are emergent readers and writers. They will be able to do and record more self-assessment and reflection, and with assistance they can take far more responsibility.

Organization of Content

There is no single way to select and organize portfolio content, as long as content relating to major developmental domains and the goals and objectives of the program are included.

Categories or Domains for Portfolio Content.   For prekindergarten children, portfolio categories might correspond to the broad goals identified by the National Education Goals Panel (Kagan, Moore, & Bredekamp, 1995): Physical well-being and motor development; social and emotional development; approaches toward learning; language development; and cognition and general knowledge. The Work Sampling System (Meisels, Jablon, Marsden, Dichtelmiller, Dorfman, & Steele, 1994), which spans preschool through fifth grade, uses seven categories or domains:

Personal and social development
Language and literacy
Mathematical thinking
Scientific thinking
Social studies
The arts
Physical development

Divisions might be the traditional developmental domains of physical, cognitive, language, and social/emotional development; or subject matter such as health and safety, social studies, science, mathematics, language and literacy. Teachers who are just beginning to use portfolios may focus on only one domain, such as language and literacy, or one aspect of literacy, such as emergent writing, where there is much information on appropriate items to collect, guides for evaluating processes and products, and excellent information to help teachers. (See Appendix A–7.)

Some items will be difficult to categorize: they may not fit any of the categories, or they may fit several. A primary student's written report of an interview with the school cooks reveals much about the reporter's fine motor coordination, thinking processes, task persistence, understanding of social roles and interdependence in the school community, as well as listening and writing competence. If the report is a result of a cooperative group effort, each child's contribution will need to be recognized. If an item is selected for a primary purpose, with other aspects being secondary, file it in the primary category. For example, if the primary purpose of the report was to check on listening and writing competence, it would be filed under Language and Literacy Development. If the primary purpose was to document children's developing understanding of the way we organize ourselves as social groups, it might be filed under Concept Development or Social Studies.

Teachers who keep anecdotal records or jottings in the portfolio sometimes simply arrange them in chronological order, perhaps coding them with colored pens or stickers as primarily related to social interaction, language, or another category.

Check frequently to ensure that all developmental or subject matter areas are adequately documented for all children. Put a copy of the goals and objectives at the front of each portfolio as a reminder. Place a list of any requirements at the front of each portfolio to help keep track of which items are in place and which remain to be collected. An example is shown in Figure 6–2. Before duplicating such a form, write in any required items, so that each child's portfolio has the same requirements. As

Figure 6–2 *Portfolio Record Form*

Portfolio Record

Grade _____ Child _____ Teacher _____

Domain	Sample 1	Sample 2	Sample 3
Physical & Motor			
Social & Emotional			
Language & Literacy			
Cognition & General Knowledge			
Approaches to Learning			

items are inserted, note the date in the appropriate cell. As optional or individual items are collected, note what they are and the date they were added.

If a portfolio has an excess of creative art and journal samples, with few entries about physical or social development, determine why, and begin to build a more balanced portfolio. The imbalance may be caused by the fact that some important school goals, such as motor and social development, do not result in an "easy to collect" product, but must be documented in other ways. Or the imbalance may reflect an imbalanced curriculum and schedule.

Because portfolios most easily lend themselves to the collection and storage of work products, make sure that children's thinking and learning processes are also documented. Even though performance samples and work products may make up the bulk of the portfolio, any classroom assessment procedures are appropriate to include and will probably be necessary in order to obtain adequate information about the goals and objectives of a comprehensive program.

Self-Reflection and Self-Assessment. Developing children's abilities to reflect on and assess their own actions and work is an integral part of portfolio development. Three- and 4-year-olds will be limited in their ability to reflect on what they have done. Older children will be more capable, particularly if they have been coached and encouraged for several years. If not, they can learn. Don't ask children to reflect on everything; they soon tire of overanalysis. When 5-year-old Monique was asked to tell why certain books were her favorites, she said of the first, "Basically, it's just a very funny book"; of the second, "It has a sad ending and then it comes out nice"; of another, "It's just nice—it's like a lullaby to me"; and then, "Can I go now?"

Older children will be more capable, particularly if they have been coached and encouraged for several years. Self-reflection and assessment start children on the long path to assuming responsibility for their own actions and learning. Appropriate prompts help children think about what they have learned or practiced during a particular activity (see Figure 6–3). Teacher or child may record the responses and attach them to the item.

Figure 6–3 *Sample Prompts for Self-Assessment and Reflection*

"Tell me what you did."
"Tell (or show) me how you did it."
"Why did you decide to . . . ?"
"What were you thinking when you . . . ?"
"Tell me more about this and your thinking (feelings) as you did it."
"What do you like about this picture (structure, painting, writing)?"
"What would you do differently if you were doing this again?"
"Why do you want this to go in your portfolio?"
"What did you learn while you were doing this?"
"What problems did you have while doing this? How did you solve them?"

Model, discuss, and practice developmentally appropriate reflection and self-assessment just as you would any other thinking process. Don't be dismayed at early responses that miss the mark. An entering kindergartner may say that what he likes about the picture he has drawn is "It's pretty 'n' stuff." A year later he may be able to spot letters that are formed incorrectly, explain why, and work toward conventional forms; another year later he may revise his own writing and justify the revisions.

Children's reflections contain insights, understandings, and delights that don't reveal themselves in other ways. One second grade teacher had worked all year to teach children the criteria for good writing and was now having children choose a piece to go in their portfolios. Anna had chosen one that met all the criteria. Delighted, the teacher asked her why she had chosen that one. Anna's response: "It reminds me of my dog." It was not the expected response, but one that captured the essence of good writing.

Relationship of Portfolios to Other Types of Assessment

A portfolio differs from a youngster's personal file and cumulative record (Paulson, Paulson, & Meyer, 1991), but its relationship to other types of assessment and documentation vary from setting to setting, as do the contents of the portfolio. In some cases, portfolios are the only systematic documentation and compilation of children's work. In others, portfolios are only one part of a comprehensive alternative assessment system. Meisels and colleagues at the University of Michigan developed such a system for children preschool through fifth grade (1994). It consists of three complementary elements: observations by teachers using developmental guidelines and checklists, collection of children's work in portfolios, and summaries of this information in summary reports. Developmental checklists "document the broad scope of a child's learning" (Meisels et al., 1994, p. 13) in relationship to established goals and national standards; portfolios contain in-depth information about how a child works, and the nature and quality of that work; summary reports integrate, summarize, and evaluate information about each child from the checklists and portfolios.

We recommend that portfolios complement and supplement other documentation, such as individual and group profiles. It is difficult to incorporate into a portfolio everything you need to know about a child, and even more difficult to determine how to plan for a group, when documentation is based solely on individual portfolios.

Increasing the Information in Each Portfolio Item

Make each item that goes in the portfolio as informative as possible: identify and annotate work products, photographs, or sketches; if the items are required, develop procedures and instructions that maximize information; and select spontaneously generated items for what they reveal about the child as well as their uniqueness.

Identify and Annotate Each Item.   Identify each work product with the child's name and the date. Whenever possible and pertinent, include the teacher's name, setting (outdoors, writing center, enrichment math), time of day, grade or group, and any other relevant information. Date items with a rubber stamp, or let children copy or generate their names and the date as functional practice in letter and numeral formation.

An annotation is a reflection, comment, or explanation that makes the significance of an item clear and adds relevant information not otherwise available. Teachers, children, or both may annotate items. Annotations might include the following:

- Reason the item was selected
- Task variables: setting, assigned or voluntary, assisted or independent, amount and type of assistance, directions, materials available, time and effort expended
- Written or dictated reflections, descriptions, remarks, and assessments
- Responses to questions or prompts (see Figure 6–3)
- Analysis of what the work shows about the child's learning and comparisons with previous work
- Explanation of why the item is significant as an example of the child's work
- Child's personal responses or observations, such as making a connection to prior knowledge and experience, pride, interest, or preference

Annotations should clarify the situation in which the item was developed and its significance. For instance, did Ben compose the simple but beautiful poem handwritten in his portfolio, or did he copy it from a bulletin board or book? Did Cory plan, research, and write her report on porcupines in class or at home, where she had guidance from her parents and computer technology for research, composition, and revision? Was the topic assigned or chosen? Children change schools, teachers change, and people other than classroom staff will have no way of knowing the situational elements that give meaning to a portfolio item unless it is recorded.

Annotations include observations by teachers. For example, in assessing fine motor skills and use of tools, teachers make observations about children's grasp, strength, and coordination. This information is not evident from the product itself, but is important in understanding the product and should be noted.

Identify and annotate, or "caption" (Kingore, 1993), the portfolio item itself, using the all-purpose record forms provided in Chapter 9 or a separate "portfolio entry slip" (see Figures 6–4 and 6–5). Staple the entry slip to the item, and it is ready to file. Affix photographs of children engaged in significant work to a portfolio entry slip with glue stick, rubber cement, or another appropriate adhesive. Identify and annotate, and then file. If there is delay between picture taking and developing, fill out the form when the picture is taken, so you won't forget the reason you took it. Half sheets of

Figure 6–4 *Informative Portfolio Item: Fall*

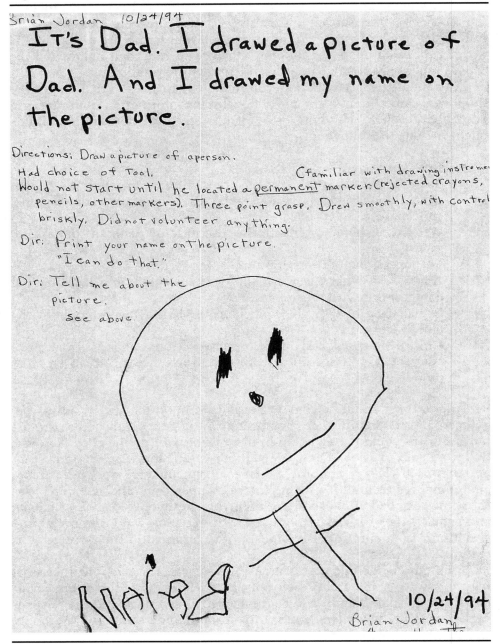

Brian Jordan 10/24/94

It's Dad. I drawed a picture of Dad. And I drawed my name on the picture.

Directions: Draw a picture of a person.
Had choice of Tool. (familiar with drawing instrumer
Would not start until he located a permanent marker (rejected crayons,
pencils, other markers). Three point grasp. Drew smoothly, with control
briskly. Did not volunteer anything.
Dir: Print your name on the picture.
  "I can do that."
Dir: Tell me about the picture.
  See above.

10/24/94
Brian Jordan

paper are adequate for most entries, but photographs need a full sheet to allow for comments and explanations.

The entry slip has several advantages. It reminds everyone to caption portfolio items; children's work is not intruded upon by analytical remarks; there is adequate space; and observers can note significant process variables (pencil grasp, use of a model, concentration, time spent) while children are working, thus saving time. Children who write can fill out some or all of the entry slip.

Figure 6–5 *Informative Portfolio Item: Spring*

Develop Instructions and Procedures to Maximize the Information Gained from Each Item.   Portfolio items can be made more informative by having children demonstrate several things in one item. For example, if you ask a child to draw a picture of a person, ask her also to tell you about the picture and then to print her name on the paper. Instead of just a picture, you will have a writing sample, language sample, coordination observation, ability to follow instructions observation, and opportunities for many other insights.

Develop consistent instructions and procedures for performance tasks. In the task above, are the children allowed to choose whatever drawing instrument they want, or are they to use a designated one? Think through these seemingly small procedures, and make a decision; they affect performance. Duplicate and attach the instructions with the portfolio entry slip, or duplicate them on the entry slip. At the least, they should be the written on the product, as in Figures 6–4 and 6–5: these simple, easily collected work products contain a wealth of information about Brian, far more than the picture alone. They reveal his familiarity with drawing instruments and their characteristics, his small muscle development, knowledge of print, understanding of his own capabilities, language, and progress from October to May. Just as important in the long run is the beginning of reflection and self-assessment shown in how he remembered the way he used to draw people and realized that he had progressed. These figures also reveal how duplicated instructions and conditions would have lessened the teacher's task. A separate entry form would also have allowed her to record observations and comments as the events occurred.

Select Spontaneously Generated Items for Information as Well as Uniqueness.   Rich and informative items for portfolios also result from children's spontaneous work and play—often revealing capabilities far beyond what we anticipate, as they are not constrained by adult direction and expectations. Look for these as priceless portfolio additions, add any needed explanations, and study them for what they reveal.

Jeremy is in kindergarten and has diagrammed the process of making cookies, which he did a week ago (see Figure 6–6). The task was a self-appointed one, done at the writing center. His work shows the following attributes:

- The sequence of steps is clear, distinct, accurate, and in order.
- Since the cookie making was done the week before, Jeremy had stored the steps in memory and was able to retrieve them.
- Left-to-right progression on the top row gives way to a flow-type representation that retains horizontal orientation.
- The product combines several types of representation into one schematic diagram—including drawing, writing, dictation, circles demarcating the discrete steps, and arrows showing the flow of the process—a more complex task than any one or two combined.
- Conceptualization of the representation was the child's; he had no model.
- Pictures and print are linked in meaning.
- Some steps are represented by print only, such as "Kut out," revealing understanding that print alone will carry the meaning.
- Clear concepts of a word are demonstrated. No words are run together.
- Abstract concepts of time, temperature, and measurement are incorporated in the correct places and linked with the correct units of measurement (cups, degrees, time). Estimation of numbers of units (2 to 3 minutes, 70 degrees) are far afield.

Figure 6–6 *Kindergarten Child's Schematic Diagram of the Process of Making Cookies*

- Invented spelling shows almost perfect sound–symbol correspondence. Conventional spelling is used in several words.
- Formation and placement of letters are still being learned. Uppercase and lowercase letters are intermingled. Uppercase *L*s are backward.
- Control of small hand and arm muscles and coordination skills show in the size of drawing and lettering, the control over placement of arrows, and the small illustrations. Such control is beyond normal expectations for kindergarten.
- Language is used to explain and inform another person; understanding that language can direct and control actions is demonstrated—the "resape" book tells you what to do.
- The entire diagram demonstrates knowledge of function of print and ability to communicate and explain intent. Trying to determine the significance of what appeared to be a book in each circle, the adult inquired about it. Jeremy answered, "We use the recipe book each time," pointing to each step in the process. Other explanations of intent were dictated to and written by the adult.

Analysis of even one work product such as this, demonstrating print literacy, representational and sequencing processes, cognitive development, and use of fine motor skills, tells far more about this youngster than a test would, especially when coupled with answers to adult requests for explanation. If comparison is needed, compare the product and its interpretation to developmental expectations in cognitive development, literacy, and fine motor skills; to school and center objectives; or to similar work the child has done previously, such as earlier drawings captioned with his own printing. By any measure, the work is high quality for kindergarten. Not every work product will offer this much insight into a child's capabilities, but usually there is more information available than we take time to understand.

Issues

The use of portfolios for assessing children's development and learning is in its infancy. Unresolved issues include the following:

- *The place of technology.* "Electronic portfolios" are a new development in creating, preserving, and storing children's work using computer technology. Software is available from several commercial companies. With a color scanner, teachers or children can enter graphics, illustrations, photographs, and pictures directly into portfolios stored and managed by the computer. Text can be created or imported, including reflections and comments by teacher and children. Sound and movement features are available for narration or for saving speeches, music, drama, and other movement performances. Selected items or entire portfolios can be transferred to videotape for viewing by parents or next year's teachers. Because the technology is so new, little information is available about young children and the use of electronic portfolios. The long-term storage and tracking possibilities could be useful for following children's progress from one grade or school to the next. However, the hardware requirements— color monitors and optical scanners, 4–8 MB RAM (lots of memory), hard disk, CD-ROM drive, printer, and microphone—are formidable and well beyond the reach of most early childhood schools. The concept and the technology bear watching. Future developments may bring into existence affordable and useful electronic portfolios.
- *Ownership.* To whom does the portfolio belong? Parents? Child? School? Who may see the portfolio?
- *Transfer and storage.* What part of the portfolio should be passed on to the next teacher or unit, and how? Storage and access over time are practical problems being addressed by computer technology.
- *Evaluation.* If the portfolio is used for evaluation (grading), who develops and applies the criteria? How is comparability attained?
- *Utility.* How can the portfolio best be used to enhance children's development and learning? What items are essential?
- *Practicality.* Like all alternative assessment, portfolios require a commitment from classroom staff. They have to experiment, learn, modify, teach the children the process, and perhaps modify their instructional procedures to make portfolios fulfill their promise.

Individual Profiles

Description and Definition

An individual profile is a written summary of a child's capabilities, integrating information from classroom assessments. Patterns of behavior, interests, attitudes, and dispositions are synthesized and then concisely written.

There are several types of profiles. In some, assessments are converted into scores and graphed on a profile sheet. These require special expertise to create and score and have limited use in the classroom. They are often difficult to translate into information useful for planning and look more like a "grade" or summary evaluation. Some teachers use a checklist to summarize assessment information. The checklist is usually broken down into categories and subcategories keyed to evaluation instruments such as report cards.

A better approach is to create a flexible, open-ended document that is tied to the planning process. These profiles consist of columns for each area of development or each curriculum area. The areas can be classroom goals that were used to plan activities. In each column, a summary statement about child status and progress is written, dated, and followed by a reference about the location of primary data records in the teacher's files that support the entry. Notations about teacher concerns, reflections, and things to monitor can also be included. As new appraisals are made, the information is integrated into the summary (see Figure 6–7).

Purposes

Individual profiles document a child's capabilities and behavior patterns, provide information for planning, and show when information is missing. They are a broad view of where the child is and where the teacher hopes the child will be, focusing on the entire forest and not individual trees—the child's general capabilities, neither isolated skills nor specific content. They chronicle an individual child's progress as information about patterns of interests, development, and interaction emerge. Individual profiles help teachers study extremes, uniqueness, and stylistic approaches that are difficult to see when looking at one assessment. In short, they help teachers know and understand each child.

Individual profiles help teachers plan to meet individual strengths and needs. A child's interest in storytelling and puppetry emerges from several assessments about "what I like to do best in school." The profile helps teachers remember to nurture that strength in the classroom. When compiling Peter's profile, the teacher notices that he never participates in art activities, but he does like numbers, counting, and manipulatives. The teacher can use this identified interest to entice Peter into the art area. A teacher can identify a child who is having trouble making friends or doesn't participate in conversations and plan activities to help.

Individual profiles also help teachers check on the classroom assessment process itself. Missing documentation is easily noted.

Figure 6–7   *Example of an Individual Profile*

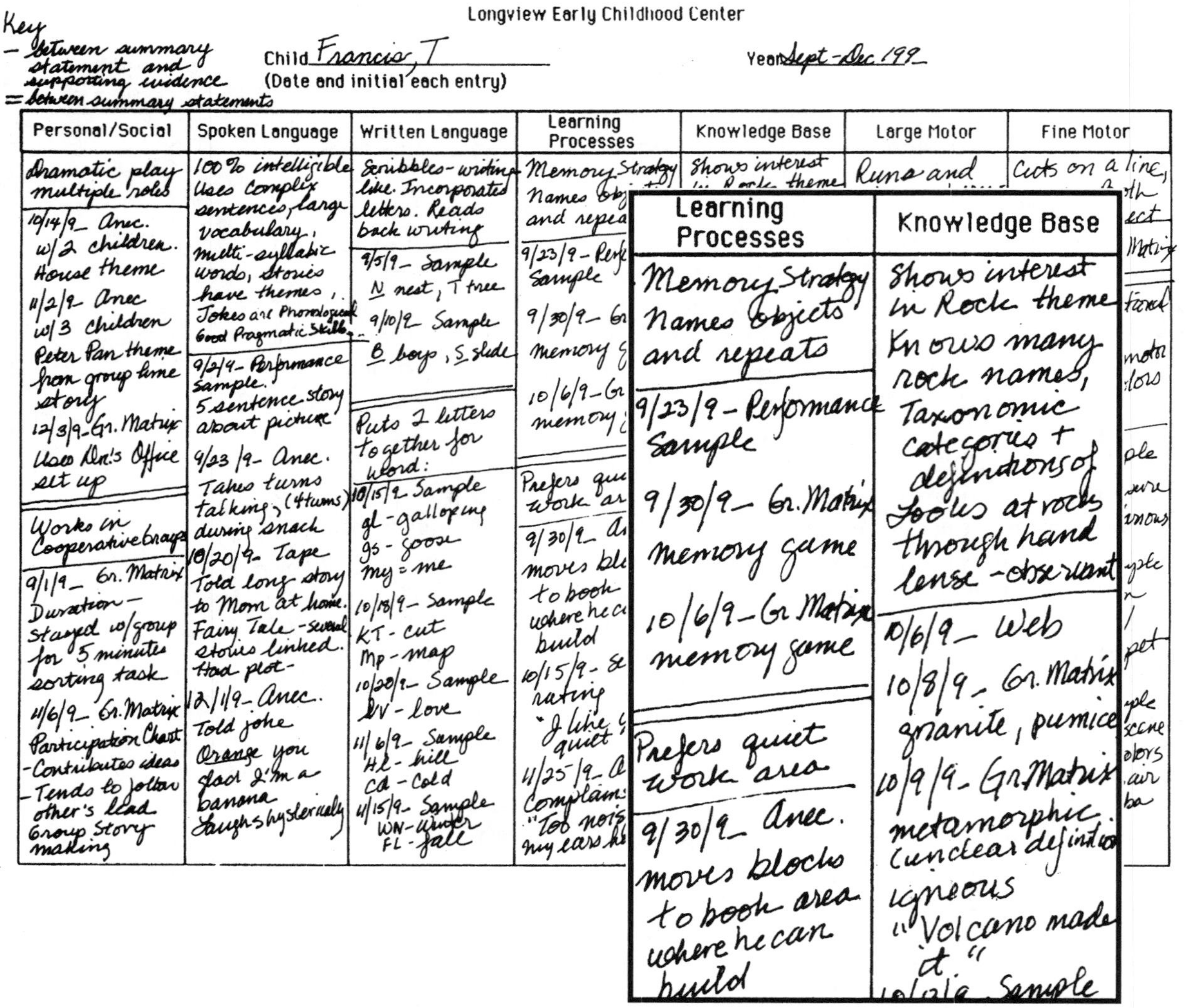

Longview Early Childhood Center

Key
— between summary statement and supporting evidence
= between summary statements

Child Francis, T
(Date and initial each entry)

Year Sept–Dec 199_

Personal/Social	Spoken Language	Written Language	Learning Processes	Knowledge Base	Large Motor	Fine Motor
Dramatic play multiple roles	100% intelligible	Scribbles – writing like. Incorporated	Memory Strategy Names objects	Shows interest in Rock theme	Runs and	Cuts on a line

(handwritten anecdotal notes in each column, with two enlarged inset columns:)

Learning Processes

Memory Strategy Names objects and repeats

9/23/9 – Performance Sample

9/30/9 – Gr. Matrix memory game

10/6/9 – Gr. Matrix memory game

Prefers quiet work area

9/30/9 – Anec. moves blocks to book area where he can build

Knowledge Base

Shows interest in Rock theme Knows many rock names, Taxonomic categories + definitions of rocks. Looks at rocks through hand lense – observant

10/6/9 – Web
10/8/9 – Gr. Matrix granite, pumice
10/9/9 – Gr. Matrix metamorphic (unclear definition) igneous "Volcano made it"
10/12/9 – Sample

Selecting and Organizing Content

Limit the Number of Educational and Developmental Outcomes/ Goals and Objectives on the Profile.   Because constructing and maintaining individual profiles for a whole class are time consuming, teachers should limit the number of areas to be tracked. Six to ten areas the same as or similar to those used for portfolios and group profiles would be sufficient for most classrooms. Use the ideas about what to assess given in Chapter 3. Create a form with the same categories for each child in the class.

Use Outcomes/Goals and Objectives That Are Similar to Those on the Portfolio Record and Summary Reports.   Plan the profile so that it helps you write the narrative summary at the end of the year. Key it to the portfolio so that the profile summarizes the information you compile.

Use a Consistent Referencing System for Supporting Primary Data Records.   Always write the date of the primary data record followed by its type and location in your files. Use the same abbreviations for type and location throughout the profiles. Keep the primary data records organized and coordinated with the profile. For example, if the primary data record is stored in the child's portfolio, then that is noted by writing "portfolio." The reference note allows anyone to go back to the original record when necessary.

Use All Available Information.   Use everything available, including work samples, group assessments, anecdotal records, performance samples, any elicited information, group and individual projects, participation charts, frequency counts, and any information contained in children's portfolios. Profile entries will vary depending on the specific child.

Compile Information One Area at a Time, One Child at a Time.   Review all of Maria's assessments and products relating to cognitive development, then her assessments for language development, continuing until her profile is complete. After finishing Maria's profile, move on to Phil's. By compiling profiles one child at a time, you gain an understanding of that child as an individual. This will not happen if you work on several children's profiles simultaneously.

Computers make coding and collating certain information less time consuming. One such program uses teacher observations and performance tasks to identify what children know and can do related to print literacy. As the teacher appraises the child, she completes a form that the computer scans, analyzes, and then uses to produce a profile of that child's print literacy directly related to the whole language, emergent-reading strategies used in the classroom.

Summarize Trends Demonstrating Growth or a Breakthrough in Learning.   Compare assessments collected at different times. Look for convergence of indicators showing a trend in development. For example, entries can summarize progress or movement from one place on the developmental sequence to another. Marissa began the semester at the level of "able to catch the ball with a body trap" and ends the semester at the level of "catching with hands." Entries might show that a child has moved from one cluster to another in a group profile. In January, Ricardo was in the literacy cluster of "drawing pictures and reciting a story" and by the end of the semester in the cluster of "drawing pictures and incorporating letters symbolizing key words." Entries can show how a pattern of behavior has changed. For example, at the beginning of the semester, Tony showed great distress when his mother left him, but by the third week in school, he no longer cries.

Summarize Unique Child Characteristics.   Describe attitudes and dispositions, such as persistence and motivation levels, that cut across different assessments. Leslie's persistence and motivation are obvious when you look at the times she tries to build a large city with blocks during one assessment. Only after the structure collapses 11 times does she settle for a smaller structure. Look for similar behaviors in different contexts. Not only is Leslie persistent in block building, but she approaches other tasks in the same way.

Include Behaviors or Areas to Monitor.   Make entries that you want to follow up on. The profile can serve as a reminder or "tickler" file. Mr. Zatus is worried because Mia is quiet and doesn't participate in class. He notes this on the profile to help him remember to check her progress in class interaction.

Update the Profile at Specific Times.   Enter information early in the year to compare with information gathered later. Review contents of individual profiles several times a year—at midyear, end of the year, and prior to parent conferences. At midyear, review additions and make new entries. At the end of the year, review the profile, adding entries to document growth since midyear and to describe status at the end of the year. The more often you update the profile, the more useful it will be in the classroom.

As patterns of behavior change, note those changes in the appropriate column. Also note your inferences and reflections. If new information indicates that an inference or behavioral trend was incorrect, cross it out and note the new interpretation.

Make Entries in Chronological Order.   To determine changes in patterns of behavior, you must compile information in chronological order.

Relationship of Individual Profiles to Other Types of Documentation

Teachers find that an individual profile is helpful when they write narrative summaries of child progress for parent reports and for cumulative files. A by-product of collecting, compiling, and summarizing assessment information is that the teacher can use it to write a more accurate narrative report based on evidence gathered throughout the year instead of only those things that the teacher remembers.

Group Profiles

Description and Definition

Group profiles show class performance on one or more items. They focus on the range of class behavior and identify clusters or subgroups of children with similar strengths and needs. They also condense information about the entire class's performance on several sheets of paper. Unlike individual profiles, group profiles do not usually cut across different areas, but summarize one area or one assessment for the entire group.

Group profiles summarize the qualitative and quantitative variations found in the behavior of individuals in a group. Qualitative variations include the following: one child throwing a ball accurately and another just throwing; one child telling a story with little sequence and another telling a detailed, sequential story; one child drawing a human figure with only a circle for a head and another drawing a body with arms, legs, fingers, and even eyelashes. There may be different levels of complexity, as in the case of a child who sorts by one attribute and one who produces a complex matrix when sorting. The range can also refer to the number of behaviors performed. In dramatic play, one child uses two themes and plays three roles, whereas another child uses only one theme and one role. One child volunteers many ideas in a cooperative learning activity, whereas another volunteers only a few.

Purposes

Group profiles are primarily planning tools used to identify needs and strengths so that appropriate activities can be planned. Instead of guessing at what children know and can do, Mrs. Meirhoff uses a group profile that shows that only two children need more guided practice, whereas the rest need more challenge. She can then plan appropriate multilevel activities and individualize classroom practices. Instead of planning an activity to provide practice for all children, she decides to plan an activity to provide challenge. She sets aside time to give one-to-one help to the two children who need more guided practice. Mrs. Meirhoff will be less likely to lose the interest of the entire group, and at the same time she can provide assistance to those who need it.

Group profiles help identify clusters of children with similar interests, strengths, needs, and levels of performance. For example, a child with a certain skill might be paired with one who needs support in a cooperative task. A child who is very interested in a subject can be placed with a child who is not interested, thus motivating both. Children with similar interests can also be paired.

Group profiles evaluate the entire class's growth and achievement. By comparing a group profile made before a concentrated emphasis to a profile made after, a teacher can gauge what children learned from the experience. Mr. Gonzales assessed children prior to a project on the solar system and compared this assessment to the profile made after the project. He found that only a subgroup of children who already knew the most about the solar system learned from the unit. The group profile helps him discover which children did not benefit and to analyze why. Group profiles help teachers evaluate their own teaching techniques and improve their effectiveness.

Selecting and Organizing Content

Determine What Will Be Profiled.   What is profiled depends on the teacher's planning needs, so a profile for interests and dispositions would be different from one focusing on knowledge or skill mastery.

Divide the Range of Behaviors.   Make divisions that have significance for teaching—what and how you are going to teach. The following are some examples:

- Use children's needs as the basis for categories, such as "needs introduction," "needs practice," and "needs more challenge."
- Use groupings that describe different levels of mastery, such as "no evidence," "developing this," and "controls this"; or "beginning to," "does this," or "has mastered this."
- Use subskills to divide the range of behavior. Examples are "can snip," "cut one whole cut," "cut on a straight line," and "cut on a curve."
- Base clusters on levels of performance, such as "expressive" or "receptive language," "recognition" and "recall," or "knowledge," "comprehension," "application," and "analysis." Consult Chapter 4 for different levels that might be useful.
- Use content as a basis for clusters, such as "addends" in mathematics.
- Use the steps identified in skill acquisition. For example, use the skill levels described in the emergent literacy research: "emergent reader," "early reader," "bridging reader," "take-off reader," "independent reader," "skilled reader" (Daniels, 1992).
- Use levels of performance identified in appropriate rubrics.

When Possible, Convert Group Matrices or Group Records into Profiles.   Use a different colored marker for each cluster or subgroup and circle or highlight performances falling within the same cluster. In Figure 6–8, Mrs. Lee is interested in identifying children who need an introduction to hopping and skipping and those who already know how to hop and skip. She shades the children in one group. By glancing down the page, she sees the range, how many children are in each group, and which particular children have similar skill levels.

When Necessary, Create a Separate Form for the Group Profile.   Sometimes information is on individual records, one record per child, but you need a group profile. This often occurs when making a group summary using work products, portfolios, or anecdotal records. Place the identified divisions or clusters in columns, and write the names of children who fall into each column. Figure 6–9 is an example.

Place a Key on Each Summary, Identifying Clusters or Subgroups.   For color coding, write the color used for each cluster at the top of the page. Keep the same color scheme to avoid confusion and misinterpretation.

Compile Group Profiles as Soon as Possible.   Since group profiles are used for classroom planning, they are of little use when they are several weeks old.

Use Group Profiles When You Plan.   Use the profile to determine activities for specific children or groups of children. Compare group profiles over time to determine needed changes.

Figure 6–8   *Example of a Group Profile from Group Matrix*

Items: *Large Muscle Skills*   Date 10 / 10 / 9_

Group: *whole class*

▨ needs challenge
▯ developing

Name	Run	Throw	Fitness Level
Akasmet, J.	Balanced Fluid at times Stops No Turns	Overhand ® Early Release No Rotation Tentative step	Fatigued before 5 min.
Bianco, A.	Balanced Fluid Stops easily Turns easily	Underhand (L) Late release No Rotation	Good 10 min
Bonilla, C.	Toe walks Run awkward	Overhand (L) Early Release No Rotation	Good 10 min.
Chang, K.	Balanced Fluid Stops easily Turns easily	Overhand step and Rotation Accurate	Good more than 10 min
Cisen, P.	Run awkward Loses balance on turns	Overhand Step and Rotation Accurate	Fatigued 5 min

Figure 6–9   *Example of Group Profile from Individual Records*

Measurement ✶	Awareness	Exploration/Experimentation; Standard, non-standard units	Inquiry/Problem-solving; Standard units and rule systems	Application/Utilization/"Real World"
Linear – such as Rulers, yard and meter sticks, tape measures; blocks, miles, kilometers, and others		Beamer	Lee Jonas Miller Hopcus Burke Yoder Epps Tomas Carling	Salazar Peake Kastiuk Lawton Washington James Lucero Brown
Weight – such as Equal arm balance, bath, kitchen, postage scales; ounces, pounds, grams, and others		Beamer Epps Tomas	Salazar Lawton James Brown Lee Jonas Miller Hopcus Burke Yoder	Carling Lucero Kastiuk Washington Peake
Volume – such as Cups, spoons, pints, quarts, liters, ounces, and others	Tomas Beamer Carling Salazar Lawton Lee Jonas Burke Peake	Brown Miller Hopcus Washington Epps	James Yoder	Lucero

✶ Levels of learning from Naeyc - Naecs/Sde (1991) "Guidelines for Appropriate Curriculum Content and Assessment in Programs Serving Children Ages 3 Through 8.

Young Children. 46, 21-38

Observer J. Alberto
Date 1/22/199–
Group Stone Prairie 2

Summary

Teachers compile and summarize information to integrate and distill information from different sources, methods, and contexts; reduce it to a manageable size; and keep past assessments accessible for continued analysis and interpretation. Three complementary ways of compiling and summarizing are portfolios, individual profiles, and group profiles.

Portfolios present a thoughtful, organized compilation of evidence documenting a child's development and learning over time. There are four basic types of portfolios: the showcase portfolio, which shows a pupil's best or favorite work; the evaluation portfolio, in which most of the contents are specified and scored; the documentation portfolio, which holds evidence of a child's work and progress selected to build a comprehensive description of the child; and the process portfolio, which contains ongoing work for a larger project. Portfolios fulfill most of the basic purposes of classroom assessment as well as documenting what has been accomplished by individuals and the group. They provide a continuous, comprehensive, multidimensional record of development.

There are four basic approaches to portfolio building: requiring specific items; requiring evidence in given developmental or curriculum areas but not specifying the items; collecting individual, often spontaneous samples from ongoing classroom activities; and combinations of the above. Appropriate portfolio items vary with the age and development of the children and the goals of the school. Good portfolio entries are informative and easy to collect. Items should be identified and annotated so their significance is clear. Helping children learn to select, assess, and reflect on portfolio items is central to the process. The information available from portfolios can be increased by identifying and annotating each item, developing procedures and instructions to maximize information, and selecting spontaneously generated items for information as well as uniqueness.

The use of portfolios in alternative assessment is popular, but still quite new. The many unresolved issues include the place of technology, ownership, transfer and storage, evaluation, utility, and practicality.

Individual profiles keep track of a child's growth relative to classroom goals and objectives, and they address broad aspects of development and learning. They summarize basic child capabilities in terms of broader educational and developmental outcomes and are not merely a catalog of isolated skill/performance/content behaviors. They summarize what a teacher "understands and knows" about an individual child. The primary purpose of an individual profile is to help teachers keep track of what they know and what they want to know about a given child. They are used to plan for meeting individual needs and encouraging interests.

Consider all current appraisals when compiling a profile. Look for patterns of behavior and trends showing growth in capabilities by comparing past and current assessments. Note areas to monitor or concerns. Update and review profiles at intervals throughout the year.

Group profiles summarize the range of behavior within a classroom and identify groups of children with similar strengths, needs, or interests. They are most useful for planning activities for the class as a whole.

For Further Study, Discussion, and Reflection

1. Suppose you were to begin now to construct a portfolio to showcase and document your own development and learning. What categories would it have? What would you want to include? Explain your reasoning.

2. Identify the advantages and disadvantages of the four approaches to portfolio building: required items; required evidence; individualized, unique samples; and combinations. In what ways might the advantages and disadvantages be different for a beginning teacher and an experienced teacher?

3. Identify three pieces of evidence you would gather to build a portfolio for a preprimary classroom in the domains of small muscle development, math and science, and language and literacy. Use the assessment and analysis guides given in Appendix A.

4. Identify three broad aspects of development and learning that you would include on an individual profile for first grade. Identify three appraisals you would use to document growth for each of these.

Suggested Readings

Clemmons, J., Laase, L., & Cooper, D. L. (1993). *Portfolios in the classroom: A teacher's sourcebook.* Jefferson City, MO: Scholastic, Inc.

Grace, C., & Shores, E. F. (1991). *The portfolio and its uses: Developmentally appropriate assessment of young children.* Little Rock, AR: Southern Association on Children under Six.

National Education Association. (1993). *Student portfolios.* West Haven, CT: Author.

Northwest Regional Educational Laboratory. (1994). *Portfolio resources bibliography.* Portland, OR: Author.

Stone, S. J. (1995). Portfolios: Interactive and dynamic instructional tool. *Childhood Education, 71*(4), 232–234.

Stone, S. J. (1995). *Understanding portfolio assessment: A guide for parents.* Reston, VA: Association for Childhood Education International.

Valencia, S. W., Hiebert, E. F., & Afflerbach, P. P. (Eds.). (1994). *Authentic reading assessment: Practices and possibilities.* Newark, DE: International Reading Association.

CHAPTER SEVEN

Interpreting Assessment Information

Assessment is of little use unless teachers know what the information means and how to use it to help children develop and learn. This chapter focuses on analyzing, interpreting, and understanding collected information. Chapter 8 suggests ways to use that understanding to make classroom activities and procedures support children's growth, development, and learning. The two steps may merge as teachers skillfully adjust materials and interactions to immediate needs of children. In other cases, it may be difficult to make sense of the information and even more difficult to decide what actions to take based on the interpretation. Both processes call for professional knowledge and judgment, as it is in these steps that a crucial blending takes place. Teachers take information that has been systematically collected, recorded, and summarized and then combine it with understandings, insights, and intuitions that come from day-to-day interactions with children.

It is in this blending of objective information and sensitive judgment that assessment of children in its truest sense takes place (Barnett & Zucker, 1990).

There are two major steps in analyzing and interpreting assessment information: (1) ensuring the authenticity and trustworthiness of the data, and then (2) understanding what it means.

Ensure the Authenticity and Trustworthiness of the Data

Teachers work to make assessment reliable, valid, fair, and adequate (see Chapters 2, 4, and 5). Before you assess, check again to make sure the following are in order:

- There are *enough* samples.
- Samples are *representative* of what is being assessed.
- Samples are *balanced*, employing different sources, methods, and contexts.
- Evidence obtained in different ways *converges*.
- Information is *consistent* over time, sources, contexts, and methods (sometimes, however, a significant inconsistency can emerge here).
- Evidence corresponds to *reality*—it is generally compatible with other aspects of the child's development and learning, and makes sense in comparison with other children of about the same age and developmental level.

As you move from documenting children's actions to interpreting what they mean, the following additional safeguards will maintain quality and trustworthiness.

To Determine Progress, Compare Performance at Two or More Points in Time

The points should be far enough apart to give development and learning a chance to show. Make sure opportunities to learn have been provided in the interval. Measurements should be comparable. Writing samples should be compared to prior writing samples, and oral reading to oral reading.

Work from Compilations and Summaries

One or two summary sheets that profile each child's progress toward major goals synthesize information from many sources and make it readily available for interpretation and further use. Use recorded information, and do not rely on memory alone (Barnett & Zucker, 1990).

Look for Patterns, Including Patterns of Errors, Rather Than Isolated Instances

As you compile information on any behavior, stable patterns will usually emerge. Attendance and tardiness are simple examples of the way patterns offer insights about children, families, and schools (Almy & Genishi, 1979). Absences on the first or last days of the week may signal a situation at home, such as weekend visitations to a noncustodial parent or weekly trips away from home. Some families may not have developed the habit of getting children to school regularly and on time, or there may be transportation difficulties. If this is the child's first year in a group, the youngster may catch every sickness that is "going around." There may be problems with resistance, stamina, or lack of medical care. Since children who are sick a lot will miss a lot, the pattern will give you clues to follow up on.

Such consistent patterns of behavior can alert teachers to children who need referral for special help.

Consider a Child's or a Group's Unique and Individual Patterns of Development, Temperament, Interests, and Dispositions

Morgan's mom told you that he was "deliberate" in his development—in no hurry to sit up, teethe, walk, talk, or do anything else. His kindergarten teacher remarked, "He does things in his own good time." This type of information can help you understand the data you have collected. Carita's tendency to be a perfectionist is evident as she avoids activities she is not good at and struggles for perfection—even to the point of tears—in things that are important to her. Children's unique interests and prior knowledge may become evident as you attempt to understand what certain information means. The children in Donna Frank's class had no interest in dinosaurs, a unit Donna always counted on to intrigue students. Looking further, she found that most of the children had thoroughly investigated dinosaurs the previous year.

Identify Areas of Concern

Consider if the child's current functioning and progress are of concern to the child, parents, you, or other school staff. If so, look in depth at the developmental or curriculum area of concern, take a broader look at all developmental areas, assess the skill or behavior in a different context, or recheck for indicators of the need for special help. Consult available specialists.

Suppose a youngster has difficulty following directions, is inattentive during story time, seldom plays with other children, either indoors or out, and responds inappropriately in conversations and discussions. Classroom staff and other children have difficulty understanding her speech. The youngster is frequently absent. Clearly, available information identifies a concern. More and different information is needed to determine the sources of the problem and develop a course of action. What do parents see at home? Are there clues in the youngster's medical records or developmental history? Are there any situations in which the youngster follows directions and pays attention or are there any situations in which she simply cannot follow what is going on? What does the speech and language specialist say?

Interpret and Understand the Meaning of Assessment Findings

Understanding the meaning of assessment information requires that teachers examine the evidence from a number of different perspectives. The first one is cautionary: generate several hypotheses about possible meanings, but hold them tentatively so that you are open to alternative explanations. The other three are basic guidelines or approaches for analyzing the information about children. The examples highlight each guideline separately, but as you work with summary and primary information, you will use them simultaneously. Think of children's understanding and performance as falling within a band or interval, rather than at a specific point on a scale; compare their understanding and performance to developmental or curriculum expectations (goals, objectives, standards); and analyze information for evidence of the learning processes and strategies they are using. All these approaches will yield information relevant to promoting children's learning.

Generate Multiple Hypotheses about Possible Meanings, but Hold Them Tentatively

Avoid thinking in terms of certainties and absolutes. There is no simplistic formula for interpretation—if a child does *X* then it means *Y* and only *Y*. Information may have several meanings, depending on what aspect you focus on. Human development is complex and not always easy to understand. Consider all aspects that are relevant to classroom decisions. Documentation of a child's efforts to solve a real-life arithmetic problem may have one interpretation if you are analyzing error patterns, another if you are judging disposition to use arithmetic, and still another if you are concerned with developmental level. Talking with other people may bring different perspectives, insights, and hypotheses.

Keep a broad view of the child. Focusing too closely on aspects of development or learning that are considered important in a given program may not reveal children's other strengths. The strong emphasis on language and literacy in most early childhood programs may conceal children's strengths in mathematics, science, the arts, or social relationships.

Interpretations should reflect only what you actually know. Children change rapidly. Our knowledge of child development changes, affording new insights into the meaning of things children do and new ways of looking at their behavior and our responses to it. Even under the best of circumstances, the assessment information we have is only a small sample of what any child can actually do—a sample based primarily on school- or center-related behavior, which may or may not reflect a child's total competence. Some of the most important information about children and their achievement may be difficult to document: motivation, drive for mastery, willingness to expend effort, and family support and encouragement.

Analyze Performance as a Band or Interval within Which a Child Is Functioning

Whatever a child has done or is doing indicates where he is within a larger band or interval that reflects the upper and lower limits of his capability at this point in time (Airasian, 1994; Gage & Berliner, 1992). Development is best thought of as a continuum, moving toward more complex and mature behavior (Bodrova & Leong, 1996; Vygotsky, 1978). There are several reasons why an interval describes children's performance better than a specific point or score: error in measurement, normal variation in development and learning, the nature of developmental processes, and the influence of the amount and nature of assistance.

Error in Measurement. Expect some error in the information you have. For example, performance or situational tasks often require children to give an oral or motor response. If the child does not respond, we cannot conclude that he could not, only that he *did* not. Accurate estimates of a child's oral language ability are difficult to obtain. The upper level of the band or interval may be higher than the samples. Children are quite sensitive to external influences such as hunger, illness, distractions, or problems at home, which can lead to measurement error. In addition, adults make errors as they document children's behavior.

Normal Variation in Development and Learning. There are wide variations of what can be considered "normal" in development and learning—normal variations in when behaviors are acquired and the rate or speed of acquisition (Berk, 1994). Child development norms and sequences are usually drawn from large numbers of children, and no individual child is expected to "fit" exactly. For that reason, published guides to children's development usually indicate a range or interval, rather than a fixed point for developmental achievement. Children have unique and individual patterns of development. "Normal" children begin walking at anywhere from 9 to 18 months—a tremendous variation in a short life span. If such differences exist in a universal, biologically linked developmental milestone, we can expect at least as much variation in other aspects of development and in children's performance relative to curriculum goals and objectives.

The Nature of Developmental Processes. Children's development is dynamic. It changes from day to day and week to week. What a child cannot do today, she may do tomorrow, especially if given appropriate assistance. Children may regress because of illness, stress, or other factors. Development may proceed unevenly, both within a given developmental domain and across domains. The pupil whose versatile vocabulary revolves around family and friends may need help learning abstract concepts. A youngster who is developing quite normally in other areas may lag in social skills.

The Influence of the Amount and Nature of Assistance. In addition to general measurement and development guides that establish the principle "think of a band or interval" rather than a point or score, consider the amount and nature of assistance a child receives to establish the Zone of Proximal Development (ZPD)—the specific type of zone described in Chapter 3. In this concept of development, the ZPD has two limits. The lower level is a child's independent performance—what the child can do alone. The higher level is the best the child can do with maximum assistance (Bodrova & Leong, 1996). Within this zone are different levels of partially assisted performance.

A child's ability to make use of suggestions and prompts gives clues to his thinking processes, level of functioning, and the range of tasks he is ready to learn (Bodrova & Leong, 1996; Campione & Brown, 1985; Vygotsky, 1978). Dynamic assessment techniques try to explore a youngster's ability to profit from assistance in doing a task (Campione et al., 1991; Cronbach, 1990; Feuerstein, 1979; Lidz, 1991). Look for development and learning that are in a formative stage and give prompts, suggestions, and hints to see what a youngster does with such help.

As an example of how a teacher gives and interprets children's use of assistance, suppose you bring in a variety of seashells for children to examine, sort, and group in whatever way they want. Some children may immediately grasp the possibilities, and then group and regroup in imaginative and perceptive ways. They don't need any hints; in fact, suggestions might stifle their creative approach to the task. Some children may perceive nothing but a bunch of shells. They are oblivious to hints and suggestions, either verbal or nonverbal. But another group may initially see nothing or only the most obvious groupings, and then quickly pick up on the slightest hint. Subtly shaded construction paper placed beside the shells will lead children into sorting and ordering by fine differentiations in color. A row of shells ordered by size will set them to grouping by size. A remark such as "Look how deep the ridges are on this shell" will lead to examination and grouping by definition of the ridges. It is these children who can benefit the most from adult assistance to lead their development (Bodrova & Leong, 1996; Rogoff, 1990). The assistance of the colored paper and hints by the teacher are in their ZPD.

Document and interpret the meaning of how children use prompts, hints, and suggestions. Those who do not pick up on the hints may need experiences at a simpler level or more assistance. Those who are beyond the hints may need amplification of the classification ideas within their Zone of Proximal Development, or tasks and assistance that will provide more challenge.

We cannot adequately understand the meaning of what a child does unless we know something of the amount and nature of assistance received.

Consider the Influence of the Total Sociocultural Context on Children's Actions

As in collecting information, we cannot interpret children's behavior apart from their sociocultural context (Goodenow, 1992). The sociocultural context encompasses the who, what, when, and where of the interaction: who the child interacts with, what materials are used, and the time and setting. Look for two things: ways the context may be hindering development and learning, and ways the context may be supporting development and learning. Both things help you understand the child's actions as well as what to do in the future.

Hindrances can include things such as placement of furniture and equipment in a way that gives children the wrong signals about what to do, such as an arrangement that encourages children to visit with each other instead of finishing tasks, or to run wildly around the gym or playground instead of using equipment. It may involve choice of materials: books, games, activities, and songs that children are no longer interested in; materials that are too difficult or too easy; materials that promote aggressive behavior. Adults may expect children to be accomplished in doing things that they are just beginning to learn.

General supports include clear guidance concerning what children are supposed to do, setting up the environment to promote desired behavior, and having enough appropriate materials ready, as well as specific supports that enable a youngster to do whatever she is supposed to: making sure children can see and hear, reducing distractions, coaching and practicing expected behavior, and providing effective mediators to help youngsters learn.

Study the context as well as the child so that you can identify hindrances and decrease them, as well as identify supports and then increase or modify them as needed.

Compare Outcomes to Developmental or Curriculum Expectations

Expected developmental and curriculum outcomes help determine "what to assess" (see Chapter 3). At this point, you will look back to those expected outcomes as a basis for comparing and interpreting assessment information.

Compare Outcomes to a Current General Sequence of Development. Developmental guides or sequences establish our current state of knowledge and understanding in basic child development domains: physical, social/emotional, cognitive, and language. The assessment and analysis guides in Appendix A summarize that knowledge for easy reference. Compare a child's or children's performance to the guidelines in the appropriate domain. Determine the child's approximate place in the sequence, which prior developments have been mastered, and which later developments are emerging or evident.

Judge if the progress the child is making is appropriate, or if opportunities to learn and develop need to be modified to accelerate progress. Many development and curriculum goals take a long time to achieve. Don't panic if a November check reveals that a youngster (or a classroom of youngsters) is a long way from year-end goals. Determine where children are on the continuum of progress to help decide if current curriculum approaches are sufficient.

Look at how checking for developmental and curriculum status and progress works, using simplified examples. Figure 7–1 shows two observations of Shana's dramatic play made approximately three months apart. Next to it is the developmental sequence for that type of play. Comparing the first observation, made on September 23, with the developmental chart, the teacher concludes that Shana's behavior seems closest to parallel play. Consulting other evidence, her teacher finds one or two examples of social play, and some turn-taking, but not much.

To determine progress over time, compare the child's performance on samples of the same type of behavior taken at two or more points in time. Look at both the entries for Shana, the first made on September 23 and the second on December 27 (see Figure 7–1). Shana talks directly to other children and interacts more in the second sample than in the first. The sample taken in September resembles parallel play. The sample from December closely matches simple social play. Shana is not yet exchanging toys, nor is she involved in complementary roles involving back-and-forth interactions. Other evidence about Shana's play and interactions on the play yard, in the block area, and with manipulatives reveals similar behavior. Shana has progressed one level on the developmental continuum, is developing at a rate comparable to her peers, and is in line with the developmental sequence.

If you are interpreting a group profile, determine the range of development and learning—the most mature or advanced behavior and the least mature or advanced behavior. Compare these two extremes with development or learning charts to see if they are in the expected age ranges. Compare clusters of behavior in the profile to the typical expectations as shown in the charts.

Figure 7–2 shows two examples of classroom appraisal of a group's status and progress in fine motor development. Evidence on cutting with scissors

Figure 7–1   *Comparison of Two Assessments of a Child's Play Behavior to a Developmental Sequence for Play*

Selected Excerpts from Social Development Records of Shana Maas.	Developmental Sequence for Peer Play 2 1/2 to 6 years of age (Adapted from Howes, 1980)
9/23—Dramatic Play Dresses as Mom. Announces "I'm going to wash dishes. I'm making dinner." Washes plate, pot, silverware and puts in drainer. Looks at child next to her, who picks up towel. S. picks up a towel, too. They don't interact.	Level 1: Simple Parallel Play Close proximity but doesn't engage in eye contact or any social behavior. Level 2: Parallel Play Mutual Regard Engage in similar activities and occasionally look at each other. May involve imitation. Level 3: Simple Social Play Direct social behavior to one another. Activities not coordinated.
12/27—Dramatic play Dressed up w/heels and purse. Chairs lined up for playing bus. S. takes first chair. "This is my bus. I'm gonna drive. Gabriella, give me your money. Go sit down." G. says "Can I drive?" S. does not respond, but starts bus, making driving noises.	Level 4: Complementary/Mutual Awareness Play Take turns with objects. No verbal exchange. Level 5: Complementary/Reciprocal Social Play Engage in complementary conversation. Back and forth turn-taking with social interaction.

Figure 7–2 *Classroom Appraisal of a Group's Status and Progress in Fine Motor Development*

Item: Cutting with scissors   Date 9/11/9–
Observer: L. Berman   Group: Fourth Street Center

Name	Snips	One complete cut	Cuts on straight line	Cuts on curved line	Cuts out figures	Holds paper correctly	Holds scissors correctly	Holds paper, scissors correctly
Atencio, Fran			✓			✓		
Bear, Danny		✓			✓			
Tytle, Gabriella		✓			✓			
Maestes, Bobby	✓							
Meese, Shana		✓		✓				
Reed, Jerry			✓			✓		

Date 12/18/9–

Name	Snips	One complete cut	Cuts on straight line	Cuts on curved line	Cuts out figures	Holds paper correctly	Holds scissors correctly	Holds paper, scissors correctly
Atencio, Fran				✓			✓	
Bear, Danny				✓			✓	
Tytle, Gabriella			✓				✓	
Maestes, Bobby			✓			✓		
Meese, Shana				✓		✓		
Reed, Jerry				✓			✓	

was recorded on a checklist. Notice that in the assessment made on September 11, the behavior ranges from snipping to cutting on a curved line. Several children have similar skills: Shana, Danny, and Gabriella cut on a straight line; Jerry and Fran cut on a curved line; only Bobby snips.

Compare the assessments of September 11 and December 18. The range has changed. In the first sample, the range was from snipping to cutting on a curved line. In the second sample it is from cutting on a straight line to cutting on a curved line. In addition, the children cluster differently. In the first sample there were three clusters: Bobby snips; Shana, Danny, and Gabriella cut on a straight line; Jerry and Fran cut on a curved line. In the second sample this has changed: Bobby and Gabriella cut on a straight line; Shana, Jerry, Fran, and Danny cut on a curved line. Work products in the children's portfolios and jottings made during observations of art and center activities provide further evidence of their progress. A third sample, taken near the end of the year, should reveal even more.

Is that progress enough, or do the children need additional fine motor experiences to see if their skills can develop faster? Several had never used scissors before coming to school. This is where interpretation comes in. The expected developmental sequence for cutting, shown in Figure 7–3, offers one piece of information for gauging progress. Another is the program goals. Should the children be able to cut out figures and move paper and scissors accurately by the end of the year? Interpreting the meaning calls for integrating all these considerations, collecting more information as needed, and making a judgment about its meaning.

Compare Outcomes to Curriculum Goals, Objectives, and Standards. To understand assessment results, compare them to expected outcomes, however they are stated. Some goals, objectives, and standards are quite broad and require further specification before assessment or interpretation of assessment results can occur. Some are stated so that direct rather than general comparisons are possible, especially if they identify specific objectives leading to the goal.

Suppose that a goal states that "children should be able to compare objects, events, and experiences in the physical and social world." This goal is a comprehensive one, encompassing language and the major subject matter areas, as well as basic learning strategies (Marzano, Pickering, & McTighe, 1993). It is relevant for learners of all ages. The specific expectations will change depending on children's age and development. If expectations for

Figure 7–3   *The Developmental Sequence for Cutting with Scissors*

Level 1: Snips. May hold paper and scissors incorrectly.

Level 2: Makes one complete cut with the scissors. May hold paper and scissors incorrectly.

Level 3: Cuts on a straight line. May hold paper correctly, scissors incorrectly.

Level 4: Cuts on a curved line. Holds scissors and paper correctly.

Level 5: Cuts out figures.

early childhood are that children will understand and use terms of contrast and comparison, such as "same as," "different from," "like," "alike," "unlike," "not the same," "similar," and "dissimilar," linked with appropriate descriptive terms (shape, size, color, number, location, function, direction, and so forth), then you know what to help them learn, what to assess, and what to compare their performances to.

Standards can be used in the same way. The National Council of Teachers of Mathematics (NCTM) designated Patterns and Relationships as one of the key categories of mathematics standards. A related *content standard* explained that

> In grades K–4, the mathematics curriculum should include the study of patterns and relationships so that students can . . . *recognize, describe, extend, and create* a wide variety of patterns [italics added]. . . .
>
> Pattern recognition involves many concepts, such as color and shape identification, direction, orientation, size, and number relationships. Children should use all these properties in identifying, extending, and creating patterns. . . . Identifying the "cores" of patterns helps children become aware of the structures. For example, in some patterns the core repeats, whereas in others the core grows. (NCTM, 1989, pp. 60–61)

Since preschool and primary children experiment, construct, repeat, and identify patterns of all types, it is fairly easy to collect evidence to compare what children do with the standard.

Let's look at an example. Leslie and the other children in her first grade class were to create ABAB (every other one) patterns on lines marked with an *X*. Leslie's paper (see Figure 7–4) indicates she has met the standard of "creating" a simple ABAB pattern in two dimensions. The next step is to ask Leslie to reflect on and explain what she has done. The recorder notes her explanation. It is clear that she can also *recognize* and *describe* the AB pattern, including pointing out that the rows of patterns alternating with a blank row make an ABAB pattern vertically down the page. A structured performance assessment with manipulatives indicates that she can *extend* the pattern as well. Comparison with the standard tells us that this child has met the standard for simple ABAB patterns and is ready for other work with varied patterns: amplification using different modalities, such as actions or sounds; challenge through introduction of more complex repeating patterns or different types, such as patterns that "grow"; application to other situations by working with material in which the pattern is less obvious, or other variations on patterns and relationships. The standard and the implied benchmark (by fourth grade, students should recognize, describe, extend, and create a wide variety of patterns) provide a basis for comparison and a guide for planning further experiences.

Rubrics.   Since most standards are usually broad and include a number of complex behaviors, educators develop rubrics to help them judge children's progress toward the standard. A rubric presents clear criteria—rules or guidelines—by which a complex performance can be judged. Such rules are typically used in judging diving, figure skating, and gymnastic competitions. A *scoring rubric* "consists of a fixed scale and a list of characteristics

Figure 7–4   *Leslie's ABAB Patterns*

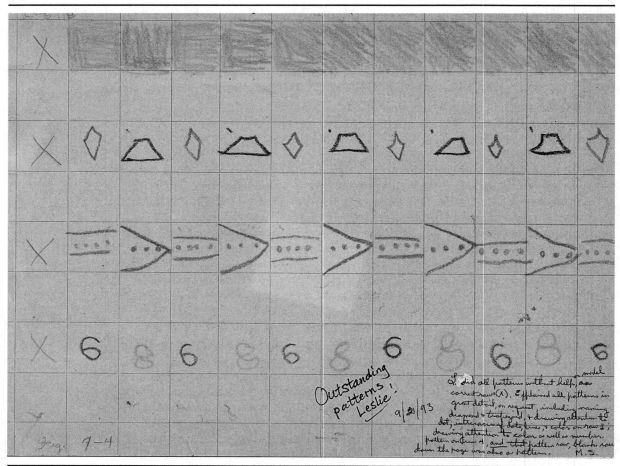

describing performance for each of the points of the scale" (Marzano, Pickering, & McTighe, 1993, p. 29). The scale often specifies what is acceptable performance. Figure 7–5 is an example of a scoring rubric for the standard "expresses ideas clearly." Teachers working with this rubric would analyze information pertinent to that standard and decide what statement on the scale best describes the child's performance at this time.

Figure 7–6 is an example of a rubric used for scoring in the Child Observation Record (COR), developed by High/Scope (1993). Teachers use evidence documented during children's daily activities to make a judgment about which statement applies.

Specifying important aspects of a complex performance presents many challenges. What is acceptable performance at a given age or developmental level, or even in relation to a standard? As with any rating scale, the intervals between points on the scale may not be equal. Attaching numerical values to children's work is difficult, at best. The items on the rubric often represent only one of many possible indicators of progress toward the standard, often the most obvious one. For example, efforts to specify various levels of classification may entirely overlook that children need to learn to

Figure 7–5 *Rubric for Scoring "Expresses Ideas Clearly"*

Rubrics for Effective Communication Standards

A.   Expresses ideas clearly.

4   Clearly and effectively communicates the main idea or theme and provides support that contains rich, vivid, and powerful detail.

3   Clearly communicates the main idea or theme and provides suitable support and detail.

2   Communicates important information but not a clear theme or overall structure.

1   Communicates information as isolated pieces in a random fashion.

Copyright © 1993 McREL Institute

Figure 7–6 *Rubric for Scoring "Solving Problems"*

B. Solving problems		Time 1	Time 2	Time 3
Child does not yet identify problems.	(1)	_____	_____	_____
Child identifies problems, but does not try to solve them, turning instead to another activity.	(2)	_____	_____	_____
Child uses one method to try to solve a problem, but if unsuccessful, gives up after one or two tries.	(3)	_____	_____	_____
Child shows some persistence, trying several alternative methods to solve a problem.	(4)	_____	_____	_____
Child tries alternative methods to solve a problem and is highly involved and persistent.	(5)	_____	_____	_____

Notes:

_____

_____

_____

©1992 High/Scope Educational Research Foundation

classify on bases they select and specify, as well as those specified by someone else.

Analyze Information for Clues to Learning Processes and Strategies

Understanding children's learning strategies does not focus on outcomes such as the ability to read a selected passage; add, subtract, multiply, and divide; or correctly interpret another's social intent. Instead, it addresses thinking and learning processes, which are difficult to capture and interpret. These learning strategies and processes—such as the ability to relate present learning to prior knowledge, construct "theories" and generalizations, transfer learning to another situation, or use prompts, hints, and clues— apply to all development and learning. For instance, many of us have tried to "unlearn" a faulty tennis or golf swing. Faulty prior knowledge interfered with learning the correct way.

As knowledge of cognitive processes and their development expands, more emphasis is being placed on helping children understand and use effective learning strategies. Learning is not always a linear, sequential process but can proceed in fits and starts. Concepts are refined and redefined as the learner progresses from being a novice to being an expert. Knowledge, strategies, and thinking processes change at different stages of the learning process (Rogoff, 1990). Many subtle cultural differences and influences are hard to interpret (Gage & Berliner, 1992). Even when a barrier in children's learning processes is identified, such as interference from prior knowledge, appropriate action is not always clear. However, commands to "try harder" and "apply yourself" are no substitute for figuring out what is causing problems for children and doing whatever is possible to help them overcome those problems.

Development and learning processes often reveal themselves in children's behavior: the errors they make; the way they use prior knowledge; the explanations they give; the way they make use of prompts, hints, and suggestions; and the way they progress from simple skills and knowledge to complex, coordinated patterns of actions and thinking.

Examine Underlying Mental Processes.   Young children are acquiring the skills that allow them to focus their attention, remember deliberately, and regulate their own cognitive and social behavior (Bodrova & Leong, 1996). They learn to be less reactive and more thoughtful and deliberate. The lack of these metacognitive abilities manifests itself across all developmental domains. For example, the 4-year-old who has a hard time concentrating in group time, waiting in line, and playing cooperatively with others, and who turns the block area into a bowling alley, may be having trouble with underlying self-regulation skills. Because he is so reactive, his attention and actions are driven by what catches his fancy at that moment. He cannot inhibit his behavior, concentrate, or act with mental deliberateness, considering the consequences of his actions before he acts. Although a teacher may work on this behavior as it appears as an isolated action in group time, play, or other activities, the underlying reactiveness is the root problem.

To determine whether a child needs help and practice in developing underlying cognitive skills, observe the child in different contexts. Compare them. Which situations tend to produce more mature behaviors, and which ones produce least mature behaviors? Children with reactive behaviors often do well when they become engrossed in an activity of their own choosing and have trouble breaking away. When they are not engrossed, they may flit from one activity to the next. They have trouble with ignoring distractions and sticking to the task at hand, and may perform better in a one-to-one relationship with objects, peers, or the teacher.

Analyze Error Patterns.   Errors should not be thought of as "random, careless, or lazy behavior of a student but . . . as rooted in a complex and logical process of thought" that is amenable to correction (Glaser, 1987, p. 333). Children make errors because they have misconceptions or partial understandings. Error analysis is regularly used in teaching reading and is helpful in any content or performance area. For example, children who are having difficulty regrouping in mathematics may make errors that show teachers the source of their difficulty.

Check the number, type, and pattern of errors to see if they fit any of the following categories (Gage & Berliner, 1992):

1. Systematic error patterns have a consistent pattern. The child makes the same mistake over and over. Systematic errors usually mean that a child does not understand a rule or fact and consistently misapplies it. Interpretation may vary with the level of development. Very young children may simply require time and experience, as in the systematic overregularizations that young children make in learning language. In other cases, skilled questioning, explanations, or appropriate material or experiences can help break a pattern that more time and experience may not correct. Think of the social skill of entering and becoming part of a group. Many children (and adults) make the same mistakes over and over and would benefit from coaching and modeling.

2. Random error patterns do not have a predictable pattern. They usually mean the child is guessing because he has no facts or rules to apply. To understand random error patterns, teachers have to sensitively probe the child's thinking. The cause of the pattern may vary depending on the child. For example, children may not have the prior experience or knowledge to enable them to respond reasonably. Some urban children may know little about plants, hills, valleys, rivers, and other aspects of the natural world. Rural children's knowledge of urban life may consist of what they see on television. Neither group will have accurate facts or rules to apply. Teachers may have to provide experiences and teach or reteach the information or skills.

3. Skip error patterns are "goofs." They are not of concern unless they become an established pattern. You can suspect that hurrying, disinterest, loss of concentration, or anxiety caused these errors.

Determine Prior Knowledge and Its Relationship to Current Understanding and Performance.   Children's beliefs, knowledge, and past experiences provide the base for current learning (Glaser, 1987). Look at Renata, whose experience with pets was limited to cats, dogs, rabbits, guinea pigs, and other furry creatures. When the teacher introduced a pet turtle, Renata described him as having "bumpy fur"—a logical extension of her prior experiences. Because of the wide diversity in young children's backgrounds and experiences, teachers cannot assume shared knowledge about anything. Probably no other aspect of children's development and learning is as subject to influence from families, communities, previous schooling, and other experiences. This prior knowledge can help or interfere with new learning (Winne & Marx, 1987). If children approach new information or skills without prerequisite skills or background, lack of knowledge will interfere.

Compare what children know to what you have taught or will be teaching, to assess their familiarity with the knowledge or skills. Analyze a "map" or "web" constructed from children's responses to identify misconceptions or preconceptions that need to be considered. Review records of skill development. For instance, children who learned one type of letter formation at home or in a previous school may show interference as they attempt to learn a new system. Study children's answers or explanations for indications of prior knowledge and understanding and whether they have linked that knowledge to present learning. Disinterest may mean either lack of knowledge or mastery. For example, children's difficulty with arithmetic story problems is related to their inability to transfer computation skills to a different situation. "Children need to learn skills in finding or creating similarity across contexts" (Rogoff & Gardner, 1984, p. 961). Adults may need to guide children to help them create links between what they already know and what they are trying to learn. "Remember when we learned how to measure and graph your growth? Today we are going to start learning how to measure and graph the growth of plants."

In analyzing learning processes, you may detect problems or facility in different types of application and transfer:

Negative transfer occurs when prior learning impedes new learning. The child uses a familiar response in a situation that calls for a different one or uses intuitive understandings that are counter to what should be learned. For example, social behavior that is accepted in the home or community may interfere with learning a different type of social behavior at school.

Positive transfer occurs when prior knowledge and skills help children learn new skills. The links between old and new learning help children remember and perform better. We may identify either positive or negative transfer as children try to apply to new situations what they know and can do.

Intuitive theories or preconceptions may also interfere with present learning (Glaser, 1987). In their efforts to make sense of the world, children construct their own theories, which can be inaccurate or incomplete, about why things are the way they are. Teachers can address some of these preconceptions directly if they can identify and interpret them accurately. Dominique was playing a computer game that presented him with simple addition problems:

$$\begin{array}{ccc} 11 & 13 & 16 \\ \underline{+1} & \underline{+1} & \underline{+1} \end{array}$$

As Dominique entered his answers—3, 5, and 8—he became increasingly upset. The computer wouldn't accept them. Only as the teacher examined the pattern of error did Dominique's "theory" about addition become clear. She was able to address it directly and help him learn how addition worked. Looking only at the number of right and wrong answers does not reveal the kind of help he needs, but analysis of errors does. Children may develop their own theories about the meaning of other people's actions—often misreading social cues or transferring the understanding of one set of social cues to a situation where that understanding does not apply. Boys who exhibit aggressive behavior may be misinterpreting friendly social cues as being aggressive (Dodge, Pettit, McClaskey, & Brown, 1986; Dodge & Somberg, 1987).

Analyze Explanations and Descriptions.   Learning involves active construction of knowledge by the learner (Bredekamp & Rosegrant, 1992, 1995; Mayer, 1992). By examining a child's explanations and descriptions, the teacher can gain insight into how children select, organize, and integrate information and experiences to construct their knowledge.

Children's responses to "How did you get that answer?" "Explain how you did that," "Why do you think that?" and other similar questions give clues to many aspects of development and learning. Children may be able to do something but not describe or explain how or why (Berk, 1994). Some children may give explanations that seem perfectly logical to them, but indicate a level of development dominated by perception and an inability to think about several variables at once. Such a situation is revealed in the following interview with a child who is experimenting with things that sink and float:

> *Teacher:* Why do you think some things float?
> *Child:* Just 'cause they have to float. A puppet would float because it's light. A fat person can float.
> *Teacher:* Can a skinny person float?
> *Child:* Yes, 'cause it's light.
> *Teacher:* But is a fat person light?
> *Child:* No, the fat person can float if it holds still. The wooden cabinet can't float 'cause it's too heavy.

Analysis of responses reveals the quality and level of children's thinking and reminds us how much children have to learn and how incomplete their knowledge and understanding are. Interviews like this one are regularly incorporated into the assessment of primary school children in England (Maeroff, 1991).

Asked "How do you know that's a male lion?" a child may be unable to elaborate beyond "I saw it on TV" and establish her level of learning at recognition. Another may immediately identify the lion's distinctive attributes, showing a higher level of knowledge. Listening to children's responses to "Why would someone do that?" or their perceptions of a classroom or playground incident can help you understand their social knowledge.

Current cognitive research (Gardner, 1991; Mayer, 1992) suggests that the difference between many poor and good problem-solvers lies in the activation of appropriate strategies and the ability to monitor the thinking process (metacognition). Poor students may have the requisite knowledge and skills, but fail to use them correctly or at the appropriate time. These students lack flexibility and may stick to one strategy even when it does not lead to successful solutions. Children's descriptions and explanations often reveal aspects of their metacognition. Requests such as "Tell me the ways you tried before you got this answer" will also help uncover these processes.

Look for Qualitative and Quantitative Differences.   Assessment information can help us understand changes in what a youngster knows and can do and how she expresses that in the journey from beginning to proficient learner. Beginning learners may be inconsistent. There are qualitative as well as quantitative differences (Glaser, 1987). For example, a beginning learner may have only a vague and incomplete understanding of a term such as *mammal*. Her fragmented knowledge, incomplete understanding, and thought process are better described as a "complex" of ideas, rather than a true concept (Hanfmann & Kasanin, 1937; Sakharov, 1990; Vygotsky, 1962). As she organizes her scattered ideas into a true concept, she can define *mammal* in her own words, apply the very specific and narrow concept correctly to novel instances, and explain the relationship of a mammal to other members of the animal kingdom.

To analyze a child's level of performance, compare the documented behavior to a breakdown of the important components of the learning. For instance, patterning requires that learners be able to match one to one, perceive similarities and differences among items, and identify the significant features of the pattern. When Steven tries to repeat an alternating pattern of two red circles and three blue squares, he gets the first two circles correct, then places a blue square, red square, and yellow square in the row. Steven has some of the essential skills. He identifies the repeating nature of a certain number of circles and squares and matches one to one, but he omits the element of color in the squares. By comparing his performance with the essential components, the teacher identifies the components he can and can't do.

We ask children to do tasks that require integrating several subskills into a complex behavior. Analysis of children's performance on the various components will aid understanding. In some cases, a child may have trouble performing one of the subskills. A child who can't catch a ball while she is standing still can hardly be expected to catch a ball while she is running. If she can't hop, she can't skip. In other cases, a child may have the subskills but be unable to combine them. He may read isolated words and identify word meanings, but can't read a passage and explain its meaning. Sometimes the number of steps required simply overwhelms the learner, and he cannot proceed. An incomplete performance may mean that the number of things the child must attend to is overwhelming.

Identify the component subskills, their relationship, and the child's performance on each. Analyze where the child is having problems, and why.

Summary

Interpretation is a high-level process that requires analysis of information, integration of that information with other data, comparison with developmental guidelines and curriculum expectations, and making valid hypotheses about what it all means. Doing so blends objective information with sensitive judgment to yield a true assessment.

To ensure trustworthiness of the information, check for fairness, validity, and reliability. Make sure there are enough representative and balanced samples; that evidence obtained in different ways converges; that samples are consistent over time, unless the inconsistency itself is of significance; and that the assessment corresponds to reality. To maintain quality during analysis and interpretation, follow these guidelines: to determine progress, compare performance at two or more points in time; work from written documentation, compilations, and summaries, not memory; look for patterns, rather than isolated instances. Consider a child's or a group's unique and individual patterns of development, temperament, interests, and dispositions. For areas of concern or where more information is needed, look in depth, look more broadly, look in different contexts, or recheck.

As you analyze and try to understand information, use these guidelines:

- Generate multiple hypotheses about possible meanings, but hold all interpretations and hypotheses tentatively.
- Think of performance as a band or interval within which a child is functioning, not as a specific point on a scale.
- Compare outcomes to developmental or curriculum expectations.
- Analyze information for clues to learning processes.

For Further Study, Discussion, and Reflection

1. This chapter suggests that the sociocultural context of the classroom can either support or hinder children's performance. Reflect on classrooms you have observed and worked in. What evidence of this principle have you seen? What are its implications for you as you document and interpret children's performance in your own classroom?

2. Look at the example of the range of performance and clustering of cutting skills shown in Figure 7–2 on page 133. What are possible interpretations of this information (a) if children are 3 years old and in their first year of preschool and (b) if they are age 5 and in kindergarten? Based on these interpretations, outline appropriate classroom strategies relating to these children's cutting skills.

3. You are getting ready to check children's progress in language development. The records include periodic samples of children's drawing and writing; lists of books they like to "read" or listen to; checklists at two points in time on their comprehension of concepts of space, time, and attributes of objects; and performance samples on tasks that required following oral directions given by an adult. What other information might be needed before you have enough representative samples to interpret children's progress in language? Outline a strategy to obtain that information.

4. Secure one or more work products from a preschool or primary child. Analyze them for information about that child. Explain and justify your interpretation. If you cannot get work products, do an

in-depth analysis of Figures 4–2 and 4–3 (see pages 59 and 60), and then compare and contrast the two products.

5. Interview both a beginning teacher and an experienced teacher who are using classroom assessment to see how they interpret the information they collect. Compare and contrast their responses. What are some implications for you at this point in your teaching career?

Suggested Readings

Bodrova, E., & Leong, D. J. (1996). *Tools of the mind: The Vygotskian approach to early childhood education.* Englewood Cliffs, NJ: Merrill.

Bredekamp, S., & Rosegrant, T. (Eds.). (1992). *Reaching potentials: Appropriate curriculum and assessment for young children.* (Vol. 1). Washington, DC: National Association for the Education of Young Children.

Bredekamp, S., & Rosegrant, T. (Eds.). (1995). *Reaching potentials: Appropriate curriculum and assessment for young children* (Vol. 2). Washington, DC: National Association for the Education of Young Children.

Levine, K. (1995). *Development of prewriting and scissor skills: A visual analysis.* Boston: Communication Skill Builders.

Rogoff, B. (1990). *Apprenticeship in thinking: Cognitive development in social context.* New York: Oxford University Press.

Tharp, R. G., & Gallimore, R. (1988). *Rousing minds to life: Teaching, learning, and schooling in social context.* New York: Cambridge University.

Wortham, S. C. (1995). *The integrated classroom: Assessment–curriculum link in early childhood education.* New York: Macmillan.

CHAPTER EIGHT

Using Assessment Information

The primary purpose of classroom assessment is to maximize children's development and learning. For the classroom teacher, this means aligning what is done in the classroom with what assessment reveals: where children are in their learning and development and what they have yet to attain. Bringing these two elements together is a challenging artistic process, not a mechanical one. Teachers can't say, "If Jeanne can't do this, turn to page 59 for activities" or "Recycle this group through Unit 8." Solutions are more complex than that. Knowing a child's strengths, needs, and interests does not always tell you what to do next. Thoughtful, sensitive, artistic planning is the best process teachers have for using assessment information in a way that directly benefits children and weaves the many threads involved in teaching into whole cloth.

Planning is essential if teachers are to respond to shifts in thinking about early childhood curriculum and practice. Curriculum is viewed as a continuum of knowledge, skills, and thinking processes.

> It is no longer viewed as a set of categories focused on content (such as reading, math, science, etc.) or on grade levels (first grade curriculum, second grade curriculum). The role of the teacher, then, becomes to match each child's developmental level of functioning, as well as individual capabilities in functioning, to the appropriate points along this continuum. (Jewett, 1992, p. 2)

Activities, content, grouping, instructional interactions, and the other elements that make up classroom learning and teaching must be grounded in children's current abilities and potential, as determined by assessment, and designed to lead them on (Stiggens, 1994). Unless teachers plan to use assessment results, the insights and information are likely to be lost in the rush of classroom events.

Teachers can link assessment with developmentally appropriate curriculum, no matter what planning process they use. The basic principles that follow apply to almost all developmental areas or curriculum goals, are drawn from the broad age span of early childhood—3 to 8 years old—and reflect the differing classroom organizations and emphases of the various levels. Suggestions and examples are representative and are neither prescriptive nor exhaustive. Our intent is to show teachers ways in which information from assessment can inform and improve classroom practice through planning strategies, individual and group strategies, and curriculum and classroom modification strategies. Specific examples of how assessment information can be linked to planning appropriate experiences for children conclude the chapter.

Planning Strategies

Planning allows for reflection on what to do with assessment results, and on teachers' possible role in those results, and it gives an opportunity to outline a course of action that may involve changes in the environment and in teaching processes and procedures.

Plan and Organize the Intended Changes

Although much planning is never written (Clark & Yinger, 1987), translation of assessment results into specific activities to help children learn probably requires more planning than teachers can carry in their heads. Projects and investigations, for example, show great promise as a way to integrate assessment results, information about how children learn, and important development and learning goals. However, projects and investigations require a high degree of planning and organization to achieve the expected results (Katz & Chard, 1989; Morine-Dershimer, 1990).

Think through what you plan to do, make a note or attach a card to remind you, revise a lesson in a science or social studies guide to incorporate the problem solving and critical thinking that assessment shows is needed, or script sample questions to ask children working on multilevel activities so that each one has appropriate interaction with an adult. Do whatever is necessary to guide and remind you and other adults in the classroom of any modifications you intend to make.

Refer to Assessment Information as You Plan

Study the summary sheets and class profiles for logical, flexible groupings and subgroupings. Review notes and children's work to remind you where they need help and where they are progressing satisfactorily. Check the assessment plan to see if you need to collect one of the core items for the portfolio, or plan a performance check on the children's abilities to estimate and measure as a part of their ongoing work in science and mathematics.

Allow Time for Reflection

Allow enough time for thoughtful consideration of and reflection on assessment results. Don't try to plan everything at one time. Make preliminary notes to provide a framework, then gradually fill in details, incorporating insights from periodic and ongoing assessment and from other people working in the classroom.

Plan Ways to Meet Children's Assessed Needs

When a particular need is identified, it is unlikely to be met through incidental learning or the passage of time alone. For instance, children who are rejected by their peers should receive help before that rejection is set in stone and the possibilities for social integration are lost (Staff, *Harvard Education Letter*, 1989). Youngsters whose backgrounds have not provided them with the experiences, language, and dispositions to tackle academic tasks are unlikely to pick them up.

Deliberately Incorporate the Wealth of Information, Resources, and Strategies Available to Support Young Children's Learning

Knowledge about young children's development and learning is expanding rapidly, but unless teachers plan to use that knowledge, they will continue to do things the same old way. Be open to trying different approaches.

Suppose you've always regarded outdoor time as a time for everyone to enjoy strictly unstructured, unplanned play. Assessment reveals that the children whose large muscle skills were already good when they entered school are getting better, and the ones who need to improve haven't. It's time to rethink the approach to outdoor time, using information which shows that children benefit from appropriate instruction in physical and motor development (Gallahue, 1993; Poest, Williams, Witt, & Atwood, 1990).

Assessment often reveals children who are having difficulty discriminating symbols important in mathematics, reading, attention, memory, and problem solving (Berk, 1994). What will help the youngster who is having difficulty discriminating mirror-image letters, such as *b* and *d*? Experiences with print in actual reading situations may make a youngster more sensitive to these and other reading-specific perceptual cues (Casey, 1986). Since this suggestion is compatible with the whole language and literacy approach the school is using, plan for it.

Theories about helping children learn through appropriate scaffolding and guided participation in the Zone of Proximal Development have enormous implications for teaching and learning in early childhood (Belmont, 1989; Berk & Winsler, 1995; Bodrova & Leong, 1996). Planning for how this will happen helps teachers implement these subtle and sensitive instructional approaches.

Plan for and with Other People in the Classroom

Many early childhood classrooms have classroom assistants, aides, parent and grandparent volunteers, older children, and specialists at given times. Extra people open up more learning opportunities, but these must be planned.

Involve parents and regular classroom personnel in long- and short-range planning. They may offer a different perspective on ways to meet assessed needs. Parents of children with special needs will be involved through the Individual Educational Program.

Using assessment results to help children learn almost always requires greater specificity in planning for other people than most teachers are apt to do. Plan where adults will be and what they will say and do to support children's learning. Some examples: As you assess, it is clear that several children need lots of help with social interaction. Classroom disruptions affirm that conclusion almost daily. You work out a plan of action designed to prevent some of the disruptions and simultaneously teach children appropriate behavior. Since all classroom adults need to be consistent if the plan is to work, coach other adults.

Assessment almost always reveals children who are at the cutting edge of some new learning and who have a range of tasks they are ready for. It shows where a child is currently functioning and perhaps gives some insights on the direction of growth and interest. Plan dialogue and activities to enable the child to move to a higher level. Pair an adult or a child who is competent in a given skill with a child who is on the verge of being competent, and show the "expert" how to assist the "novice" as they work together. For instance, children might not be able to set a table or prepare snacks on their own, but can do so with assistance. Children who are still learning the social and organizational skills to dramatize a favorite story can benefit from adult assistance. Planning ensures that props, space, time, and a coach are available.

Balance What You Might Like to Do with What Is Possible

Set priorities for individual children and the class. Make easy changes first. Changing time schedules in a self-contained classroom to be more compatible with children's development and ways of learning is relatively easy. Changing the teaching of reading from a long-established basal reader approach to an integrated whole-language approach may take longer.

Start with obvious and critical needs. If assessment reveals that the youngster you thought was comprehending English is not, an obvious and critical need exists. If assessment reveals that a youngster frequently disrupts or is rejected in classroom activities, an obvious and critical need exists.

Individual and Group Strategies

Authentic assessment usually reveals many strengths and many things "yet to learn." There will be developmental or curriculum areas in which only individual children need challenge or assistance, areas in which several children could benefit, as well as areas in which all children will benefit from additional opportunity to learn and develop. Balancing the needs of individual children with those of the total group is one of a teacher's most challenging tasks. Current instructional practices and research offer many guidelines and clues, but no definitive answers. We will look at situations in which one or two children may need specific attention, when several children would benefit, and when the entire group will benefit, as well as mixed-age classes.

For One or Two Children

Sometimes one or two children require specific help, either because they lack proficiency in an age and developmentally appropriate learning or because they need challenge. Usually their needs can be met by providing opportunities for learning with the entire group, in a small subgroup, or by providing multilevel activities. It is seldom necessary to remove children from the group. You might plan a specific activity that would be appropriate for several children, including the one or two that need help. Sit beside the youngster(s) who need attention, and as you work with the entire group, give appropriate help. Maybe that consists of counting balls of modeling clay, when the others are well into understanding "fewer" and "more." A few opportunities for individual attention will often work wonders with a child who is just on the verge of grasping an idea.

Sometimes opportunities must be closely tailored to needs and interests. If a child is having difficulty, analyze assessment results for clues to the problem. If a second-grader is having difficulty alphabetizing words because she does not fully understand *before* and *after* as they apply to position in a sequence, help her learn those terms, going back to experiences with concrete materials if necessary. If the difficulty stems from uncertainty about the order of letters in the alphabet, provide practice to make alphabetical order automatic.

Children who need challenge deserve the same thoughtful consideration. Multilevel activities, project work, and cooperative groups enable them to enjoy the benefits of group interaction. Individual activities can challenge, extend, broaden, and elaborate their development and learning into areas they might not otherwise explore: creative problem solving, scientific investigation, composing music or poetry, mastering games of strategy and skill. Amplification (Zaporozhets & Elkonin, 1971) of children's knowledge may bring depth and breadth of understanding at their own level of development. A youngster need not move into working with symbols prematurely, but can "amplify" his development with sensory-motor or other developmentally appropriate activities. "Challenge" need not be synonymous with acceleration.

Sometimes individual children are reluctant to participate in activities such as vigorous outdoor play, art, dramatic play, focused skill development, or oral presentations. Look first for obvious reasons: Is the play too boisterous and competitive? Are the skills beyond the child's developmental level? Are there gender signals that keep a boy or girl away? Is the reluctance simply this youngster's initial reserve in entering into a new activity? Are sociocultural differences operating? Evaluate the child's current level of functioning and skill for possible clues to the reluctance. Plan activities the child likes and in which she is successful, and relate or extend them into other areas, such as gradually combining the block area and dramatic play area or setting up attractive, versatile art, science, or writing materials that engage the child's interest. Perhaps your observation confirms what others have found—that children may be not be engaged in large muscle activities, even though they are outside (Poest et al., 1990). Rearrange active physical play apparatus and put it in a prominent place on the play yard. Plan noncompetitive games and activities to discourage inappropriate competitiveness, often disheartening to the children who need the most encouragement. Select or alter activities so children do not have a long wait for a turn. Join in to guide and provide a model.

In all situations, provide support, guidance, informal instruction, and encouragement, but also help the youngster improve skills that will make participation easier (Bodrova & Leong, 1996; Rogoff, 1990). Help children who can't throw and catch learn how to. Teach oral presentation skills gradually, and let children practice with one other person or a small group until they are comfortable, gradually assuming more responsibility for their own performance (Rogoff & Gardner, 1984). Adapt classroom interaction processes to recognize community and cultural practices, such as allowing more time for responses or time for pauses in speech (Gage & Berliner, 1992).

For Several Children

Class profiles usually identify several children who are having difficulty with the same skill, who need more opportunity to practice, or who need challenge because they are quite proficient. Use a variety of flexible grouping strategies. Some of the options are friendship groups, interest groups, achievement groups, interdependent cooperative groups, work and study skills groups, self-selected groups, informal skill groups, formally assigned skill groups, random groups, groups of one or two, and others. For instance, groups of two can form author/editor pairs in which each child learns important writing, reading, editing, and discourse skills. Two children can "pair and share" to give an opportunity to discuss, report, or share without the deadly routine of round-robin "show and tell" or reporting. Children who write can be paired with children who are still dictating. If children are having difficulty entering a peer group, let them play and work with some younger children. Aggressive children may be less aggressive with older or larger children. Pair a shy child with a friendly, outgoing one, and form small groups in which less outgoing children feel welcome (Wittmer & Honig, 1994).

Avoid assigned, unchanging ability or skill groups that may stigmatize and track children by narrowing their opportunities to learn, influencing motivation (Manning & Lucking, 1990; Oakes, 1991; Slavin, 1987). Group children on functional competence and need related to specific developmental or learning areas, not on overall perception of ability or achievement (Warger, 1988). With skillful planning, subgroups can be formed, accomplish their purposes, and proceed to another activity unobtrusively.

Interdependent cooperative learning groups deliberately mix children with differing skills and knowledge so children learn from each other; the group itself becomes a way to learn both social and academic skills.

"Choice" activities can be geared to the needs of one group, and others can participate if they wish. Children who have mastered a certain development or learning often enjoy and benefit from repetition, just as they reread favorite books. If the activity involves adult–child interaction, adults can vary the level of interaction to the child's need. For example, in a game designed to help children learn the concepts "more," "less," and "equal," some children might simply be hearing and repeating the terms, whereas others would be using them spontaneously or in conversational interchanges.

Mixed-Age Classes

Typical early childhood groups are grouped by age. Mixed-age classes open up new possibilities for meeting children's assessed needs. There are indications that social development, particularly leadership and prosocial behavior, is enhanced. Interaction between less able ("novices") and more able children ("experts") may have academic and social benefits for both. Children who are slightly older and more proficient may be operating in another child's Zone of Proximal Development and thus be able to provide just the appropriate amount of modeling and guidance to help the learner (Katz, Evangelou, & Hartman, 1990). Children will need some specific guidance if the benefits of this approach are to be realized. Katz and associates (1990) suggest that children be helped to ask for and give assistance; that teachers guard against exploiting older children as helpers and discourage stereotyping by age; that children be sensitized to their peers' emotional needs and help them know how to respond; and that children be helped to know their peers' interests, needs, and capabilities. The opportunity to help another student can increase the "expert's" motivation as well as the actual learning (Webb, 1983). Many of these same strategies will work in any group, which will always have mixed abilities and interests.

For the Entire Group

Sometimes almost all children in a group will benefit from experiences provided to a total group: class meetings, group or circle time, music, dance, movement, aerobic exercise, group discussion and problem solving, listening to books being read aloud, and many other activities. Even activities traditionally thought of as self-selected or individual may have components that involve the whole group. For example, some physical development experts suggest that outdoor playtimes begin with a group "warm up," with everyone walking, then walking briskly, before children proceed to their chosen activities. Everyone should also participate in a "cool down" as a transition from outdoor play to the next activity. An "individually appropriate" activity does not mean that children do everything as individuals.

Attractive, interesting learning centers are another way to make learning experiences available to every child. Children work in these as they are interested and have time. Monitor participation. If some children don't participate, try modifications in placement, materials, competing activities, time availability, and adult involvement and encouragement before deciding the approach doesn't work. Participation doesn't have to be daily, but can be over a period of time.

As an alternative, children can be expected to participate in certain learning centers sometime during each day. For instance, children who are learning to express themselves in writing might be expected to write in their journals or work in the writing center sometime during the day. The choice of when and what to write is theirs. Children involved in project work can be expected to solve certain mathematical problems related to the project. They may not all do it at one time or in the same way, but all will have the experience.

Child-selected or free choice activities can also reach all the children in the group, provided they are interesting enough and children have an extended period of time to work through their choices. Monitor participation to make sure children who need the experience get it.

Children can also be assigned to groups that rotate to appropriate activities at set intervals, although it is difficult to make such groups flexible enough to accommodate young children's varying interest levels and task orientations.

Children can participate in "everyone needs to do this" as individuals. Choose interesting and intrinsically rewarding activities, and offer them often. Computers, tricycles, reading or looking at books, writing, puzzles, art, scientific observations, and many problems based on manipulatives can be individual activities.

Curriculum and Classroom Modification Strategies

Making the curriculum responsive to children's strengths and needs as determined by assessment requires modification of classroom activities.

Allocate Time and Space in Different Ways to Achieve Different Results

Teachers make most of the decisions about how much time to spend on a goal, subject, or activity. They decide on the space arrangement in the room. These easily manipulated variables can help make the classroom more responsive to children's needs. They are one way to give more or less emphasis to a particular activity or curriculum area. However, the effect of time and space on children's involvement and learning has to be carefully monitored so that more does not become "too much."

Suppose assessment indicates that most of the children would benefit from extensive work and play with math manipulatives. You decide to leave 1-inch interlocking cubes out for children to use whenever they want. Monitoring reveals that use increases immediately, then falls off as the cubes blend into the shelves. Replanning, you try another approach. Interlocking cubes, attribute and pattern blocks, and other math manipulatives will be rotated, with the time for rotation guided by the level of use.

To solve problems created by crowding during the opening class meeting, you spread the children out so they can't possibly nudge, push, or bother each other, and inadvertently create a different problem. The children are so scattered you cannot maintain their attention, they can't see visuals—even "big books"—and the feeling of being a group is lost.

A related problem is that of too little time. Integrate learnings so children learn several things simultaneously. Children do not distinguish one area of development or one subject matter from another. Reading, writing, listening, speaking, and literature can be learned simultaneously. Science, mathematics, problem solving, symbolic representation, physical development, and other learnings are merged as children work, play, and experiment with manipulative equipment, water and sand, weighing and measuring, cooking, music, movement, and art. Such integration, combined with the use of learning centers, individual activities, and small flexible groups, allows teachers to do away with rigid time periods and creates a classroom that allows children to work at their own paces and explore a topic "in-depth" both within a day and over longer periods of time. Children who need plenty of time and practice for mastery of key concepts and skills are not left behind.

Select and Arrange Materials in Response to Assessment Results

Equipment, supplies, and activities should encompass the range of capabilities found in the group. A group profile reveals the range: Three children don't grasp the idea of pattern; two can copy and extend almost any pattern and also create their own. Two children are reading; two cannot recognize any letters, not even the first letters of their names. Four children can construct and read their own maps; three don't know what maps are. The other children are at all points in between.

Fortunately, almost any activity, content, or process in which young children are involved can be made either simpler or more complex (Hendrick, 1994). Multilevel activities and materials enable each child to achieve success and continued learning. Some of the very best material for children's learning is open-ended: Cuisenaire rods, counting cubes, blocks, pattern and attribute blocks, modeling clay, books, drawing and writing materials, movement, music, art materials, and many others. Plan to adapt the same basic material and activities to meet the assessed needs of particular children. Teachers often have to open up different possibilities for children, such as supplying accessories, signs, and suggestions for extended block play.

Any classroom with children who need language and literacy development should have a prominent, changing, and varied display of books, functional signs, posters, and other written material keyed to children's interests and backgrounds. Youngsters who are learning to sort and classify need many opportunities to explore a wide variety of structured and natural materials on their own and to solve specific classification problems. Emerging literacy—at whatever age—calls for writing instruments and paper of all kinds to be placed strategically around the room. Children who are learning to share resources in a cooperative learning group shouldn't each have a box of crayons, a pair of scissors, and identical books. Materials and activities should be gender-neutral or clearly include both boys and girls. Plan procedures that ensure equal access to computers, science and math apparatus, dolls, blocks, challenging physical games, and any other activities that may be gender-stereotyped.

Use Any Apparent Sequence

Although not everything can be sequenced, it makes sense to give children experiences to help them understand a concept before they are expected to comprehend and then say the words that stand for that concept. Make sure children understand directions before they are expected to follow them. Show children how to share and take turns before admonishing them to do so.

Some sequences are fairly evident from the way children develop. Larger manipulatives (beads, pegs, interlocking blocks, parquetry) are usually easier to use than small ones; mixing, pounding, squeezing, and rolling modeling clay directly with the hands is easier than with tools. Tracing inside a cut-out template is easier than tracing around the outside. Whole-hand fingerplays are easier than ones calling for individual finger movement, which in turn are easier than complicated, two-hand coordinated ones. Many adults have difficulty alternating index finger and thumb to make the eensy beensy spider climb! Printing large letters without regard for lines is easier than printing on lines. Cutting out a circle is easier than cutting out an angled figure.

By understanding the direction and sequence in which a skill develops, teachers can provide scaffolding to ensure that children grow increasingly independent. The term *scaffolding* refers to the support that teachers, materials, other children, or interactions between the child and others provide to help the child perform the task. But just as we remove scaffolding from a building as its walls are able to stand alone, so the teacher must plan ways of making the child gradually responsible for performance of the task. Scaffolding has another implication—that the teacher knows what the end skill is going to look like and how to get to it. Thus the support is given in such a way that it fosters the child's ability to eventually perform by himself. Both the support and its removal are provided in a conscious manner (Bodrova & Leong, 1996).

For example, a teacher provides a scaffold for a child's counting by holding her hand and showing her how to move it as they point and count together. As they work, the teacher begins to "fade out"—to omit a number to see if the child can say it on her own. When the child seems able to say the numbers by herself, the teacher only points with the child. In the next step the teacher doesn't point but just watches the child point and count aloud, progressing from assisted, or scaffolded, counting to independent counting.

Children can provide scaffolds for each other, too. A second-grader who is having trouble remembering the story he is trying to write may have a buddy whose job is to help him remember what he wants to say. By talking through the story with the "say-back buddy," he is able to write a more complicated story than he would have by himself. As this second-grader becomes a more fluent writer, he will need less scaffolding by his buddy. He will have moved from assisted, or scaffolded, writing to independent writing.

Look at the Need for Possible Change in Procedures

Suppose participation charts show that well over half the children seldom talk during class meetings, group discussions, circle time, or any teacher-led activity—not an uncommon finding. Before starting to work with the children, examine adult patterns of interaction—calling on volunteers or those children who readily respond, answering our own questions, or allowing so little wait time that thoughtful children are still thinking when the next question comes. Plan interaction techniques to get more children participating, such as beaming questions to the group, calling on all the children, and valuing their responses.

Rethink and Restructure to Meet Children "Where They Are"

Many children don't match the curriculum guide, activities handbook, or expected sequence of goals and objectives. We've got different kids! Professional teachers must know curriculum theory and child development well enough to simplify, delete, extend, elaborate, and embellish curriculum content and processes so they are developmentally and individually appropriate. They have to know how to construct curriculum when no guides exist.

Examples of Using Assessment Information to Guide Instruction

Examples of ways teachers use assessment information to inform and guide instruction are given throughout the previous chapters. The intent is to show possibilities, not to prescribe a single approach. The examples that follow are chosen from typical goal areas in early childhood education to show additional possibilities. For other examples, see the research and instructional strategies in the extensive literature available on children's learning. Guides for nurturing children's emergent literacy are particularly rich in their implications.

Play

Mr. Frankel's assessment during dramatic play revealed that Tony, LaTessa, and Jerry sometimes engaged in play that became angry and sometimes physically violent. His attempts to let the three of them work it out usually led to crying and disintegration of the play. If he were to remove all the props they argued about, the playhouse would be bereft of any props at all. When asked what they could do next time to avoid an argument, all three children seem to be able to state reasonable alternatives: "We should use our words"; "I shouldn't hit him." But once they are at play, fighting stops only when Mr. Frankel enters the dramatic play area and directly intervenes. These youngsters need to learn better strategies for interacting with one another instead of practicing inappropriate ones. Without intervention it is likely that they will *not* learn or practice positive social skills. Mr. Frankel considers two options: child planning and "social tutoring."

Children can plan their play before they begin (Bodrova & Leong, 1996). As they plan, the children develop a common theme, choose the props they will use, and identify their roles. The children can do this on paper, by drawing (not in detail, but just as a reminder) what they plan to do, as shown in Figures 8–1 and 8–2. Have the children who plan to go to the dramatic play center decide what they will play and what props they need. Assist the planning if children need coaching on how to pick an appropriate theme or divide up roles without arguing. If they can plan independently, have them show and explain the plan after it is done. We have yet to see children plan to fight! They always plan to work together and to have fun.

Planning avoids many of the arguments that children have over objects or roles. If there is only one ballerina costume, children can work out a solution. When children enter the play area with a solution to the "one costume" problem ahead of time, they usually do not fight or argue when they get there. Planning avoids conflict over roles, such as everyone wanting to be the doctor. Roles can be decided ahead of time with alternatively appealing roles created or the idea that we can have several doctors—a surgeon, a heart doctor, and a x-ray reader.

Planning allows the teacher to stay out of arguments when children get upset. Asking "Was this part of your plan?" is often enough to stop the fight and get everyone back on track.

More important in the long run, planning helps children learn to think ahead, interact, solve potential problems, and make their own play more productive. They begin to imitate and practice the advanced social skills that the teacher wants them to learn. This thoughtful, deliberate approach will lead to advanced cognitive skills as well (Bodrova & Leong, 1996).

The teacher can also pair Tony, LaTessa, and Jerry with other children who have more advanced social skills or with an older child from another room. Each child can play separately with the "social tutor" so they do not overwhelm him or her.

Large Muscle/Gross Motor Development

Suppose that analysis of the children's level of performance shows that Martin, Megan, and Chris need introduction, instruction, and practice in catching objects—an important skill in a school and neighborhood where

Figure 8–1   *Child's Plan for Play—Dictated*

play with horses
at blocks

softball, basketball, and "playing catch" are social activities. You decide to implement these ideas:

1. Have a short time every day for children to learn to catch, in addition to other regularly offered catching opportunities.
2. Begin with easy-to-catch items and gradually progress to regular playground balls. The sequence you decide on is (a) 6-inch-diameter-beanbags, (b) 6- to 8-inch yarn balls, (c) 6- to 8-inch sponge or fleece balls, (d) lightweight 6- to 8-inch playground balls. These items are

Figure 8–2   *Child's Plan for Play—Dictated*

play babies
in play house

not only easy to catch, but they also minimize the chance of the children's being hurt if they are hit.

3. Coach the children on obvious techniques by demonstrating, modeling, and guiding: "Keep your eyes open and watch the ball (beanbag)."

4. Combine this direct instruction with movement exploration activities, giving the children ample opportunity to toss and catch, roll and catch, bounce and catch, and experiment as they like. Keep the emphasis on catching. Just because there is a ball or beanbag involved doesn't mean there will be lots of catching. Children are just as likely to throw, toss, or kick a ball, especially those children who have difficulty catching.

5. Plan for an adult or older child to throw the beanbags and balls to the children until they have learned to catch. Have them stand as close as necessary to enable the children to successfully catch the object and very gradually move farther away; toss gently and accurately; and tell the children what they are doing successfully. The expert serves as a model when the object is tossed back. We know from the developmental sequence and from observation that the ability to throw usually precedes the ability to catch, so the children will probably be able to return the object. If not, this is a perfect time to learn. Why not let the children simply play catch with each other? Few young children are able to throw accurately or gauge the distance and force at which a learner can successfully catch an object.

6. Let other children join in the activities planned for children needing special practice, but don't let them take over. Have several extra objects to throw. An adult can play with several children at once.
7. Progress at the children's rate, as determined by day-to-day observation.

The group profile that identified Martin's, Megan's, and Chris's need showed several children who "need challenge" in catching. Let these youngsters practice with each other. Let them catch a ball from different body positions: kneeling, squatting, even walking and running. Let them catch balls at different levels: waist level, knee level, eye level, overhead, and "grounders"; experiment with balls of differing sizes, weights, hardness, and resilience. These and other problem-solving activities provide challenge in catching within the basic structure of the total group.

Small Muscle/Fine Motor Development

Assessment of kindergarten children's fine motor development identifies several who are having difficulty cutting. They can't hold either paper or scissors to make them work. One parent explained that crayons, pencils, markers, and scissors were off limits to the children in their house because they marked on the walls and messed up the house. Other parents had difficulty providing food, let alone scissors and paper.

Plan opportunities for all types of fine motor development. Incidental learning, such as is made available in unplanned manipulative play or art, probably will not be enough. Have a center or area that focuses on needs, or incorporate skill development into appropriate existing functional areas or centers. Develop an office area with rotary and push-button telephones, paper and pencils, scissors, a keyboard, and other office tools. Develop a center with writing, drawing, and cutting tools. Vary the manipulatives area to provide needed skill building. Incorporate "real-life" materials to add interest, variety, choice, and practice with a variety of fine motor motions—paper punches and fasteners, nuts and bolts, wrenches, screwdrivers, hand drills and egg beaters, all types of fasteners and closures—any appropriate tools to help develop strength, dexterity, coordination, and control.

Plan specific assistance for those youngsters who are still learning to use scissors. Show them how to hold both scissors and paper "thumbs up" and to say "thumbs up" to remind themselves. Put a dot on the paper in the place where the thumb is supposed to go. Start with strips of paper, gradually making them wider as children learn. Make essential practice interesting and functional. When children need practice to advance from snipping to a smooth single cut, have them cut straw for the horses and cows, or pretzel, carrot, and celery sticks for a pretend snack. Let children snip or punch confetti for a parade or collage. The paper strips they cut can be used by the whole group for a special collage, three-dimensional representations (strips pasted on top of strips to make their own creations), or bulletin board decorations. The adult's job is not to withhold assistance, but to coach those children who need help in learning certain skills and then to let the children take over. There is quite enough for children to learn on their own.

Watch the awkward way many adults write with pen and pencil, and providing young children guidance and practice in fine motor skills will take on more meaning.

Memory Strategies

"If only they would pay attention and remember!" may be a teacher's interpretation of a whole group's progress on specific items. Since almost everyone, including adults, can benefit from help in identifying important information, paying attention, and remembering, a teacher may decide to work with the total group on memory strategies, giving reinforcement, reminders, and practice to those children who use memory aids consciously, and teaching the others how. Doing this is not to facilitate "rote memory" but to help children learn cognitive strategies to help them remember, and to use those strategies to aid further learning. Memory is intelligent activity applied to a reconstruction of the past and relates to children's ability to organize and make sense of material, and to use it in reasoning (Jackson, Robinson, & Dale, 1977). Teachers often expect children to remember things (what they learned yesterday, what they were supposed to bring from home, what they were to tell their parents), but seldom teach memory strategies. Share with parents what you are doing, and provide them with some ideas to help at home, such as helping children pack their schoolbag or backpack at night and place it right beside the door they leave to go to school.

Find out what strategies the children you are working with know about and use, practice and support those, and teach them others. There is no need to have a separate focus on "how to remember." Teach and remind children to use cognitive memory strategies to help them achieve other content and process goals. For example, the whole class may discuss ways to remember what ingredient each is to bring for stone soup. (This would be an excellent assessment activity. Record the suggestions on an experience chart or web.) Let the youngsters then choose which memory strategy they want to use. While eating the soup, find out which strategies worked for whom. Some items, such as what to bring for stone soup, require remembering for a short time. Others are for longer-term memory and understanding.

Help children use external mediators to symbolize what they are to remember. Very young children may draw a picture or scribble a "list" before they can write a list or check an item they are responsible for. A washable stamp or dot on a child's hand can remind them to tell parents something, or to put an item in their schoolbag to bring tomorrow. Older children can develop their own memory "jogs."

Give practice in verbal rehearsal by having children remember something they did that day that they want to discuss with their parents. Children identify where they store what they want to remember (memory bank, head, brain), and then tap it as they repeat the item five times, either out loud or to themselves.

Have children visualize, think about, and name what it is they want to remember. The mental picture helps "fix" the image and the name in memory if the item or information is new.

Use several learning modalities. All too often, children are simply told and expected to remember. Actual physical involvement, such as with math and science manipulatives and apparatus, can enhance memory. Pictures, drawings, dramatizations, and other representations of past events can help children reconstruct and re-create the event.

Mnemonic devices, such as associating materials with something already known, can help children. The "ABC Song," for example, is a mnemonic device for learning and remembering alphabetic order. Making sentences, rhymes, and jingles out of material to be remembered is a time-honored approach that still works.

Help children relate new learning to what they already know—their prior knowledge. Make the relationship explicit. Help children construct relationships, develop concepts and categories, and "fit" one element of learning into a larger scheme. Such a scheme should be evident in all integrated curriculum experiences.

Use known learning principles to help children organize and remember important concepts, skills, and knowledge. Present information in small steps; have children learn and say the names of things they are to remember; repeat information and provide learning experiences in several different contexts as needed; organize information so that it is comprehensible and familiar, and its relationship to other information is clear.

Teach children to try to remember. Remind them to use the strategies they know. Build memory tasks into other learnings. For example, elementary school children can make drawings of a display they have created, or plan to create, and then use the drawings to set up the display another time. Remember, memory is an integral part of children's cognitive processes. It should grow and develop along with the children, but is unlikely to do so without deliberate attention.

Summary

Teachers can use assessment information to help children develop and learn by employing a combination of thoughtful planning, meeting individual and group needs in a variety of ways, and modifying the classroom and curriculum to be more responsive to assessed needs. Plan intended changes and adjustments; refer to assessment files and summaries during planning; allow time for reflection; plan strategies and activities to meet children's assessed needs; incorporate current knowledge and resources; plan for and with other people in the classroom; and balance what you might like to do with what is possible.

Meeting the needs of individual children within the context of a classroom is a challenge. A variety of approaches are needed for using assessment results when one or two children need specific attention, when several children would benefit, when an entire group would benefit, and for using assessment results in a mixed-age classroom.

Modify and adjust the curriculum and classroom to meet children's needs: select and arrange equipment, materials, and supplies in response to assessment results; use appropriate sequences for simplifying or increasing complexity; consider the need for possible changes in classroom procedures; and rethink and restructure curriculum if needed.

Within the context of a developmentally appropriate curriculum, plan specific activities to help meet children's development and learning needs because they are unlikely to be met by incidental learning alone. Several examples showed how this can be accomplished.

For Further Study, Discussion, and Reflection

1. Making full use of aides, assistants, and volunteers is suggested as a strategy to meet instructional needs identified by assessment. Reflect on your own knowledge, attitudes, skills, and feelings regarding planning for, guiding, and coaching other adults in the classroom.
2. Interview one or more teachers to learn how they plan to meet the assessed needs of children in their classrooms. Within your adult learning group (college class or staff development group), interview representatives from both preschool and primary levels. As a group, or as individuals, analyze their responses. What conclusions can you draw?
3. Assessment has revealed several needs within a kindergarten group: three children are having difficulty entering a play or work group, either indoors or out; four youngsters are obviously lost when discussion turns to comparisons of likenesses and differences. Specifically, they neither comprehend nor use the terms *the same as* and *different from*; two children are having difficulty classifying objects or pictures of objects on any basis except observable attributes (color, shape, size). Select one of these needs, and plan a course of action to help children within the context of a developmentally appropriate curriculum.
4. After conducting several assessments, you find three clusters of children with similar skills. Cluster 1 needs practice hopping, cluster 2 has already mastered the skill, and cluster 3 cannot hop at all. Discuss how you might develop multilevel activities that will benefit all of the children. Describe several ways you could work with children.

Suggested Readings

Berk, L. E., & Winsler, A. (1995). *Scaffolding children's learning: Vygotsky and early childhood education.* Washington, DC: National Association for the Education of Young Children.

Bodrova, E., & Leong, D. J. (1996). *Tools of the mind: The Vygotskian approach to early childhood education.* Englewood Cliffs, NJ: Merrill.

Bredekamp, S., & Rosegrant, T. (Eds.). (1992). *Reaching potentials: Appropriate curriculum and assessment for young children.* (Vol. 1). Washington, DC: National Association for the Education of Young Children.

Bredekamp, S., & Rosegrant, T. (Eds.). (1995). *Reaching potentials: Transforming early childhood curriculum and assessment* (Vol. 2). Washington, DC: National Association for the Education of Young Children.

Hollifield, J. (1989). *Children learning in groups and other trends in elementary and early childhood education.* Urbana, IL: ERIC/EECE.

Johnson, D. W., & Johnson, R. T. (1991). *Learning together and alone: Cooperative, competitive, and individualistic learning.* Englewood Cliffs, NJ: Prentice-Hall.

Katz, L. G., Evangelou, D., & Hartman, J. A. (1990). *The case for mixed-age grouping in early education.* Washington, DC: National Association for the Education of Young Children.

National Association for the Education of Young Children & National Association of Early Childhood Specialists in State Departments of Education. (1991). Guidelines for appropriate curriculum content and assessment in programs serving children ages 3 through 8. *Young Children, 46,* 21–38.

CHAPTER NINE

Organizing for Assessment

Knowing what to assess, when to assess, and how to collect and record assessment information provides teachers with different options to use when appraising children. How do you pull all of these things together to create a workable classroom assessment process? This chapter discusses three elements that will help you get started:

1. Integrating assessment with teaching
2. Developing an assessment plan
3. Files and forms

Integrating Assessment and Teaching

The key to authentic classroom assessment is embedding it in classroom activities. The following guidelines outline a general, practical approach, followed by tips about specific assessment opportunities found in most preschool and primary classrooms.

General Guidelines

Assessment can be overwhelming if you attempt everything at once. Schedule activities so you have time to assess. Begin gradually, starting with easy assessment techniques that are appropriate for the children. Stay organized and current. Make assessment a regular part of classroom living, and enlist the aid of other people.

Schedule Activities So You Have Time to Assess.   Help children learn to work and play on their own as well as in interaction with an adult. Teach them how to move to their next activity, get help, regulate their own behavior, and solve problems on their own or with a classmate.

Help children understand that assessment is part of teaching. One team of primary teachers brainstormed with the children to list all the things that teachers do. The list was long, but there was nothing related to observation and assessment. Then the teachers explained about "kid watching" and enlisted the children's help. Each teacher developed a visible signal that showed she was documenting learning—a pair of old sunglasses perched in the hair, a bright bandanna around the neck. When the children saw these signals, they knew an important aspect of teaching was going on and did not interrupt.

Begin and Proceed Gradually.   It is easy to attempt too much. Only you can know your other personal and professional commitments, prior knowledge and skill, teaching load, and center, school, and parent expectations. Start with one developmental or curriculum area, and focus on it until you are comfortable with the process. Or start with four or five children, adding more as you learn. Don't try to get an anecdotal record on each child every day, but get one on two or three children per day.

Start with Easy, Appropriate Techniques.   Start with assessment techniques that are relatively easy and developmentally appropriate. Children who are reading and writing will produce many products to provide evidence of their learning. Collect and work with these while you are learning how to analyze reading and writing processes—a more challenging task.

Stay Organized and Current.   Many teachers take a few minutes at the end of each day to file notes, completed charts, and other information. Certainly it should be done once a week. Summarize when there is enough information to warrant it. Keep information current enough to be useful in the classroom. Last month's notes are needed to document progress but are not much help in planning tomorrow's or next week's activities.

Make Assessment a Normal Part of Classroom Life.   One of the big advantages of classroom assessment is that activities do not have to be suspended for a week of testing—whether screening, readiness, or achievement. Information is collected along the way. The intent is to have gathering and recording information "seem so much a part of the ongoing classroom procedure, so focused on [children's] learning" that the children are hardly aware of it (Almy & Genishi, 1979, p. 9).

- Place supplies for recording in each activity area. Keep a stack of paper or prepared checklists near areas where routines are carried out. If parents bring children to school, put paper and pen in the transition spot. Slip a pencil, index cards, or a small spiral-bound notebook in your pocket when you go outdoors. The spiral wires of the notebook make a convenient storage place for a short pencil. Keep well-organized supplies near learning centers where children write subject matter journals, maintain reading logs, plan projects or play, or write or dictate stories; they will do much of their own documentation. Have your own recording supplies in several places so it is easy for you to make a note, mark a checklist, or fill out a rating scale as you supervise and work with children.
- Gather information regularly so everyone gets used to it. If you teach primary grades and plan to use short paper-and-pencil tests, give them frequently, not just before report card time. If performance samples are used as evidence of learning, use them often in interactive teaching, not just at "assessment time." Interview and have conferences with children routinely, so they don't feel put on the spot.
- Be unobtrusive. Learn to gather and record information deftly; sit or stand nearby rather than hovering. When appropriate, fade into the background. Store recording forms in key places where you can sit or stand to see the whole room. A few minutes of recording while the children are working and playing will yield much useful information.
- Be matter-of-fact when children ask what you're doing. "I'm writing what we do and say so I can remember." "I'm keeping track of what we've learned and have yet to learn." "I do this to help me teach better." Keep an extra clipboard with scrap paper on it for those children who want to scribble or write their own records in imitation. Some children may do their first functional "writing" that way—a nice example to go in a portfolio.
- Maintain "dual focus" (Kounin, 1970) so you can monitor the activity of a group of children as you record or play a learning game while simultaneously checking length or level of participation. Maintaining dual focus is the ability to attend to two or more things at once—a skill that will improve with practice. It helps keep the classroom going while a teacher documents what a small group is doing. Some helps: face into the room or play yard, place yourself so you see as much of the space as possible, scan the area frequently, and keep your ears and other senses attuned to the tone of the group.
- Establish the habit of retaining some work products early in the year, helping parents and children understand the reasons. Exhibit some in the classroom, halls, and display cases; keep some for portfolios;

send some home. If a child feels strongly about taking something home, it's probably wise to let her. We have no way of knowing what an item means to a child, and one of the advantages of having many examples is that undue importance is not attached to any one. If necessary, make a photocopy.

- Maintain credibility. Don't retain a number of items only to dump them in a wastebasket that children or parents will see. If you dispose of some, do it discreetly.

Enlist the Aid of Other People.   Specialists, classroom aides and assistants, volunteers, parents, and interns can be an integral part of the assessment process, gathering information from their own perspectives. Coach all nonprofessionals on confidentiality as well as what they are to do. Only professional school personnel should handle confidential information, but volunteers can check how far children can kick a ball, throw a beanbag, count objects, or "count on." Aides or volunteers can write a brief, objective description of several children a day to help get acquainted and to contribute their perception of the children. They can take dictation, observe small groups, help children record reading samples, check type and level of participation in almost any activity, and do other assessment tasks. They can help with classroom activities while you are assessing a small group of children. They can bridge language and cultural differences between the classroom, home, and community.

Children can record their own attendance and their participation in learning activities; identify, date, and place portfolio items in a basket or work folder; check spelling and arithmetic; keep reading logs; and perform numerous other assessment-related tasks. More important, they are beginning to take responsibility for their own learning.

Develop a Plan

Teachers need a plan for incorporating assessment into teaching activities. Planning keeps assessment systematic and makes it easier to embed appraisals in ongoing activities. It allows teachers to spread the assessment process out over the year and gather information gradually. By planning, teachers avoid arriving at parent conference time with a lot of information about some children and nothing about others. There will be no hurried effort to get adequate information. Good opportunities for gathering information will not be missed. Planning assessment also allows you to key collecting, compiling, and summarizing assessment information to end-of-semester and end-of-year evaluations. Records will accumulate that will help you with parent conferences and end-of-year reports.

Figure 9–1 shows one way of planning. Teachers systematically work through the basic assessment decisions: why, what, and when to assess, and how to collect and record information. At first, you will need to consciously consider and write the plans. As assessment becomes routine, some of the steps will be done mentally and more quickly. Experienced

Figure 9–1   *Sample Assessment Planning Form*

ASSESSMENT PLAN _____ 199__ TO _____ 199__

PURPOSE OF ASSESSMENT: _____

AREA OF DEVELOPMENT/CURRICULUM: _____

What to Assess	When	Assessment Window and Recording Procedure

teachers find that some steps always have to be written—either noted on monthly or weekly classroom plans or on a shorter form than the one presented here. For example, what to assess and the assessment window to be used are usually written.

Considerations in Planning

Purpose of the Assessment.   Write the purpose of the assessment at the top of the planning form (see Figure 9–1). Since assessment can serve several purposes, choose one primary purpose, because this will influence other choices for the plan. For example, if the primary purpose is to keep track of individual status and progress, then several pieces of information from the same child must be collected at different times. If the purpose is to plan an upcoming unit or theme, then information will be collected before, during, and immediately after the theme. The purpose listed does not preclude using the information for other functions.

Development and Curriculum Domains.   Identify the general area of development or curriculum that you plan to assess. Identify a specific area of focus, and then subdivide it into the specific learnings to assess. These are the indicator behaviors that will be documented on the primary data record.

For the model form, the process of arriving at specific items to assess begins by identifying the general goal or objective—the area of development or of the curriculum to be assessed. Write this at the top of the page on the line *AREA OF DEVELOPMENT/CURRICULUM.*

Have at least one assessment planning form per area; if the domain is large, you may need several. For example, language may be divided into spoken and written, receptive and expressive, or pragmatics.

What to Assess.   Next, identify specific categories or child capabilities to focus on, and then further break these down into specific learnings or indicators. For example, literacy includes knowing that symbols and print have meaning; a knowledge of words, letters, and other symbols; and recognition of story elements. Cognitive development can be viewed from the aspects of cognitive processes, such as representation, attending and remembering, or as problem solving; or from knowledge of subjects, such as science, geography, or history. Capabilities in the area of social development might be positive peer interactions, friendship-making skills, and cooperative learning skills. Sometimes these specific areas are found in curriculum guides or child development and educational texts.

Next, specify the observable behaviors, indicators, or specific learnings that would help a child reach that goal or would indicate growth. These are the items you will watch for and document on the assessment record. Think of several behaviors that can be used to appraise the same capability. Map knowledge in geography can be appraised by seeing if a child "points to street on a map," "draws own fantasy maps," or "draws representational maps." In social development, cooperative learning skills might be assessed by "accepts another's ideas," "contributes to the group," and "rejects an idea diplomatically."

Specific outcomes and a sequence for development are identified in the research, curriculum guides, and work of national professional organizations, and "standards documents" (such as the National Council of Teachers of Mathematics, 1989). State and local standards and curriculum frameworks are other guides. In other areas, specific learnings have been identified, but no sequence of development is apparent, as in the case of self-esteem. Examples of areas with identified specific learnings are given in the assessment and analysis guides in Appendix A under *Examples of Things to Look for*.

When curriculum and development sequences or specific learnings have not been defined, teachers have to identify specific learnings from general goals.

Write the categories or child capability and the specific learnings in the column *What to Assess*. Leave space between capabilities so that you can add specific learnings as the year progresses and as you adjust teaching to meet child needs. Add new capabilities at the end of the column.

When to Assess.   In the next column, identify approximate times or "collection periods" for assessment. Write either the actual month of the assessment or the general schedule. Keeping track of children's progress requires continuous, day-after-day assessment, in addition to focused assessment periodically.

Consider what you have already identified as the purpose, the area, child capabilities, and specific learnings. For example, documenting progress requires spreading assessment over a period of time and taking more than one measurement. Assessment designed to help you plan a specific unit or theme may require appraisals before beginning the unit and then at least one follow-up.

Verify completion of assessment by checking the item when you have assessed it.

Assessment Window and Recording Procedure.   In this column, describe the assessment window you will use—the source, method, and context—and the recording procedure. Decide on the assessment window first. Consider how you will embed the assessment in your classroom activities, and pick a source, method, and context that are appropriate given the resources you have in your room. If putting together a complex obstacle course is not possible unless you buy new equipment, then this is not the appropriate assessment window for your classroom. Be practical! (For more guidance, refer to Chapter 4.) Write the assessment window in the column *Assessment Window and Recording Procedure.*

Figure 9–2 on pages 171–173 gives examples of assessment windows that could be used to gather evidence about major goals in early childhood classrooms (Airasian, 1994; Gage & Berliner, 1992; Meisels & Steele, 1991). Some of the sources, methods, and contexts are appropriate for preschool, others for primary classrooms.

Next, pick the recording procedure that you will use to document the information (see Chapter 5). Write the procedure next to the assessment window. Examples of typical recording procedures for different assessment windows are given in Figure 9–3.

Sample Assessment Plans

Figures 9–4 to 9–7 (pages 174–177) are examples of assessment plans that might be developed in preschool and primary classrooms. Figure 9–4 shows a plan to document status and progress in the area of language development for a preschool through first grade classroom. Figure 9–5 is an assessment plan to use in planning a multicultural unit. A plan to document status and progress in the area of classification (cognitive development) is shown in Figure 9–6, and in the curriculum area of mathematics, in Figure 9–7. Note the variety of assessment windows—sources, methods, and contexts—as well as the variation in the timing of assessment.

Using the Plan

Consult the assessment plan often as you organize and plan classroom activities for the week or day, just as you would for a semester or unit classroom plan. Look at the *When to Assess* column. Should you be planning an assessment of a specific area? Look at the activities and themes you are considering. Ideally, assessment fits into the theme, project, or topic of study that is under way.

Systematically review and revise the plan as necessary. Do not become tied to a familiar but inefficient or ineffective system.

Figure 9–2 *Assessment Windows Used to Appraise Major Early Childhood Goals*

Large Muscle/Gross Motor
—Systematic observations of child in movement during movement activities, outdoor play, physical education
—Self-reports or elicited information about a child's favorite games, activities, or apparatus and why they are favorites
—Systematic observations of a child's skill level
—Evidence of participation in large muscle activities
—Performance sample of an obstacle course combining several skills
—Performance sample of one specific skill
—Evidence of the length of participation in active physical exercise without tiring
—Performance sample of mimicking of progressively harder patterns of movement (following a song, videotape, or teacher)
—Descriptions of after-school and weekend physical activities from parents

Small Muscle/Fine Motor
—Systematic observations and examples (products) of a small muscle skill, such as fingerplays or use of writing instruments, modeling clay, manipulatives, crayons, paints, pencils, chalk, clay, paste, or other material that requires small muscle use (these can be spontaneously generated or elicited by the teacher)
—Spontaneously generated work products and performance samples of cutting
—Spontaneously generated work products and performance samples of scribbling or printing of letters and numerals
—Examples of constructions with small manipulatives (products), such as cubes, Cuisenaire rods, pattern blocks, pegs, seeds
—Computer printout of child's work with a draw/paint program (product)
—Systematic observation of child's ability to use keyboard, mouse, and accessories
—Samples of child's stitching (product)
—Systematic observations of use of hand tools and implements (may be videotaped)
—Child sketches of own constructions
—Performance samples of constructions (build a bridge from this side of town to the other, build a tower that is this high)
—Self-portraits drawn at the beginning and end of the term
—Systematic observations of self-help skills made by the teacher
—Reports from parents about self-help skills seen at home

Cognitive Development
—Elicited information about a child's knowledge or thinking processes (using a web or semantic map to record information)
—Elicited information or self-reports of what a child was thinking in a particular operation, project, or process (Why did you sort the shells that way?)
—Self-reports, elicited information, or work products showing child's ability to present information in graphic form
—Systematic observations or performance samples of puzzles, problems solved, and how they were solved
—Work samples from different subject matter areas
—Performance samples of a child's ability to carry out basic cognitive processes—classify, pattern, seriate, think, and represent using symbols; sequence; use number concepts and operations; observe; compare and contrast; and others
—Self-reports or elicited descriptions of memory strategies (e.g., list made by child)
—Self-reports or elicited descriptions of child's understanding of a process, such as how a favorite food is made

continued

Figure 9–2   *continued*

—Performance samples of specific knowledge or skills
—Work products, such as reports, practice papers, displays, presentations, models, or other end products of project work
—Performance samples of problem solving with teacher- or child-recorded information
—Self-reports of games the child has made up or played and how to play a known game (knowledge needed, strategies used)
—Systematic observations, elicited descriptions, or self-reports of things child uses to aid own thinking (use of fingers, self-talk, monitoring thinking processes)
—List of hints at different levels that helped the child solve a problem; list of hints that were not helpful
—Descriptions of error patterns found on practice papers and performance samples
—Descriptions of child's favorite problem-solving games and puzzles from home
—List of the "How does this work?" and "Why?" questions children ask their parents

Language and Literacy Development
—Systematic observations and performance samples showing communication competence
—Evidence of comprehension and use of specific concepts, vocabulary, constructions
—Evidence of time spent reading or looking at books, times in book center
—Self-report or record of books read or books read to child at home or school
—Self-report or elicited listing of favorite books
—Performance sample of child reading aloud to another child, parent, an aide, a volunteer, or the teacher (may be recorded on audio- or videotape)
—Evidence of child's understanding of functional uses of print (e.g., signs, maps, letters, newspapers, lists, books, teacher recording, photographs)
—Work products such as copies of final and draft copies of child compositions—songs, poems, stories, recountings, samples of journal entries
—Drawn or written responses to "prompts"
—Performance samples of storytelling, retelling, or reading of own writing (recorded on tape)
—Performance samples of writing—successive drafts or stand-alone samples
—Group compositions or experience charts
—Performance samples showing child's conceptions about print
—Parent reports of favorite books or reading activities at home

Personal and Social Development
—Teacher observations and recordings of specific aspects of child's interactions with peers
—Evidence of friendship and affiliation abilities
—Self-reports or observations of a child's skills in cooperative work groups, class projects, and outings
—Evidence of child choices of activities for a specified time
—Evidence of participation in and contributions to various activities requiring peer interaction
—Evidence of child's ability to organize self and others to accomplish task
—Evidence of child's uniqueness and personal style, interests, and dispositions
—Elicited information about friendship (what it means to be a friend and have a friend) and social problem solving (How would you handle this problem?)
—Observations of positive initiations with others or of negative, inappropriate interactions
—Descriptions from parents of the child's friendships and affiliation abilities at home
—Elicited or self-reports of child's conception of self (Who am I?)
—Systematic observations and self-reports of child's level of motivation during different types of activities

Attitudes and Dispositions (about almost everything)
—Evidence showing time spent at a given activity or task
—Evidence showing a child's choices of activities, books, projects, food

Figure 9–2   *continued*

—Elicited information and self-reports of "favorite" activities, books, songs, subjects, things to do at home and on playground—and why
—Evidence of a child's uniqueness in approach, attitude, and disposition
—Self-reports or elicited information of the number of books read, puzzles completed, maps made, pictures made, skills mastered
—Knowledge and skill in a particular developmental or subject area
—Parent reports, reports from other teachers about a child's attitudes and dispositions
—Description of motivation levels, attitudes, and dispositions observed during performance samples in a specific area

Specific Content Areas
—Performance samples of child's ability, designed to elicit specific skills, concepts, or processes
—Practice papers and other work products: science, math, or integrated project journals or reports
—Evidence of the relationships between concepts, processes, and strategies for use (may be documented by webs or semantic maps)
—Descriptions of specific skills, concepts, and processes

Other Important Assessment Windows
—Attendance and tardiness records
—Child's reflections on own development
—Observations of who sleeps at nap time and for how long (preschool)
—Observations of who is tired or hungry in the morning
—Observations of child's preferred study time (morning or afternoon), quiet time, reactions to noise or new situations, and other learning style characteristics

Figure 9–3   *Typical Recording Procedures for Different Assessment Windows*

Type of Window	Recording Procedure
Observations, elicited responses, self-reports, descriptions, performance samples	Jottings, checklists, expanded checklists (with jottings), frequency counts, timed samples, videos and audiotapes, diagrams and sketches (webs or semantic maps), descriptive narratives, and anecdotal records
Evidence of participation or time spent doing activity	Participation chart, duration sample, checklist, room scans
Work products	Product itself, checklists, sketches, diagrams, rating scales, self-assessments, videotapes, audiotapes (record supplementary information about behavior or processes with jottings or narrative)
Information from parents and other adults	Descriptive narrative, jottings, rating scales, audiotape, parent responses to prepared questions

Figure 9–4 *Example Assessment Plan to Assess Status and Progress in Language Development for Preschool or Primary Classroom*

ASSESSMENT PLAN ____August____ 199__ TO _____June_____ 199__

PURPOSE OF ASSESSMENT: Document Status and Progress

AREA OF DEVELOPMENT/CURRICULUM: Language Development

What to Assess	When	Assessment Window and Recording Procedure
Pragmatics—Use of language as a tool when communicating with others 1. Takes turn during conversations. 2. Expresses own opinion in positive manner. 3. Rejects another's opinion in a positive manner.	Beginning, midyear, end of year Continuous for some children	1. Cooperative learning groups, document on group matrix jottings 2. Dramatic play with a small group of children, document on group matrix or anecdotal record
Literacy Skills 1. Book handling: Knows front and back of book, holds book right side up, turns pages. 2. Understands function of print: Notices words and letters, attempts to read logos and signs, distinguishes pictures from words. 3. Recognizes letters and words: Can put fingers around a letter, put fingers around a word, point to letters in name, point to letters in a word, identifies letters by name, reads name, reads some words partially or completely. 4. Written forms: Dictates stories or explanations for drawings, scribbles own writing, incorporates letters in writing, forms letters, invents words, makes sentences.	Continuous on a weekly basis—at least one aspect	1. Performance samples during daily small-group literacy activities. Document on group matrix, checklists for items 1, 2, and 3. 2. Work products for item 4 with notes and jottings about child's reactions, including Journals.

Organizing Files and Forms

Being well prepared and organized helps teachers appraise children as an integral part of teaching. Workable, efficient filing and storage systems save time and keep valuable records from being misplaced, lost in a stack of papers, or accidentally tossed out. Few teachers use all available recording forms and organizational systems; they pick, choose, or adapt those most appropriate or preferred by a center or school. Experiment to see which systems work best. Consider the age of the children, the expectations of the program, what recording is required and what is optional, and personal preference. Representative examples follow.

Figure 9–5 *Example Assessment Plan in Social Studies for Preschool or Primary Classroom*

ASSESSMENT PLAN ___October___ **199__**

PURPOSE OF ASSESSMENT: ___Plan Classroom Activities___

AREA OF DEVELOPMENT/CURRICULUM: ___Social Studies Theme: My Family___

What to Assess	When	Assessment Window and Recording Procedure
1. Knowledge base about the family: Has studied families before? Can identify who is in own family including extended family (grandparents, uncles, and aunts). Can discuss similarities and differences.	Before theme After theme	1. Large-group activity—brainstorming what we know about families. Document on a web. 2. Elicited responses to open-ended questions about families. Document on group matrix, checklist.
1. Knowledge base about family artifacts: Can describe what an artifact from daily life is and how it is used. Can discuss similarities and differences between family artifacts.	Before theme During theme	1. Parent questionnaire before activity asking for help in finding an artifact with child and describing child's understandings about family artifacts. 2. Work product from an activity in which children draw a picture about their artifact. Include jottings.
Attitudes and dispositions 1. Pride in own cultural identity. 2. Curiosity, enjoyment, and empathetic awareness of cultural differences and similarities. 3. Appropriate responses triggered by cultural differences.	During theme As occurs	1. Several activities around the artifacts theme. Document child participation using a participation chart. 2. Observe specific instances when children voice pride, enjoyment, curiosity, and empathy. Document on individual anecdotal records.

Theme and ideas from Derman-Sparks, L., & A.B.C. Task Force (1989). *Anti-bias curriculum: Tools for empowering young children.* Washington, DC: National Association for the Education of Young Children.

Notebooks, Files, and Portfolios

Notebooks and files help keep track of different types of information.

Notebooks and Record Books. Class roster and attendance record books are usually issued by the center or school. Most have a place for children's names on the left and day and week divisions across the page. Daily attendance is marked in the appropriate column.

Loose-leaf notebooks are a convenient way to organize some records for individual children, as well as summary information about a group. Label the dividers and tabs alphabetically according to the things you are going to keep track of, such as social development, literacy, mathematics, large muscle development, or dramatic play. When the summary sheets are prepared, punch and place them in the binder in chronological order with latest entries to the front. To store recording forms for individual children, tab the dividers with children's names and alphabetize them according to last names.

Figure 9–6 *Example Assessment Plan to Assess Status and Progress in Cognitive Development—Classification for Preschool Classroom*

ASSESSMENT PLAN __September__ **199__ TO** _____June_____ **199__**

PURPOSE OF ASSESSMENT: __Document Status and Progress__

AREA OF DEVELOPMENT/CURRICULUM: ___Cognitive Development—Classification___

What to Assess	When	Assessment Window and Recording Procedure
1. Classifies objects into two groups: Classifies spontaneously using consistent attribute; can say attribute. Classifies given an attribute; can say attribute. Can reclassify into another grouping spontaneously; can say attribute. Can reclassify given new attribute; can say attribute.	Every two months: Sept, Nov, Jan, March, June	1. Performance sample. Documented on a group matrix with jottings. 2. Work products, such as drawings or descriptions of the child's classifications.
1. Makes patterns: Makes simple ABAB pattern spontaneously; can voice pattern. Copies simple ABAB pattern; can voice pattern. Makes more complex patterns spontaneously, ABCABCABC or a pattern rotated in space. Can graphically express pattern on paper.	Beginning, midyear, end of year As occurs	1. Performance sample. Documented using a sketch with notes. 2. Patterning activities. Documented using anecdotal records for children who participate.
Attitudes and Dispositions 1. Enjoyment of classification and pattern making.	During activities: beginning, midyear, end of year	1. During selected ongoing classification and patterning activities. Document using a participation chart or duration sample.

If you use notebooks, you'll want either two notebooks or a thick notebook with two major divisions, one for individual children's records and one for group records. You'll want a suitable bound or loose-leaf notebook to keep a journal of your own reflections and development.

Files. Some administrative files are kept in a central office. What teachers keep in the classroom varies. At the least, you'll need personal files and portfolio files for the children.

Keep personal files for each child in a file drawer or cabinet that is not accessible to children or unauthorized adults. Contents vary, but this file is the place for results of any standardized screening or diagnostic tests, reports from specialists or other teachers, sensitive information from parents, medical information (if not in a separate health file), lunch payment status, social security number, custody arrangements, and any other information that could be construed as private in nature. Set up files alphabeti-

Figure 9–7 *Example Assessment Plan to Assess Status and Progress in Math for a Primary Classroom*

ASSESSMENT PLAN ____March____ 199_ TO ____June____ 199_

PURPOSE OF ASSESSMENT: __Document Status and Progress__

AREA OF DEVELOPMENT/CURRICULUM: ___Math__

What to Assess	When	Assessment Window and Recording Procedure
Counting 1. Rote counting: to 10, 20, highest number? 2. Meaningful counting: to what number? Has cardinal principle (last number=total number). Has abstraction principle (can count any objects). Can count starting on any object.	Every month for those who can't count ten objects; beginning/end for others; March, April, May, June	1. Performance samples. Documented for group matrix with jottings describing highest level on own and highest level with hints given (note hints). Use a tape recorder as backup.
Addends 1. Addends: up to 4, 6, doubles (2 + 2, etc.). Recognizes number of objects up to four no matter how arranged (one object with three objects grouped near each other).	For specific children only: March, April, May, June	1. Performance samples. Documented for group matrix with jottings describing highest level on own and highest level with hints given (note hints). Use tape recorder as backup. 2. Practice papers/work products from activities and learning centers. Document common errors made on jotting matrix.
Attitudes and Dispositions toward Math 1. Enjoyment of counting and adding activities. 2. Spontaneous use of skills. 3. Problem solving.	One activity March, May, June, Two times: beginning and end of year	1. Daily math activities. Document participation on a participation chart. 2. Way child handles frustration found during daily math activities. Document using anecdotal record for each individual child.

cally by children's last names. Leave plenty of space so that items can be added, with the most recent entry toward the front. Some teachers keep all assessment information in standard file folders.

If you plan to make notes and records on index cards, and wish to keep them separately, you'll need a card file with blank tabbed dividers.

Portfolios.   Portfolios require at least two storage systems for collecting and organizing children's work: a "work folder" and a more permanent portfolio. The distinction between these influences the handling and storage systems. Children temporarily store work in progress or completed work that a teacher needs to see in a work folder. Younger children put their work in labeled baskets or shallow "tote" trays. By kindergarten or first grade, children can do their own filing in folders that are clearly marked and accessible. File folders in a open file holder work well (see Figure 9–8). Place it where children can easily reach their own files. Teachers quickly review children's progress daily or weekly, note observations, discuss them with children, make decisions about items or information that should be transferred to the portfolio, and send the remainder home. Because items are not personal or private, work folders are left out so teachers and children can add to them.

Portfolios require more space and flexibility. Legal size (11 × 14 inches) hanging files organized in an open portable stand work well (see Figure 9–9), as they can store the larger items young children generate. They come with plastic indexing tabs. Roll-away racks and some plastic file "crates" hold letter-size folders (8½ × 11 inches) one way and legal size (11 × 14 inches) the other (see figure 9–10). Have extra files for supplies such as checklists, address labels, and portfolio entry forms. Include a "to be filed" folder, at least one folder for group work, and a miscellaneous file. Different-colored file folders are highly visible dividers for developmental or subject matter domains.

Bins provide easy access but fill up quickly (see Figure 9–11). Some teachers use a large expanding file envelope for each child (see Figure 9–12). They are available in both standard and legal sizes. The fold-over flap and enclosed sides keep items from getting misplaced.

If the budget allows for none of these, strengthen with tape the corners of a corrugated cardboard box—one that reams of paper come in is ideal—and fold large construction paper to make file folders. Leave an inch sticking up on one side for children's names. Smaller boxes, such as pizza or shirt boxes, can store an individual child's portfolio. Roll and store group projects such as murals, maps, or graphs in a map cylinder or with rubber bands. Or fold and place them with other documentation of group projects in files behind the portfolios.

Figure 9–8 *Open File Holder for Working Portfolio*

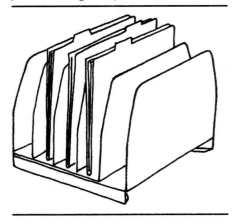

Figure 9–9 *Portable Stand for Hanging Files*

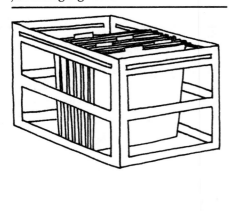

Figure 9–10   *Roll-Away Racks for Hanging Files*

Figure 9–11   *File Bin*

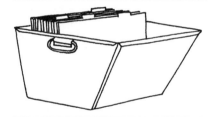

Figure 9–12   *Individual File Envelopes*

Forms

Examples of several forms and charts that teachers use are on the following pages. A school or center may have prepared recording forms that match their goals and objectives. Select two or three you think will be most useful, and prepare enough for several weeks' trial, after which you can make modifications or try others. Try starting with blank half-sheets and grids. Make copies of the forms you plan to use, file them, and then put them in several convenient places close to the point of use. Use small notepads, gummed labels, self-sticking notes, or "recycled" office paper cut in fourths for quick jottings.

Prepare a standard heading for forms, including a place for the child's name or group's designation (Pueblo Primary School, second year), observer's name, the date including year, and setting (see Figure 9–13) on page 180. Add time of day if that is important. The slash marks on the date line help people remember to include the year. If codes or marks will be used,

Figure 9–13   *Sample Full-Sheet Recording Form*

Mankota Early Childhood Center

Child _____   Date ____/____/____   Time _____

Observer _____   Setting _____

Group _____ (if needed)

add a place for a key. You may remember what the symbols "X," "/," or "+" meant, but someone else won't know.

The consistent format helps people learn what information goes where and reminds them to fill in complete information. A note without a child's name or a date is useless. All observers and interviewers should initial or sign records. An alternative is to have a rubber stamp to make the heading. This is especially useful for small sheets of recycled office paper.

Half-Sheets of Paper.   Use half-sheets of paper (see Figure 9–14) with a heading at the top for anecdotal records, quick notes, sketches, notes about performance tasks, portfolio entry slips, and information from other adults about individuals or a small group.

Index Cards.   Copy the standard heading on index cards, and keep several stacks available to use for notes or sketches, or punch a hole in one corner and place a stack on a bookring. For a more systematic use of index cards, prepare them using a different color for each area of interest—developmental or content areas, activity centers, experiences, or whatever you are documenting. Place one card for each child for each area on the ring.

Figure 9–14   *Sample Half-Sheet Recording Form*

Mankota Early Childhood Center

Child _____ Date ____/____/____ Time _____

Observer _____ Setting _____

Group _____ (if needed)

When one or more observations are made, remove the card and file it. The remaining cards act as a reminder of children yet to be observed in a particular area. Duplicate simple forms such as participation charts or columns directly on large index cards. Index cards are convenient because they are stiff enough to write on, but they are costly.

Grids, Matrices, Charts, and Checklists.   All-purpose grids, matrices, charts, and forms for checklists save time. Grids are especially useful for recording or profiling information about the whole group or profiling a lot of information about an individual child. A sample blank grid is shown in Figure 9–15 on page 182. Simply change the heading to use for an individual child.

Children's names, usually in alphabetical order by last name, go down the left side, and the behavior being checked is listed across the top. Or names go across the top and behavior down the left side. Stick with one or the other for consistency. Leave a blank space for comments. Modify the spacing of rows and columns to accommodate the recording procedure you want to use. For abbreviated notes or jottings, enlarge the cells to approximately 1 × 1½ inches, as shown in Figure 9–16 on page 183. The extra space

Figure 9–15   *Sample Blank Grid for Group of Children*

Item(s) _____   Date ____/____/____

Group _____

Observer _____

Figure 9–16 *Sample Blank Grid with Large Cells*

Child _____   Date ____/____/____

Observer _____   Group _____

means that more than one page will be needed for all but the smallest groups.

Instead of copying the class list by hand on each of these forms, use a computer to make the form and list simultaneously. Or make a master with spacing identical to the grid or chart, and make several copies. Tape one to each of the forms, and copy as many forms as you need. Keep the list on a computer disk, delete or add names as children depart or enter, while still maintaining alphabetical order. Some people use such a class list to make sure they are gathering information on each child. They focus on specific items for one or two children each day, check off the children they have information on until all have entries, and then start over focusing on other items. Consider using a grid, with the items being tracked noted along the top spaces. As information is collected, check the appropriate square. That way, you can monitor several types of information simultaneously. Tape the list to a counter, desktop, side of a cabinet, or other convenient spot as a reminder of who is left to observe.

Columns.   For recording some types of information about individual children, full sheets of paper with columns are useful. Figure 9–17 shows one setup for major child development areas. Change the column headings to reflect content areas (literacy, art, science) or learning processes (representation, communication, classification) that might be emphasized in various programs. This form lends itself well to abbreviated notes or jottings.

Still and Video Cameras, Audiotape Recorders, and Computers

Still and video cameras, audiotape recorders, and computers are powerful tools for capturing information about children. Before school begins, find out which, if any, are available to use in your classroom. If you don't know how to use the equipment, learn how on simple cameras or tape recorders. Then learn to use another. Learning one tool a year will rapidly boost your confidence and skills. These tools will be most useful if they can be kept in the classroom.

Still Cameras.   Automatic focus and exposure ("point and shoot") cameras make capturing a block building, intricate pattern with geometric shapes, or three-dimensional art project quick and easy. Keep the camera ready to go, loaded with fast film suitable for both indoor and outdoor use and with charged batteries. An instant print camera enables immediate feedback, display, or storage. Store the camera and extra film on a convenient shelf out of children's reach. Make sure the budget provides for the expense of film and finishing.

Video Cameras.   Small and simple video cameras are within reach of most school budgets. Usually they are shared among several classrooms. Those that display the date and time are probably worth the price. Standard quality videotape is adequate and can be reused. If the school does not have a hand- or shoulder-held video camera, see if a parent who has one will come

Figure 9–17 *Sample Columnar Recording Form*

Longview Early Childhood Center

Child _____   Year _____

(Date and initial each entry)

Personal/Social	Spoken Language	Written Language	Learning Processes	Knowledge Base	Large Motor	Fine Motor

in to tape occasionally. Make a tape for each child, plus one for analysis and documentation of classroom events. Parents are usually willing to supply a tape for their child in return for a priceless record of that child's year in school.

On a blank piece of paper, write the name of the child or group, the date, and what the child or group is doing, such as "dramatic play," "block construction," or "reading sample," in large block letters. Children enjoy making these. Run a few seconds of blank tape, and then hold up the "title" in front of the camera for 10 seconds before you begin taping the child. This will enable you to identify each segment and easily find it when fast-forwarding. Leave a little blank tape at the end of the segment, too. Some cameras rewind for a few seconds before beginning to tape new footage and may erase important information. It is unlikely that you will run out of tape, so leaving 5 to 15 seconds blank between segments is not a problem.

Audiotape Recorders.   Portable tape recorders are simple enough that many 3- and 4-year-old children have their own. A separate plug-in microphone helps capture children's voices during a group meeting or activity. A chance to hold the microphone may entice some otherwise reluctant children to speak or read aloud or to sing and dance. Have a tape for each child if you plan to record individual progress.

Cassette tape comes in different lengths. The length printed on the box includes both sides, so a 60-minute tape has 30 minutes of recording time on each side. Longer tapes are thin and may break. Get a tape cleaner cartridge, and periodically clean the recording heads to prolong the life and quality of the machine.

Begin each taped segment with the name of the child or group, date, and what the child or group is doing—similar to the "title" for videotaping. If children or parents are taping, have a script for them to follow as they begin. Allow a few seconds of silence before and after each segment so that you can find the place you want at a later time. If possible, start each tape at the beginning and push the counter button to zero, then fast-forward to the spot you want and note the counter number on the outside of the cassette. This will help you locate a particular segment.

Computers.   Computers quickly generate grids, checklists, and other forms. They keep the class roll current and alphabetized, so it can be printed on frequently used forms, charts, and address labels. They can keep a copy of all paper forms and charts filed and ready to print out. Some programs organize, compile, and store information about children, as well as printing out progress reports for parents.

Other Aids

Teachers have developed ingenious and practical ways to organize for authentic assessment. Here are a few of their ideas.

Clipboards.   Get a couple of full-size or several half-size clipboards, tie a pencil or pen to the clip, insert a stack of blank forms, and you have a portable recording surface for indoors or outdoors. Metal box-type clipboards have storage space inside for extra paper, forms, pens, or pencils. Hang the clipboards on the wall or on the end of a cabinet, and they will be readily accessible but out of the way. Have an extra or two for the children to use.

Self-Sticking Notes and Labels.   Self-sticking notes and gummed address labels are convenient for short notes about a child or group. Some teachers use sheets of computer labels with each child's name already printed, an automatic check on whether or not you have made a record for each child. Make notes during class time, and then later stick them to the appropriate product, folder, or form. For long-term storage, staple or tape self-sticking notes so they don't come off.

Writing Implements.   Keep sharpened pencils or working pens beside the blank forms and index cards. Some teachers wear pens on a long yarn loop around their necks or attached to their belts, or wear smocks, aprons, or shirts with pockets for paper and pencils. If you plan to use colored pens or pencils to designate separate development or learning domains or children who need certain experiences, have a good supply.

Rubber Stamps.   Use a rubber stamp to quickly date children's work or teacher recordings. If printed headings are not feasible, a rubber stamp can put the same information on any size paper or card, or the back of a photograph.

Counters and Timers.   Counters, stopwatches, and timers are useful for tallying and timing behavior. Wrist "clickers" are available at most teacher supply houses.

Self-Reports.   If children are to mark their own participation in centers or activities, they need appropriate forms. Figure 9–18 on page 188 shows an efficient one. While children are learning to recognize their names, use symbols or pictures beside the names. Mount the backing separately in each center, and change the listing of children—every day for young ones and once a week for older ones who can manage different daily headings. To keep track of each child's activities, prepare something as shown in Figure 9–19 on page 189 for each child to complete daily. Change the listing to correspond to the major areas in each classroom and outdoor play area. Older children need plenty of paper and implements to record what they have done. Have journal paper, forms for reading logs, and entry slips for portfolio items readily available.

Other.   Have colored dot stickers or highlighters to designate different developmental or curriculum areas on children's products, photographs, or notes.

Figure 9–18   *Sample Form for Child Reporting of Participation, by Center*

Art Area

Make a check beside your name if you worked in this area today.

Armano, Tony _____
Bustos, Seri _____
Curtis, Sarah _____
Dawson, Carl _____
Foreman, Akala _____
Kubiac, Jody _____
Lucero, Angie _____
Makaves, Sierra _____
Markum, Josh _____
Namaste, Ashley _____
Poste, Alfonso _____
Ramirez, Jana _____
Rostukus, Paul _____
Rutledge, B.J. _____
Shonka, Troy _____
Tran, Kwan _____

Summary

Teachers learn to integrate assessment with instruction by scheduling activities so that they have time to assess, proceeding gradually, staying organized and current, making assessment a regular part of classroom activities, and enlisting the aid of other people.

Use an assessment plan to record decisions about what, when, and how to assess. Identify the purpose of the assessment first, and then decide what will be appraised and when. Identify some possible assessment windows and recording procedures. Consult the assessment plan as you create daily and weekly materials and activities. Review and modify the plan as you proceed.

Figure 9–19   *Sample Form for Child Reporting of Participation, by Child*

	Mon.	Tues.	Wed.	Thurs.	Fri.
Art					
Blocks					
Computer					
Dramatic Play					
Language Games					
Manipulatives					
Reading/ Listening					
Writing					
Science					

Child_____   Week_____

Preparing and organizing files, forms, and other necessary aids for systematic storing of information about children makes classroom assessment easier. Teachers choose file systems and forms to suit the purpose for which the information is being collected, the age and developmental level of the children, school and center expectations, and their own preferences.

For Further Study, Discussion, and Reflection

1. Authentic assessment can be overwhelming if you try to begin everything all at once. Review the general guidelines for integrating assessment with teaching on page 165. Examine your own comfort

level and competence related to assessment, and decide how and where you will begin. Justify your decisions.

2. Mr. Stanley is interested in assessing how children communicate and use language as a tool in his classroom. Suggest how this assessment could be integrated into the routines of daily living, outdoors, and while the teacher is interacting with the children. Which of these would be the best context? Why?

3. Ms. Tan is interested in assessing her kindergartners' familiarity with books. Give suggestions as to how can she integrate assessment of these skills during the routines of daily living, when children are working or playing on their own, and when she is interacting with children. Which of these would be the best context? Why?

4. Develop an assessment plan for social development in a preschool. Using Appendix A, identify two skills that would be appropriate for children of 3 and 4 years of age. With documentation of progress as the purpose, fill out an assessment plan giving two assessment windows that are appropriate. What recording procedures would be best? Why?

Suggested Readings

Almy, M., & Genishi, C. (1979). *Ways of studying children.* New York: Teachers College Press.

Bennett, J. (1992). Seeing is believing: Videotaping reading development. In L. Rhodes & N. Shanklin (Eds.), *Literacy assessment in whole language classrooms, K–8.* Portsmouth, NH: Heinemann.

Hendrick, J. (1994). *Total learning: Curriculum for the whole child* (3rd ed.). Columbus, OH: Merrill.

National Education Association. (1993). *Student portfolios.* West Haven, CT: Author.

Stenmark, J. K. (Ed.). (1991). *Mathematics assessment: Myths, models, good questions, and practical suggestions.* Reston, VA: National Council of Teachers of Mathematics.

CHAPTER TEN

Communicating about Assessment Processes and Results

A lthough the primary purpose of classroom assessment is to help children learn, assessment has other purposes that extend beyond the classroom.

Teachers must routinely report assessment results to students and to parents or guardians. In addition, they are frequently asked to report or to discuss assessment results with other educators and with diverse lay audiences. If the results are not communicated effectively, they may be misused or not used. To communicate effectively with others on matters

of student assessment, teachers must be able to use assessment terminology appropriately and must be able to articulate the meaning, limitations, and implications of assessment results. Furthermore, teachers
will sometimes be in a position that will require them to defend their
own assessment procedures and their interpretations of them. At other
times, teachers may need to help the public to interpret assessment results appropriately. (American Federation of Teachers et al., 1990, p. 5)

Assessing and guiding young children also has potential for enriching
teachers' professional and personal lives as they attempt to understand children and themselves and help both develop and learn.

Communicating with Others

Communicating with Children

Teachers and children have conferences to discuss children's progress as an
integral part of assessment and teaching. Assessment is not something administered to children, with the results returned from some distant place
weeks later and then reported to their parents. Children edit and revise
their writing in conference with their teachers. They are congratulated
specifically on the restraint they showed by using verbal conflict resolu-
tion. Happy faces or saying "O.K.," which convey only general approval,
give way to knowledge of exactly what they did that was appropriate and
productive and what remains to be learned.

Some progress reports use pictures and simple words so children can
easily understand them. Children help build portfolios and explain their
contents to teachers, parents, and others. Children assess and reflect on
their own progress, as this youngster did as she was preparing to leave second grade (see Figure 10–1). Many schools have a policy of including children in all conferences with parents. However it is done, children should
know what they have achieved and what they have yet to learn.

Communicating with and Reporting to Parents

Communicating with parents about classroom assessment begins long before a parent conference is held or a progress report sent home. If changes in
assessment or reporting are being planned, parents should be involved from
the very beginning through task forces, planning committees, advisory pan-
els, open forums, or other means. Such involvement is especially important
if changes in reporting are involved. Moving from letter grades or other
rankings to a narrative progress report, for example, requires the understanding and support of parents. In the planning process, parents can advise
on what is and isn't important to them and to the larger community.

Inform and involve parents all along the way. Solicit and consider their
reactions to drafts of reporting forms and formats of parent conferences. Explain the reasons for alternative assessment and the potential benefits to
them and their child. Demonstrate the way changing concepts about how
children learn to read, write, compute, and solve problems influence how
teaching and assessment are done. Show and explain a portfolio and the reasons some items will be kept for the portfolio. Anticipate and deal with

Figure 10–1   *Self-Assessment by Second Grade Child*

Name Torrey Stenmark	**Key:**	1. Needs improvement		
Date 6/92		2. Developing		
School Jackson—RE 6		3. Doing well, confident		
		4. Exceeds expectations		

Reading	1	2	3	4
Initiates own reading				4
Chooses variety of materials			3	
Participates in discussion			3	
Uses comprehension strategies				4
Requests appropriate help			3	
Reads at or above expected level				4

Writing	1	2	3	4
Initiates own writing			3	
Participates in conferences			3	
Edits/revises as needed				4
Requests appropriate help				4
Writes at or above expected level			3	

Teacher comments:
Torrey's confidence, initiative, and desire to learn have increased her reading and writing skills. This self-assessment is quite accurate. —R. J.

Pupil comments/goals:
I don't really need much help in reading or witeing.

Parent comments:
Torrey really enjoys reading and writing.
P.S.

questions and concerns before they arise. If you're going to be pilot-testing a performance task, tell parents and ask them to report back anything their children said or did at home related to the task.

Involve parents in assessment. Not only are they a valuable source of information (see Chapter 4), but they also can assist both at school and at home. Your purpose is to build parent understanding and support for authentic assessment and to have home and school work together for the benefit of the child. This requires coaching so the purposes and procedures are clear. Otherwise parents may push too hard, fail to give appropriate help, or not know when to stop.

Reporting to parents takes many forms, both formal and informal. Formal reports include parent conferences, written progress reports and letters, report cards or forms, summarized and interpreted children's portfolios, and test scores. Informal reports include sample work displayed or sent home, programs and exhibitions, informal conversations or notes, telephone messages, folders of sample work and reports sent back and forth between home and school at least once a week, short notes or "happy-grams," and others. Most programs use a combination. Formal reports are usually given more weight than informal ones, but anything communicated by teachers is likely to be taken seriously by parents. Informal reciprocal exchanges convey much useful information (Powell, 1989).

Prekindergartens and kindergartens rely heavily on parent conferences, samples of children's work, and informal communication, although many have formal rating scales. Primary grades usually have a report card or progress report, even when it is called by another name. Parent conferences are typically scheduled at least once or twice a year and are always available on request.

Regardless of the reporting methods used, judgments and conclusions communicated to parents should be substantiated and grounded in valid and reliable appraisals. Early childhood teachers often report on many things other than reading, arithmetic, and other "subjects." They judge dispositions and skills such as attention span, confidence, participation in group activities, social interaction, and work habits. Teachers should know what reporting forms they will use and develop ways to assess child progress on all items. When reporting time comes, adequate information will be in each child's files and portfolio to make fair and valid conclusions and to have examples to discuss with parents.

One of the advantages of authentic assessment in communicating with parents is that the documentation often speaks for itself. Evidence of a child's growing control over small hand muscles, writing and arithmetic samples, increased participation in group discussions, and the ability—or lack thereof—to work with written symbols in mathematics doesn't need a lot of translation. There are no confusing "percentiles," "means," "norms," "developmental age versus chronological age," and other statistical terminology to interpret. Parents perceive such information from teachers to be as informative as more formal measures (Diffily, 1994; Shepard & Bliem, 1993).

A well-organized portfolio, written records, and progress summaries provide focus for a parent–teacher conference. As parents and teachers go through the documentation together, opportunities for explanation, questions, and responses arise from the records, work products, and other materials. The conference becomes a shared reflection and look to the future, rather than a cut-and-dried evaluation of a youngster's performance. If parents and teachers have jointly prepared goals at the beginning of the year, evaluation of progress toward those goals is part of the progress report and conference. If video- or audiotapes of a child's progress in selected areas have been made, watching or listening to excerpts is powerful documentation. At the end of the year, when selected documents go with the child to the next level or setting, the ones that go home are a precious record of an important year in a child's life.

Relationship of Classroom Assessment to Summary Reports

In some early childhood settings, teachers are required to make *summary* or *summative* evaluations of children's progress. These evaluations compare a child's cumulative status, general strengths and weaknesses, or progress toward program goals and objectives to a criterion or to other children (Gage & Berliner, 1992). When teachers compare a child's performance to a goal or objective, they are making *criterion-referenced* evaluations. Wendy has made satisfactory progress toward the goal of being responsible for her own work in the classroom. In *norm-referenced* evaluation children are compared with other children of the same age (as in using a developmental continuum or pattern) or to the other children in the class. Wendy's self-management skills are similar to those of other children her age, but better than the average found in this second grade class. Comparisons can also be made between past and current performances.

Many teachers find summary evaluations difficult and distasteful and would gladly do away with them altogether. They fear, rightly, that ratings and reports can be disheartening for children and parents and encourage unhealthy competition (Juarez, 1996). "Putting less emphasis on comparisons is fine, but at some point a child and his parents have a right to know whether the child's progress is reasonable for his or her age and experience" (Maeroff, 1991, p. 276). The questions that early childhood teachers and schools face are (1) when that point is and (2) how progress shall be communicated.

Types of Summary Evaluations Found in Early Childhood Programs

Two types of summary evaluations are used in early childhood programs: narrative reports and grades or ratings. Some programs require both, others only one, and some require none at all. Teachers report a great deal of autonomy in deciding what information goes in narrative reports. Some simply write essays, others have forms with headings for major goals or developmental areas, and some have no written reports (Leong, McAfee, & Swedlow, 1992).

Narrative reports are considered the most appropriate way to summarize preschool and primary children's progress (see Figure 10–2). They contain statements about achievement, effort, attitude, and behavior (Hopkins, Stanley, & Hopkins, 1990).

Good narrative reports emphasize strengths, but also communicate concerns and recommendations. They usually do not summarize all areas of growth but only the most significant. Typically, comparisons are made between the child's capabilities and program goals and objectives, universal patterns of growth and development, or the child's previous performance.

Figure 10–2 *Typical Narrative Progress Report*

Progress Report   Date: 6/15/9–

Child: Turner, T

Tina has made great progress in all areas of development. Most notable were gains in the areas of written language, thinking skills, knowledge base, and social development. At the beginning of the year, Tina was just beginning to label her drawings with scribbles that were horizontal, had repeated features, and spaces for words. Now she has begun to incorporate letters and has written words interspersed between the scribbles. I would expect her to increase the number of written words. She has begun to read back some of her stories, but for the most part, what she reads is not yet tied to what she has written—a normal developmental step.

In thinking skills, Tina is experimenting with numbers and with the idea that numbers remain the same even though the objects are arranged in different groupings. For example, she figured out that 4 + 1, 1 + 4, 3 + 2, and 2 + 3 all make 5.

Her knowledge of math facts has also grown during the year. Early in the year she was counting meaningfully by 1's to 20. She is now counting by 2's and enjoys experimenting with adding different one-digit numbers. I anticipate that this interest and enjoyment of math will continue.

Tina has also grown in her social skills. Her dramatic play is full of fantasy and very complex, showing both intellectual development and social development. She has shown instances of empathy and social problem-solving skills. She enjoys being with her friends and plays primarily with Tania, Mark, and Sonia. She participates in cooperative learning activities.

Comparisons with children in the same class are kept to a minimum. Narrative reports seem to lighten the "impact of comparisons among students and give the teacher an opportunity to bring up important areas to parents" (Hopkins et al., 1990, p. 325).

The second type of evaluation is a rating. To rate or grade a student, the teacher converts the child's performance on key items into a letter (A, B, C, D, or F) or some other rating scale: 1, 2, 3, 4; satisfactory–unsatisfactory; needs work, satisfactory, or excellent; or some variation of these.

The summary reports developed by Meisels and his colleagues (1994) report progress "as expected" or "other than expected." All the different numbers, letters, and phrases are efforts to solve the difficult problem of reporting children's progress as a rating.

Using Classroom Assessment Information in Summary Evaluations

Narrative Reports. Recorded and summarized classroom assessment information is essential to accurate narrative reports. Summarize and use information that reveals the child's progress toward major classroom goals and objectives, as well as information on the individual child's uniqueness. Because other people will read and be influenced by your statement, it must be fair, accurate, and impartial; report only what can be substantiated with data.

A consistent format helps organize the report, so that important information is included and easy to find. If the school or center does not supply a format, you may wish to develop one. Programs have developed a wide variety of reporting forms. Figure 10–3 shows the only "report card" issued by one primary school using portfolio assessment. Teachers fill out the academic and social sections with succinct statements about what and how well the child is doing and the child's strengths. Any concerns are noted on a separate sheet of paper. During parent conferences, the concerns are restated as goals (the last item) for parents, teachers, or pupils. Home and school each get a copy of the entire report.

Other elementary schools have lists of achievement items in categories such as "learning attitudes and behaviors," "mathematical concepts and processes," "self-esteem and respect for others," "critical-thinking, problem-solving, and decision-making skills," and "cultural, scientific, and technological literacy." Teachers rate each child's progress on the major items and sub-items, but also have a space for narrative comments on each major item.

A kindergarten classroom uses the report form shown in Figure 10–4 for end-of-year reporting; the first report is an essay. Some forms give a brief summary of what development and learning are being discussed in each section. This is particularly helpful to parents who may not know what the school means by "symbolic representation," "critical thinking and problem solving," "cognitive development," or "emergent literacy." The important thing about all of the progress reports is that parents, teachers, and administrators know and agree on what is being assessed and reported. For additional information on writing narrative reports, see Sattler's *Assessment of Children.*

Ratings: Grades, Scales, and Ranks.   Since the primary purpose of classroom assessment is to provide information to help children in their efforts to learn, the relationship of that information to traditional ratings—grades, scales, and ranks—is still in process of development. To give some idea of the issues involved, consider the case of successive drafts of a piece of writing. What should be considered in grading? Only the final product? Progress made from the first to the last draft? The number of drafts? The teacher's judgment of the child's insight into the writing process? Originality? Progress toward conventional forms in punctuation, usage, and spelling? What will be considered satisfactory progress in performance assessments of mathematical problem solving? The challenge involved in making criteria explicit for children, teachers, and parents is formidable (Herman, Aschbacher, & Winters, 1992; Maeroff, 1991).

Criteria for assigning ratings should be clear. Many schools make this simpler by developing criterion-referenced items that are fairly clear-cut, such as "recognizes own name in print" or "matches letters." Less specific information is communicated in narrative reports. Rubrics make criteria for ratings clear and descriptive, but only in relation to the specific complex performance being rated, such as "expresses ideas clearly" or

Figure 10–3 *Narrative Semester Report, Primary School*

**CAMPBELL ELEMENTARY
PRIMARY SEMESTER REPORT**

CHILD'S NAME _____ TEACHER _____

ACADEMIC

   FIRST SEMESTER

   SECOND SEMESTER

SOCIAL

   FIRST SEMESTER

   SECOND SEMESTER

GOALS

   FIRST SEMESTER

   SECOND SEMESTER

"effectively communicates in a variety of ways." How these and other rubric ratings might be compiled for an overall rating for communications skills or any other broad developmental or curriculum domain is less clear. For more information on weighing and evaluating different

Figure 10–4   *Narrative Report Form*

WASHINGTON SCHOOL

Kindergarten Progress Report

Date: _____

Name of Student:

_____

_____

Teacher Signature

Intellectual Development
Language:

Mathematical and Scientific Thinking:

Creative Development

Social and Emotional Development

Physical Development

Work Habits

General Comments (See back of page)

---

pieces of evidence to derive a cumulative grade, consult Gage and Berliner's *Educational Psychology* (1992) or Airasian's *Classroom Assessment* (1994). Many primary schools are attempting to move away from letter grades (Alexander, 1993).

Reporting Progress to Parents

The best communication with parents about a child's status and progress takes place as teachers and parents, and sometimes pupils, consider, discuss, and exchange evidence, thoughts and feelings face to face. Schools and centers using alternative assessment try to arrange parent conferences for reporting.

Communicate with Parents, Not to or at Them.   The process is one of people interacting with other people. Parents are a primary source of information about their children, and teachers listen as well as report. Even better is mutual sharing of information and insights. Parent conferences are ideal, but telephone conferences, voice mail, progress letters, home visits, informal sharing, and many other forms of communication achieve similar results.

Give Parents a Written Progress Statement That Reports on Major Developmental and Learning Areas.   In some schools and centers, parent conferences are held from teachers' notes, and parents receive nothing in writing. If forms for reporting show scaled indications of the child's progress, take time to write comments, too. These mean more to parents than all the check marks and circles put together.

Keep Language Clear, Simple, and Free of Jargon.   Use terms that everyone can understand instead of "perceptual–motor," "auditory memory," "cognitive processes," and the many other terms we as educators use. "Sometimes we deliberately use jargon to befuddle or hide behind; more often, we use it without thinking" (McAfee, 1987, p. 196). Use no labels. Concentrate on what the child does. Offer enough explanation that parents see the significance of what you are discussing. For example, unless the clarity and organization in a child's report or journal are pointed out, a parent may focus on poorly formed letters or misspelled words. If the parent or guardian speaks a different language from you, arrange for a translator to be present.

Be Selective.   The amount of documentation you have about a child requires that you summarize and select what parents will want and need to know. Some children may wish to help in this process. Select only a few portfolio items to make your points clear.

Be Clear, Straightforward, and Supportive.   With the documentation that good classroom assessment provides, you can share children's strengths and needs in a way that parents can respect and accept. It is no kindness to gloss over problems and concerns. In fact, if real concerns exist, you, the administrator, or the appropriate specialist should be working with parents immediately, so there are no surprises at conference or reporting time (Abbott & Gold, 1991).

Be Prepared to Answer Parents' Questions.   Many schools send out preconference forms to parents to ask what they would like to discuss at the conference. Almost every parent, at some time or other, will want to know their child's relative standing in the class. Schools have worked hard to find alternative ways of reporting about children, but this question inevitably arises. Be prepared to tell or show what the typical child of that developmental level can do, and make your comparison to that hypothetical child, rather than to other children in the class. A different way to accomplish the same purpose is to save samples of typical work from past years that show parents the variations within the range of normal.

If parents have questions about the program, be prepared to answer them. Sometimes parents wonder why children are not being drilled on the "ABC's," phonics, or "the basics." Be ready to explain and show how children are progressing toward school and parent goals.

Be Sensitive to the Impact of What You Are Saying.   Judgment of what is appropriate to say will vary with the family and child. Altered expectations, pressure, and even punishment can result from insensitivity to family dynamics. Teachers sometimes expect parents to give more help with school behavior problems than any parent can. If a child's parents knew how to keep her from disrupting class, they would doubtless do it. Indeed, sometimes there are no problems at home (Tuma & Elbert, 1990).

Use Assessment Results as the Basis for Home Activities.   One of the most effective home–school collaborations is helping parents learn how to help their children (Epstein, 1987). Assessment results tell you what children need help with. You can get beyond "give her some help when she has trouble" or "help him with his homework" to being specific about what this family can do (Coleman, 1991; Gotts, 1984). Assessment results may also help you with the parent who needs to ease up on the child—an equally valid aid to some children's development.

Communicating with Other Professionals

Communication with other professionals or staff takes many forms: communication and coordination within the school or center; communication with other centers and agencies that deliver child services; and communication with other teachers and agencies to ease the transition from prekindergarten to kindergarten or from kindergarten to first grade. Chapter 4 has guidelines on using other professionals as sources of information about children. Chapter 11 gives suggestions for working collaboratively with specialists and other members of assessment teams.

Administrators in schools and centers usually require certain minimum reports from teachers: attendance, potential concerns, permission slips for special activities, and others as determined in the individual setting. Teachers involved in alternative assessment are almost always working with the support and understanding of the administrator, who should be kept informed. Do this indirectly, through displays, bulletin boards, exhibits, invitations to hear reports, and other public ways children show what they have done (Katz & Chard, 1989; Kneidek, 1991). Direct ways are also appropriate: a well-done portfolio explained by a child, outstanding progress by a child or group in any developmental or content area, a new form or way of documenting children's work that you think might be helpful to others, or simply an informal conversation about how it's going—what's working and what isn't. Especially appropriate are reports on what is working and why.

Teachers, aides, assistants, specialists, administrators, and other school or center staff do not always agree on children's needs and how to respond to them. Often these disagreements are the result of deeply held convictions about how children learn (Smith & Shepard, 1988), but sometimes they happen because each person has only part of the necessary information. A classroom teacher may focus on a child's total functioning, a specialist may focus on deficiencies or strengths that become obvious in one-to-one therapy, whereas the teacher down the hall may know that part of the child's behavior which shows itself in play yard disputes. Although some elements of truth are present in all these perceptions, no single one is complete. Basic information from each source, discussed objectively and professionally, can help staff arrive at appropriate courses of action.

As children move from one setting to another, teachers should send and receive summarized information about those children. Transition strategies almost always involve transfer of records. Some forms, such as the California Learning Record (California State Dept. of Education, 1989), have a section designated "information for the receiving teacher," to ensure that information for the receiving teacher is up-to-date and helpful. Health and social service staff can use existing information as a discussion point to ensure continuity of services for children and families (Administration for Children, Youth, and Families, 1986; National Association of State Boards of Education, 1988). Efforts are under way to identify and develop workable and appropriate procedures to convey assessment information from one setting to another (Regional Educational Laboratories' Early Childhood Collaboration Network, 1995; Love, 1991; Love, Logue, Trudeau, & Thayer, 1992).

Reporting to Funding and Regulatory Agencies, Governing Boards, and Citizen Groups

Traditionally, communicating with funding agencies and governing boards has been done by administrators. However, with "site-based management" and other ways of empowering teachers and local centers and schools, teachers may participate more fully in reporting.

Programs may be expected to provide evidence of what they are doing as a condition of being funded. All too often, standardized tests are thought of as the only way to document effectiveness. Scores make headlines in local and national newspapers, television, and magazines, as districts, funding agencies, and even whole states publicize the results. Alternative assessment may moderate this overemphasis on test scores (Eisner, 1995; Kneidek, 1991).

Summative data about groups are often used for reporting to funding agencies and governing boards. This is different from the summarizing of children's work that is done to guide planning or report to parents. Depending on the situation, there may be requests for pre- and postevaluations of children's progress, case studies, parent interviews, and other reports of progress. In today's social and educational climate, such tasks are an integral part of teaching.

"The challenge for policy makers is to craft approaches to accountability that give decision makers the data they need but that minimize the unintended consequences for the teaching and learning of young children" (Schultz, 1989, p. 128). Some states and school districts postpone the use of any standardized achievement tests until third or fourth grade, in line with recommendations from many national organizations. Some states and agencies limit testing to representative samples of children, thus avoiding comparison between districts, programs, or groups of children—and greatly reducing testing costs. Some are attempting alternative assessments involving samples of student work, teacher observation, performance in classroom settings, case studies, videotaping, and other techniques (Arter, 1990). States and school districts are working to devise ways to aggregate and compare alternative assessment data across classrooms, schools, and school districts (Cizek, 1995; Maeroff, 1991). Using alternative assessment for accountability or comparison purposes in the way test scores have been used presents many problems (Mehrens, 1991).

Doing away with requirements or expectations for standardized achievement testing in early childhood will not lessen expectations for assessment and reporting of progress. In fact, alternative, authentic assessment using a variety of techniques will require greater teacher understanding of and skill in the whole assessment process, and the ability to communicate results to a wide and varied audience.

Professional and Personal Development and Learning

Self-reflection and self-assessment are part of classroom assessment, for both teachers and children. Teachers keep logs or journals that record their reflections on events of the day or week, their frustrations, joys, triumphs, and hopes in their professional and personal growth and development (Brandt, 1991; Hebert, 1992). Classroom assessment places great responsibility and demand on teachers for selection and development of appropriate approaches; for collecting, recording, and organizing information; and for interpreting and using it. It is not a "system" but a way of thinking about how children learn and how teachers can help in that process. The development and use of alternative, authentic assessment should be a learning experience for a reflective educator.

Professional Development and Learning

Authentic classroom assessment of children, and the use of that information to modify curriculum, is professionally and personally demanding but equally satisfying and rewarding. Teachers have the opportunity to expand and upgrade their professional role as they systematically assess what children know and can do, their attitudes and dispositions, and their interests and abilities. No standardized test, achievement battery, or diagnostic evaluation can bring to children's development and learning the breadth and depth of knowledge that teachers can. Increased expectations of teachers for assessment is a challenge and an opportunity. It can bring back the centrality of a group of children and adults working together to learn and allow them to discard the idea of education as a prescriptive, lock-step process.

Modifying, creating, augmenting, or simplifying curriculum experiences to meet children's needs and help them learn is enormously satisfying. To have personal knowledge, intuitions, hunches, and insights become a legitimate part of the assessment process—humanizing scores, grades, and percentiles—deepens the satisfaction.

Personal Development and Learning

Learning more about children and their development, uniqueness, and individuality and the ways they respond to and interact with people, objects, events, and activities is emotionally and intellectually satisfying. It is also humbling, as teachers begin to appreciate the complexity and mystery of human life and learning and the distressing problems that confront many young children.

On a more personal level, teachers may have to confront and face themselves to understand why it is so difficult to accept this child as she is, why it is easy to deal with a high-spirited child but difficult to help a passive youngster—or the reverse (Humphrey, 1989; Jersild, 1955). Personal values, beliefs, and convictions come to the fore as teachers decide what is important for children's growth and development, a teacher's role in that process, and how they can fulfill that role. As teachers work to help children develop and learn, they also develop and learn.

Summary

Responsibilities relating to assessment go beyond the classroom—to parents, other professionals, funding and regulatory agencies, and citizen groups. Teachers may be expected to prepare variations on two basic types of reports: narrative progress reports and ratings. Both types should be substantiated by valid and reliable data.

The skills and attitudes that create successful communication with parents involve preparing written progress statements; using simple, easy to understand language that is free of jargon; being selective about what is reported; being clear and supportive; answering questions; and being sensitive to the impact of what you are communicating. One of the most effective uses of assessment results is to help the family help the child develop and learn.

Teachers should keep administrators informed in a variety of ways. Schools and centers may require specific information from teachers for official administrative purposes and for reporting to funding and regulatory agencies, governing boards, or citizen groups. Increased emphasis on authentic, classroom-based assessment may increase the responsibilities teachers have for such reporting.

Finally, increased expectations for assessment conducted by teachers in the classroom present both a challenge and an opportunity for professional and personal growth. In understanding and responding to children lies the opportunity to understand more about ourselves.

For Further Study, Discussion, and Reflection

1. Reflect on the opportunities and challenges this enlarged professional responsibility for assessment offers you personally. Write a short paragraph describing them, perhaps in your teacher's journal. Share your reflections with others in your study group or class.
2. Evaluate and reflect on your current attitudes and skills in communicating assessment results to parents by comparing what you know how to do with the suggestions given in the chapter.
3. Put yourself in the role of a parent of a preschooler, kindergartner, or second-grader. (Some of you may be those parents.) List the assessment information you would like to have from your child's teacher.

Suggested Readings

Brandt, R. S. (Ed.). (1991). The reflective educator. *Educational Leadership, 48,* 6.

Burns, R. C. (Ed.). (1993). *Parents and schools: From visitors to partners.* Washington, DC: National Education Association.

Clift, R., Houston, W., & Pugach, M. (Eds.). (1990). *Encouraging reflective practice in education.* New York: Teachers College Press.

Coleman, J. S. (1991). *Parent involvement in education.* (OERI, Order No. 065-000-00459-3). Washington, DC: U.S. Government Printing Office.

Herman, J. L., Aschbacher, P. R., & Winters, L. (1992). *A practical guide to alternative assessment.* Alexandria, VA: Association for Supervision and Curriculum Development.

Lawler, S. D. (1991). *Parent–teacher conferencing in early childhood education.* Washington, DC: National Education Association.

Powell, D. (1989). *Families and early childhood programs.* Washington, DC: National Association for the Education of Young Children.

Stone, S. J. (1995). *Understanding portfolio assessment: A guide for parents.* Reston, VA: Association for Childhood Education International.

CHAPTER ELEVEN

Contemporary Considerations in Assessment

Social and Educational Context

Assessment in early childhood schools and centers is not just another activity teachers do in their classrooms, much as they might read a story, prepare an art activity, or plan a field trip. It is central to the way society cares for and educates children.

> Societal changes have hit the schools [and early childhood centers] with full force. . . . Schools that were designed to educate a relatively stable student body are straining to adapt to students who are increasingly diverse, with great differences in racial and cultural heritage, language, health, family situation, and preparation for schooling. (Committee for Economic Development, 1991, p. 8)

Fair, continuous, authentic assessment of all children is essential if early childhood schools and centers are "to help children become educated no matter what their social, economic, or cultural background" (Committee for Economic Development, 1991, p. 5). Within that overall task are special challenges and concerns that stem from sociocultural and individual differences. To differences in "racial and cultural heritage, language, health, family situation, and preparation for schooling" (Committee for Economic Development, 1991, p. 8) could be added gender, place of residence, economic resources, educational level of parents or guardians, genetic inheritance, and the many other influences that shape human development and make each person unique.

Those differences are part of the rich diversity of teaching in contemporary classrooms. Make a distinction between "differences" and "deficits" or "disabilities." Differences are "dissimilarities, uniqueness, and distinctiveness" (Guerin & Maier, 1983, p. 373). The concept of differences is neutral, suggesting neither good nor bad and is the best term to describe variations among groups and individuals. "Disability" refers to a "deficit in learning that occurs in spite of persistent instruction or from an inability to participate in ordinary instruction due to physical, mental, or emotional reasons" (Guerin & Maier, 1983, p. 373).

Teachers' responsibilities in coordination, collaboration, and referral relating to contemporary needs conclude the chapter.

Sociocultural Differences in Assessment

Young children in the United States come from incredibly diverse backgrounds. They vary in race and ethnicity; culture and degree of acculturation; language dominance and fluency; socioeconomic and educational level; rural, urban, suburban, inner-city, or rural–isolated home location; family structure and values; and prior school experience. So do their teachers. And whether they recognize it or not, both bring those differences to the classroom assessment process. Teachers, families, and children are often unaware of cultural differences that may influence children's performance (Phillips, 1983; West, 1992). In a fast-changing cultural setting such as the United States, acculturation occurs at varying speeds, and our knowledge of the powerful and subtle ways home, community, and culture influence children's development is incomplete.

Standardized tests are criticized for lack of sensitivity to sociocultural differences and those differences' influences on children's learning. Alternative assessment holds the promise of being more sensitive. This will not happen automatically, or even easily. In practice, the challenge of developing equitable assessment processes for children from diverse backgrounds may be the classroom teacher's. Efforts to devise "culture-fair" or "culture-free" means of measuring children's development, achievement, and learning potential have not lived up to expectation (Cronbach, 1990). Teachers must acknowledge and understand the influence that sociocultural background has on classroom assessment, ranging from such a simple thing as whether the child is used to answering "test-like" questions to deep-seated family attitudes—supportive, nonsupportive, or indifferent—toward anything connected with educational institutions. For example, some families may help their children in anything connected with schooling, coaching them on how to behave and respond. Others may not know how to help children bridge that gap.

Teachers also have to face the fact that they, too, are products of a particular sociocultural background, often with little conscious knowledge of why they have certain values, expectations, or ways of acting. When they interact with people who speak languages or dialects other than theirs, or act in different ways, they may have a tendency to judge those people's behavior by their own standards. Most teachers have to learn more about their own backgrounds as well as those of the families and children they are dealing with. Understanding their own sociocultural values will help them become more sensitive to sociocultural differences in children and families.

Local sources offer the best guidance about cultural, language, and other differences in a given community. Families, a family coordinator, a school–home liaison, or a cultural or language specialist, if available, should have local and current information that will increase understanding. Schools, centers, and human resource agencies often distribute printed information or conduct workshops on significant differences likely to be found among minority groups in a particular area. Economic, language, ethnic, or cultural groups are not monolithic in their attitudes and practices (Suro, 1992), and particular generalizations may or may not apply to particular individuals, families, or communities. The characteristics of local groups and individual families as they relate to classroom and assessment procedures are what a teacher needs to know. Sweeping generalizations are of little help and may actually perpetuate stereotypes.

It is easy to equate sociocultural differences with skin color, ethnic origin, name, or economic status, but reality is not that simple. Many families have mixed ethnic, racial, and religious backgrounds through marriage, adoption, and other circumstances. Some families have definite preferences and choices about the cultural orientation and education they want their children to have—regardless of family background.

Cultural characteristics most relevant to school behavior and progress include "learning style, relations between children and adults, attitudes toward achievement, the role of the home and the school, and behavioral styles" (Guerin & Maier, 1983, p. 297).

Cultural Differences That May Influence Assessment

Children's backgrounds have a profound influence on their knowledge base, vocabulary, and skills. Knowledge about fish, the ocean or the desert, street games, families, holidays, computers, or anything else will be related to the importance of that knowledge in a particular culture. Rules for expressing opinions, discussing, and taking turns in conversation may differ from one culture to another (Gumperz & Gumperz, 1981). Politeness and respect are communicated in different ways: averting the eyes, looking "straight in the eye"; silence or response; saying or not saying "Yes, ma'am," or "No, sir." "Yes" may be expressed by eyes wide open, "no" by squinting (New, 1991). Even "thinking seriously" is communicated in different ways. When asked a difficult question, children from one culture may look up, whereas children from another culture may look down. Teachers filter this behavior through the school or their own culture to determine its meaning. Chances are that the child looking up will be assessed as "trying harder" than the child who looks down, unless the teacher is aware of the cultural difference. One culture may emphasize fine motor skills so that children may be advanced in cutting and drawing and behind in jumping, kicking, or running. Another may emphasize and give opportunity for gross motor development so that children's physical development is far ahead of expectations.

Children from one cultural group may have learned ways of responding to questions that put them at a disadvantage in school. One researcher found that African American children's responses were more likely to describe objects and events in relation to themselves or their experience rather than to name the object or event (Lawson, 1986). The expected response in most school settings is the name of the object or event. Studies of Athabaskan and Warm Springs Native American communities found "participant structures"—rules that govern conversations—that differ from what is expected in school. Participant structures involve such things as turn-taking and pace in conversations, pauses and silence, and who asks and answers questions. Imagine the miscommunication, even when everyone is speaking English (Gage & Berliner, 1992).

The thinking processes and learning styles that children develop and use are closely linked to the sociocultural environment in which they develop, as those processes are nurtured in collaboration with others or in social arrangements of children's activities (Bodrova & Leong, 1996; Rogoff, 1990). Learning processes, such as memory strategies, classification processes, and approaches to problem solving, are not developed solely within the individual, but "are intrinsically related to social and societal values and goals, tools, and institutions" (Rogoff, 1990, p. 61). For example, taxonomic classification—putting things together in abstract categories on the basis of their presumed relationships—is emphasized in school and some cultures. Perceptual categories—how things look the same or different— are emphasized in others (Ceci, 1991). As schools and centers aim to assess and teach higher-level cognitive processes, as opposed to simpler notions of reading, computation, and recall of facts, the influence of sociocultural differences may be more, not less, important. The emerging body of literature on sociocultural contexts of development and learning is beyond the scope of this book, but the evidence is compelling; see the suggested readings at the end of this chapter.

Assessment that occurs in school settings is subject to the biases of the school culture. All schools have a "culture," including certain values, rules for interaction and behavior, and expectations (Gage & Berliner, 1992). All children must make some adjustments to being away from home. For most youngsters, these adjustments expand their world and the repertoire of behavior and skills they have at their command (Powell, 1989). However, children from some ethnic, cultural, and community backgrounds must make more, often difficult adjustments (Kagan, Moore, & Bredekamp, 1995). They may not be used to following oral directions, performing on demand, or the restrictions of the setting. They may base their answers on social cues rather than on what they "think" or know (Sattler, 1992). These children may need more explicit directions and support to make the adjustment.

Efforts to lessen the discontinuities between home and community culture and that of the school have been found effective in improving children's school performance. For example, the Kamehameha Early Education Program (KEEP) developed a culturally compatible language arts program for kindergarten through third grade children of Hawaiian ancestry in Hawaii (Tharp & Gallimore, 1988). The focused work of this program—that is, working with Hawaiian children in Hawaii—may well have clues for local programs hoping to address the complexities of sociocultural and regional diversity.

Implications for Assessment

"Assessment . . . presents a formidable problem for teachers of children outside the economic and cultural mainstream" (Bowman, 1992, p. 136). Little definitive research exists on the way assessment should be done to be sensitive to sociocultural differences. More research and guidance should become available as assessment processes stabilize and research is conducted. Whenever human judgment is involved, the potential for human bias increases. Teachers should take extra care to overcome that possibility. The following guidelines are based on available information, older research that has implications for current practices, strategies particularly suited to working with young children, and personal experience in assessing and teaching young children.

Assume there will be sociocultural influences on children's actions in the classroom. If nothing more, there will be differences among expectations of the home and community, previous schools, and the current setting. Children coming from a preschool that stresses individual choice, initiative, creativity, and much peer verbal interaction may be sized up in initial assessment differently from children who are quiet and wait for direction. These differences may be present across all cultural, social, or economic backgrounds. Assume, also, that there may be lack of congruence of the school culture with the sociocultural setting of the home and community. Competitiveness and cooperation, gender-role differentiation, the importance of schooling in the life of the family or community, the relationship of the child to adults, and many other aspects related to learning and teaching may be involved. If you suspect that cultural, language, or other differences may be operating, check it out. Use this information to understand why children may be having trouble, and then gradually help them learn whatever it is they need to know. However, don't make the mistake of blaming all problems on a child's home background.

Involve parents, the community, and any language, cultural, and social specialists to determine specific similarities and differences that may help explain a youngster's actions. All too often, we focus on the perceived differences and overlook the similarities (Jones & Derman-Sparks, 1992; Rogoff, 1990). The latter may give points of entrance for assessment and instructional activities and be a reminder that all families, all children, have their own sociocultural approaches to living and learning.

Manipulate assessment situations to allow children to demonstrate their full capabilities. The freedom to do that is one of the big differences between alternative assessment and standardized tests. "Most children in low-income and minority communities have mastered [developmental tasks similar to those expected of all children], but their mastery may be displayed in unfamiliar dress" (Bowman, 1992, p. 134). Make full use of available multiple assessment windows and approaches, including informal ones. If one approach is not appropriate, another may be; one provides a check against the other, so that a youngster who is unable to respond in one context or to one method of assessment has some options (Villegas, 1991). Children who are unable or unwilling to respond to structured performance tasks may be able to demonstrate their knowledge in informal "real-life situations." When she was asked to name colors, 4-year-old Leila simply refused to respond. Less than a half-hour later, during informal lunchtime conversation with her teacher, Leila said all the color names correctly, linked with examples and incorporated into functional, real conversation. Which is Leila's true competence level? Assessing in noncontrived "contextualized" situations—informal, comfortable, and familiar—may enable children to perform at higher levels (Cazden, 1988).

If possible, learn how adults and older children in a particular sociocultural setting help children learn, and add these to the repertoire of dynamic assessment techniques you use. Do adults demonstrate, and then let children try? Do they provide elaborate oral interpretation or only key elements? Do they involve children in every facet of ongoing daily life, with guided participation at every step? Little is known of how these various sociocultural patterns might be used by teachers to help dynamic assessment, but there seems to be promise. Dynamic assessment of young children involves far more than words.

Be prepared to rephrase, restate, or recast a task or expectation in terms that might be familiar and sensible to the youngsters. Change the assessment context to a more familiar one. Assess using children's interests and activities, which should, in turn, be linked to their homes and communities—the sociocultural setting. Above all, do not assume a lack of ability or potential based on sociocultural or language differences (Hakuta & Garcia, 1989).

Individual Differences

Assessment will reveal many individual differences among children. Acknowledging and trying to provide for differences has been a concern of educators since the 1920s, when the testing movement revealed great disparity among children's achievement in the typical classroom (Gage & Berliner, 1992). Multidimensional alternative assessment makes us aware of individual differences in all developmental and curriculum domains. Three types of individual difference are of particular concern to early childhood educators: children with special needs, children and families "at risk," and children who need challenge. Inclusive education is a way of acknowledging the many things children have in common, as well as their individual differences.

Children with Special Needs

Probably no area of child assessment has received more attention and criticism than the process of identifying children with special needs—disabilities or developmental delays. Research and theory on identifying and educating these youngsters is expanding. Terminology changes in response. Many children with special needs do not fit any categories, or fit several. Children who have severe hearing or vision impairment or severe neurological, orthopedic, muscular, or multiple handicaps are usually identified and diagnosed before they enter the classroom setting. Less obvious needs, such as learning disabilities, speech and language problems, emotional disturbance, attention deficit disorders, or mild mental retardation may first be detected by a classroom teacher. The developmental "red flags" in Appendix B will alert you to possible need for referral.

Even as teachers are sensitive to possible problems, they must be careful not to overidentify. Many school "problems" are perfectly normal behavior for children of a given age, developmental level, or cultural group (Armstrong, 1995; Gage & Berliner, 1992). For example, young children are unlikely to pay attention to something that is not interesting (McAfee, 1985). Listening and attending are not the child's problem alone, but are shared with adults, other distractions, the activity, time of day, and innumerable other variables. Inappropriate educational programming or classroom guidance may result in child behavior that is distracting or disruptive or in failure to learn. For instance, active young children who are asked to sit and work at tasks beyond their developmental level may seek unacceptable outlets. Children who need to manipulate, arrange, rearrange, and solve problems with objects may fail to learn if the same task is presented with symbols only.

Developmentally and individually appropriate programs lessen unrealistic expectations of young children and allow identification of children who truly have special needs. To do this, use the recommended assessment process: describe and document the child's behavior using multiple sources, methods, and settings; compare it with developmental expectations and with other children; talk with parents; study, discuss, and interpret the information, including any information on the classroom environment that might contribute. Then decide whether the situation is something that you can handle or if consultation with a specialist is in order. If there is any doubt, always consult. Most schools, centers, and agencies have multiple safeguards to ensure that children's and families' rights are protected, including clinical evaluations to check out any referrals. Evaluations that lead to placement in special programs are considered "high stakes," and teachers work with many other people in making those recommendations.

Children at Risk

Early identification and intervention with children and families "at risk" is increasing, as educators and policy makers realize that kindergarten or first grade may be too late for many children. The first of the major educational goals of the National Governors' Association is that every child should enter first grade ready to learn and able to benefit from an appropriate education (National Governors' Association, 1990). Further definition of this goal calls for attention to physical well-being and motor development, social and emotional development, approaches toward learning, language development, and cognition and general knowledge as factors that make a difference between being "ready to learn" and "at risk." How does this relate to assessment? First, selection of children and families to be in programs for children "at risk" calls for sensitive, multiple validations of need. Indicators that allow for assessment of the dimensions of readiness are only now being developed (Kagan, Moore, & Bredekamp, 1995; National Educational Goals Panel, 1991). Second, assessment of children's status and progress as a guide to educational programming is imperative. Third, teachers in such programs may need to be vigilant for indicators that call for evaluation and possible intervention by a specialist. Even the best screening will miss many children who may need a closer look, just as it may wrongly identify children who actually have no problems of any kind. Children with subtle, intermittent, or inconsistent problems may be missed (Patterson & Wright, 1990). In addition, problems may develop after screening. Teachers must always be alert for signals to "look again" (see Appendix B).

Children Who Need Challenge

Young children may need special challenge for many reasons: the richness and variety of their educational and family experiences, early learning of basic skills, precocious development in a particular area, generally advanced development, being older than other children in the group, or being gifted, talented, or of "high potential." Classroom assessment can identify those children who need challenge, the areas in which they need it, and some guidance for appropriate activities to nurture their interests and abilities. Not all children who need challenge are gifted or talented, but teachers should be as alert to these children's needs as to those who have difficulty. Gardner (1985) suggested seven types of intelligence: linguistic or verbal, musical, logical–mathematical, spatial, bodily–kinesthetic, intrapersonal (self-knowledge), and interpersonal or social. Children may excel or have special needs in any or several of these types of intelligence.

As with any other assessment of young children, the potential for error is great. It is easy to mistake rapid learning, early maturation, or special training for true giftedness. Teachers are likely to confuse conformity, neatness, and good behavior with giftedness (Gage & Berliner, 1992). Giftedness and talent take many forms, but early childhood schools frequently recognize only intellectual prowess—being "smart." Parental pressures to have children in gifted programs can have negative effects on the child. Designating a youngster as gifted, talented, or of high potential should be done with all legal and ethical safeguards.

Two highly respected psychologists compiled the following signs as guides for teachers and parents:

- Demonstrated talent in performing or creating
- A wide variety of interests and information
- Ability to concentrate on a problem, task, or activity for long periods

- Ability to engage in abstract thinking and to construct relationships between problems and solutions
- Independent thinking characterized by creative ideas
- Extensive curiosity
- Early reading ability
- Use of a large vocabulary
- Rapid learning of basic skills (Gage & Berliner, 1992, p. 222)

Inclusive Education

"Inclusive education" implies the inclusion of youngsters with special needs as fully as possible in all aspects of education and community life. In an ideal situation, teachers receive the specialized help they need to assess special needs and implement appropriate curricula. This does not always happen, and teachers may find themselves taking much responsibility for assessment and educational programming. Even when specialized help is available, teachers need accurate descriptions and adequate documentation to participate in development and education decisions with other specialists. At one time, children with special needs were usually taken out of the regular classroom and placed in self-contained "special ed" classrooms. Once children had been identified, the regular teacher's responsibility ceased. Now, all children are included in the regular classroom as much as possible. Likewise, many schools that once provided programs for developmentally advanced children—whether called gifted, talented, or high potential—are no longer doing so, and teachers have responsibility for identifying those children and developing programming to match their capabilities.

Strategies for Classroom Personnel

No teacher or group of teachers can have all the knowledge necessary to deal adequately with the diversity of children and the high expectations of parents and the larger society. In assessing and using assessment results to help children learn, three strategies are feasible for all teachers: be sensitive to and knowledgeable about cultural and individual differences and their possible impact on assessment and curriculum strategies; work with local resources— parents, other school personnel, and specialists from other disciplines—to augment teacher knowledge and skill; and be alert to clues and indicators that say, "Check this out."

Work with Specialists from Other Disciplines

Schools and centers do not have all the resources to serve the diverse children and families they work with. Coordination and collaboration with other schools and centers, other public and private community resources and agencies, and other disciplines are essential (Committee for Economic Development, 1985, 1991; National Association of State Boards of Education, 1988). Work with professionals from other disciplines, with different orientations, priorities, and possible constraints on what they can do, is part of the role of today's early childhood teacher. In certain areas of diversity, such as cultural, ethnic, or language, reaching out to other community resources may be the only way to get essential information.

Teachers in many classrooms will be fortunate enough to have specialists with relevant knowledge and skills. Such specialists are not always employed by the school or center, but may be from another public or private agency or group, such as a mental health center, public health agency, local hospital, or nearby university. They help with identification, diagnosis, and the development of Individual Educational Plans (IEPs) and Individual Family Service Plans (IFSPs), the required plans for delivery of services to children with special needs.

The three major approaches to working with specialists are *interdisciplinary, multidisciplinary,* and *transdisciplinary* (Bagnato & Neisworth, 1991; Taylor, Willits, & Lieberman, 1990; Wolery & Dyk, 1984). These approaches are not mutually exclusive, but may occur simultaneously and complement one another. A fourth approach in which one person from one discipline makes the total assessment is seldom used.

Interdisciplinary approaches bring together specialists from various disciplines, including teachers, parents or parent representatives, and, where appropriate, cultural specialists, to work as a team outside the classroom. They contribute their unique perspectives on a particular child or problem, and then consult and work together to develop an appropriate course of action. Probably the best example of this approach is the "staffing" process used to consider evidence and deliberate on its meaning for children with special needs.

Multidisciplinary approaches depend on specialists from several disciplines who usually assess and evaluate a child independently and submit separate reports. An in-depth medical or psychological evaluation and diagnosis of a child might well be of this nature. It is left to others to fit the various pieces together into a workable program for a child or center.

Transdisciplinary collaboration takes place "across," and involves all, relevant disciplines. The approach minimizes disciplinary boundaries and promotes interactive collaboration and team consensus (Bagnato & Neisworth, 1991). "Play-based" assessment for children with special needs (Linder, 1993) is an example of transdisciplinary assessment.

Transdisciplinary approaches can be likened to team teaching, with the classroom teacher and one or more specialists working together to assess, plan, and carry out appropriate activities. The specialists may be in the classroom full or part time, depending on availability and need. Boundaries between the various specialties are minimized as the team works together. Advantages of transdisciplinary assessment include the following:

- Several professionals see and relate to children in the real-life setting of the classroom. Their observations and findings will complement each other's.
- Two professionals in the classroom make authentic classroom assessment more feasible.
- Interpretation of the meaning of results benefits from joint deliberation and consideration.

Unfortunately, the transdisciplinary approach is usually justified only when children with special needs are enrolled.

Roles and Responsibilities of the Teacher in Team Assessment.   The roles and responsibilities of the teacher are slightly different in these three approaches, although some aspects remain the same. In all approaches, teachers should:

- Know what each specialist does and what their unique contributions are likely to be. Titles and areas of expertise of typical health specialists are listed in Figure 11–1. Depending on the situation, there might also be a cultural and language specialist, home–school liaison, or parent coordinator. Some communities have public health nurses who survey, screen, and manage family and community health care or case managers who coordinate a variety of services for individuals and families. Teachers trained in special education may have their own specialties, such as teaching children with hearing loss.
- Remember that classroom teachers, too, are specialists, with knowledge of how children develop and learn both as individuals and in groups. Teachers know more about setting up, planning, and implementing developmentally appropriate activities for a group of children than any other members of the team. With well-done classroom assessment, the teacher has documented, authentic evidence of children's everyday functioning.
- Compile, summarize, and write classroom assessment information to help present and discuss the items under consideration. If necessary, point out how the evidence relates to the concern, as others may not have the classroom perspective that enables them to see the relationship.
- Be open and receptive to suggestions from other disciplines. In meetings, practice active listening. If reports are written, read them with an open mind. Even when you disagree, look for and recognize the perspectives that the other discipline brings. Almost always some aspect will contribute to understanding and helping the child or situation.
- Respect the other discipline or specialty and what it can contribute. Expect that same respect in return. There is no place for "just a teacher" or "just a parent." Teachers and parents have unique information.
- Recognize that you can't know and do everything. Seek out information and help from whatever sources are available.

Interdisciplinary and transdisciplinary approaches may require additional skills:

- The teacher may be the leader/facilitator of the team. This role includes getting people together on a regular basis to consult, evaluate, and maintain cohesiveness. Sometimes teachers and parents are the only members who are present consistently. Acting as a leader/ facilitator is particularly important in transdisciplinary approaches,

Figure 11–1   *Titles and Areas of Expertise of Typical Health Specialists*

An **allergist** is a medical doctor with special interest and training in diseases of the immune system including allergies (certified by the American Board of Allergy).

An **audiologist** is a specialist in hearing problems.

A **dentist** is a specialist who cares for and treats the teeth and gums.

A **neurologist** is a medical doctor with special interest and training in brain and nervous system disorders.

A **nutritionist** is a professional with interest and training (a master's degree) in nutrition, who evaluates a person's food habits and nutritional status. This specialist can provide advice about normal and therapeutic nutrition, feeding equipment, self-feeding techniques, and food service.

A **occupational therapist** evaluates and treats children who may have difficulty performing self-help, play, or other independent activities.

An **ophthalmologist** is a medical doctor who evaluates, diagnoses, and treats disease, injuries, or birth defects that limit vision.

An **optician** advises in the selection of frames and fits the lenses prescribed by the optometrist or ophthalmologist to the frames. An optician also fits contact lenses.

An **optometrist** examines the eye and related structures to determine the presence of visual problems, eye disease, or other problems.

An **orthopedist** is a medical doctor who evaluates, diagnoses, and treats diseases and injuries to muscles, joints, and bones.

An **otorhinolaryngologist** (E.N.T. doctor) is a medical doctor who screens, diagnoses, and treats ear, nose, and throat disorders.

An **otologist** is a medical doctor who screens, diagnoses, and treats ear disorders.

A **pediatrician** is a medical doctor who specializes in prevention and management of childhood diseases and problems (certified by the American Board of Pediatrics or the Osteopathic Board of Pediatrics or English or Canadian equivalents).

A **physical therapist** evaluates and plans physical therapy programs and equipment to promote self-sufficiency primarily related to gross motor skills such as walking, sitting, and shifting position.

A **psychiatrist** is a medical doctor who screens, diagnoses, and treats psychological, emotional, behavioral, and developmental or organic problems. Psychiatrists can prescribe medication. They generally do not administer tests.

A **psychologist** screens, diagnoses, and treats people with social, emotional, psychological, behavioral, or developmental problems.

A **social worker** provides services for individuals and families experiencing a variety of emotional or social problems. These services may include individual, family, or group counseling; advocacy; or consultation with programs, schools, clinics, or social agencies.

A **speech–language pathologist** screens, diagnoses, and treats children and adults with communication disorders. This person may also be called a **speech clinician** or **speech therapist.**

From: *Mainstreaming preschoolers series* by U.S. Department of Health and Human Services, 1978. Washington, DC: U.S. Government Printing Office.

where assessing, planning, evaluating, and working together is essential, but some team members may be in the setting only part of the time.

- Know how to ask for advice and suggestions that can be integrated into a particular classroom or situation. Specialists may not always have a sense of a developmentally appropriate classroom setting. Some specialists are excellent working with one or two children, but may need help to transfer their expertise to a classroom of 20 or more children. Sometimes teachers have to adapt suggestions.
- Ask for clarification of anything you don't understand, and politely persist until it is clear. Reflective listening will help: "Now, let me see if I can put what you're saying in my own words."
- Be clear and specific about who is going to do what. In transdisciplinary planning, make written assignments.
- Support, respect, and, if necessary, coach parents who are team members or involved in staffings so they can contribute their extensive knowledge of the child and can benefit from the expertise of the other team members.

Working with Specialists Individually.   Teachers also work with specialists individually—sharing concerns, seeking advice, consulting, and working together to plan programs that are integrated and complementary. These relationships are often far more informal. A specialist may be able to help with an appraisal, confirm a concern, or come in the classroom to try out some activities. There is no need to wait until you have a full assessment done and summarized, but do have some documentation so consultation is fruitful.

Working with Community Resources.   Many private preschools and child care and child development centers do not have specialists, or even a set process to get specialists for consultation. Teachers at these centers have to know and depend on public and private community resources, such as Child Find or local health agencies. If assessment reveals a special concern, have some possible course of action for parents to take, even if it is no more than saying, "Talk with your pediatrician, and get a recommendation and referral from her." School districts usually have defined processes.

"Alert" Indicators and How to Use Them

Classroom teachers are often in the best position to see early indications that children may need specialized assessment and help. Teachers know about normal growth and development, have experience with many children of a given age and developmental level, and are with the children on a regular basis. There are lists of specific behavioral indicators or signs that help teachers know when to observe more closely, gather more information, consult with parents, and consult with specialists to make sure that everything is all right. It is not always easy to know what is a normal difference and what patterns of behavior should raise a "red flag." It is always better to check out a possible problem and find there is none than to let one go too long. Even mild hearing or vision problems can impede children's learning. A practical guide for helping teachers identify developmental concerns for preprimary children is in Appendix B. For older children, use school district or state guides.

Summary

Fair, impartial, and objective classroom assessment of all children must take into account the diversity found in most schools and centers. Of particular concern in contemporary society are sociocultural differences and individual differences.

To develop schools and communities that regard language, cultural, and ethnic diversity as an opportunity, appropriate assessment is essential. Teachers must be sensitive to the way children and families from different cultures and backgrounds respond to the assessment approaches used, and make appropriate adjustments or changes. The wide variety of classroom assessment methods and contexts makes this possible. Obtain information from families and communities in culturally sensitive ways.

Three types of individual difference are of special concern to early childhood educators: children with special needs relating to disabilities and developmental delays, children and families "at risk," and children who need challenge. Inclusive education keeps most of these children together in the classroom and the community, whenever possible..

Diversity in preparation for school; in physical, emotional, social, cognitive, and language strengths and needs; in family, community, and economic circumstances must also be considered in assessment. Young children at risk of being unable to achieve their full potential may need experiences to help them with physical well-being, emotional maturity, social confidence, language development, and general knowledge. Assessment concerns include selection of children and families to be in such programs, assessment of children's status and progress as a guide to educational programming, and vigilance for indications of possible need for the help of a specialist.

Coordination and collaboration with community resources and with specialists in other disciplines are usually essential to meet assessed needs. The three major approaches are multidisciplinary, interdisciplinary, and transdisciplinary. Teacher roles and responsibilities in the three approaches vary somewhat, but all require that teachers know what each specialist does, remember that teachers are also specialists, compile and present assessment information professionally, be receptive to and respect other disciplines, and recognize that teachers must work collaboratively with other people to fulfill their responsibilities. Additional skills and attitudes are needed to implement interdisciplinary and transdisciplinary approaches, to work with specialists individually, and to work with families and communities.

Early childhood teachers should be alert to indicators that signal the need to gather more information and consult with parents and specialists. A guide to those indicators for children of ages 3 to 5 is in Appendix B. Use state or school district guides for older children.

For Further Study, Discussion, and Reflection

1. Reflect on your own experiences, knowledge, attitudes, and skills in coordination and collaboration. What experiences have you had that may help or hinder you? What do you have yet to learn?

2. Gardner's theory of multiple intelligences (1985) suggests seven different types of intelligence: linguistic, musical, logical–mathematical, spatial, bodily–kinesthetic, intrapersonal, and interpersonal or social. In what ways might the idea of multiple intelligence help schools and teachers deal with contemporary considerations in assessment and education?

3. You are teaching in a school that is a cross-section of the cultural diversity found throughout the United States, and most of the children have cultural backgrounds different from yours. Explain how you might go about selecting and using available assessment approaches to take full advantage of this educational opportunity. Justify your response.

4. Children who need challenge are sometimes overlooked in the regular classroom. What are some reasons for this? What could you, as a teacher or future teacher, do to respond to those children's assessed strengths and needs?

Suggested Readings

Au, K. A. (1993). *Literacy instruction in multicultural settings.* Chicago: Harcourt Brace.

Barona, A. (1991). Assessment of multi-cultural preschool children. In B. A. Bracken (Ed.), *The psychoeducational assessment of preschool children* (2nd ed, pp. 379–391). Boston: Allyn and Bacon.

Bredekamp, S., & Rosegrant, T. (Eds.). (1992). *Reaching potentials: Appropriate curriculum and assessment for young children,* (Vol. 1). Washington, DC: National Association for the Education of Young Children.

Chandler, P. D. (1994). *A place for me: Including children with special needs in early care and education settings.* Washington, DC: National Association for the Education of Young Children.

Derman-Sparks, L., & A.B.C. Task Force. (1988). *Anti-bias curriculum.* Washington, DC: National Association for the Education of Young Children.

Education and Human Services Consortium. (1991). *What it takes: Structuring interagency partnerships to connect children and families with comprehensive services.* Washington, DC: Institute for Educational Leadership.

Kendall, F. (1996). *Diversity in the classroom: New approaches to the education of young children.* New York: Teachers College Press.

McCracken, J. B. (1993). *Valuing diversity: The early years.* Washington, DC: National Association for the Education of Young Children.

Taylor, R. T., Willits, P., & Lieberman, N. (1990). Identification of preschool children with mild handicaps: The importance of cooperative effort. *Childhood Education, 67,* 26–31.

Wolery, M., & Wilbers, J. S. (1994). *Including children with special needs in early childhood programs.* Washington, DC: National Association for the Education of Young Children.

APPENDIX A

Assessment and Analysis Guides

The following assessment and analysis guides include selected examples of developmental patterns that can be extracted from child development textbooks, educational psychology textbooks, and books and journal articles addressing specific areas of development and curriculum. References are given at the end of each guide.

Remember that some children may skip steps in the sequence. Others may stay at one level for a period of time. Use the guides following the cautions and suggestions in Chapters 7 and 8.

Appendix A-1: Assessment and Analysis Guide: Large Muscle Development

Appendix A-2: Assessment and Analysis Guide: Small Muscle Development

Appendix A-3: Assessment and Analysis Guide: Cognitive Development—Knowledge Base

Appendix A-4: Assessment and Analysis Guide: Cognitive Development—Memory

Appendix A-5: Assessment and Analysis Guide: Cognitive Development—Logical Thinking

Appendix A-6: Assessment and Analysis Guide: Language Development—Oral Language

Appendix A-7: Assessment and Analysis Guide: Language Development—Written Language

Appendix A-8: Assessment and Analysis Guide: Personal–Social Development—Personal Development

Appendix A-9: Assessment and Analysis Guide: Personal–Social Development—Social Development

Figure A–1 *Assessment and Analysis Guide: Large Muscle Development*

Examples of Things to Look For	Developmental Pattern
Walking: Placing one foot in front of the other while maintaining contact with floor. *Watch for:* heel–toe progression; placement of arms as child walks (smoothly in opposition to feet); length of stride; balance. Walking on a straight line is easier than on a curved line; forward is easier than walking backwards; spontaneous is easier than in rhythm to music or a drum beat.	By 2–3 years most children can walk in a heel–toe progression with arms in opposition; up and down steps with one foot leading, then with alternating feet (3 yrs). By 3–4 years most children can walk backwards; a straight path (1″ wide); up and down short stairs with alternating feet; a balance beam (2–3″ high) with help. By 4–5 years most children can walk on balance beam (2–3″ high); up and down ten or more stairs alternating feet with hand rail; on a circle. By 5–6 years most children can walk in time to music; across balance beam (2–3″ high); up and down ten stairs alternating feet; use roller skates.
Running: Placing one foot in front of the other with a brief period of no contact with floor. *Watch for:* placement of arms (should move smoothly in opposition to the feet, should not flail around, should not be stiff); balance; fluidity; speed; ability to start and stop with balance; ability to run and turn with balance.	By 2–3 years most children can run (length of stride, balance, and smoothness begin to improve). By 3–4 years most children can run more smoothly (even stride but may lack mature arm movements and form). A few children can turn, stop suddenly, or run around objects easily. By 4–5 years most children can run with improved form, speed, and control (stopping, starting, and turning without falling). By 5–6 years most children can run in an effective adult manner (arms across midline in rhythmic pattern, elbow bent at a right angle); combine run and jump. By 6–8 years most children can run with longer stride; coordinate run with other motor skills (e.g. kicking); increased speed and agility.
Jumping: One or two foot takeoff, landing on both feet. *Watch for:* takeoff and landing, including placement of the arms on takeoff, landing, and as the jump is being made (arms aid in jump and don't flail around); bending of knees (should not be stiff); balance and fluidity. Jumps increase in distance and height. Jumping down is easier than jumping up onto something.	By 2–3 years most children can jump off a step with both feet; jump in place with minimal crouch, may land on one or both feet (one foot ahead). By 3–4 years many children can jump well in place; jump over a small object leading with one foot. By 4–5 years most children can jump well in place; crouch for a high jump of 2″; do standing broad jump of 8–10″. A few children can jump over a barrier. By 5–6 years most children can jump over barriers; make a vertical jump; do a running broad jump. By 6–7 years most children can jump rope in a simple pattern; jump onto a target. By 7–8 years most children can do jumping jacks; jump rope in complex patterns; a standing broad jump with deep crouch (arms swing further back behind body and continue until body is fully extended, and synchronized); jump and catch ball.
Hopping: One foot takeoff and landing on the same foot.	By 2–3 years most children cannot hop; make irregular steps instead of a hop. Some children attempt a hop.

Figure A–1   *continued*

Examples of Things to Look For	Developmental Pattern
Watch for: takeoff and landing; placement of arms (arms swing and aid in takeoff and landing, no flailing); isolation of the hopping side; balance; fluidity (should not be stiff); preference for one foot.	By 3–4 years most children can hop once or twice on preferred leg (by 3); execute ten hops in a row on preferred leg. By 4–5 years most children can hop a distance of 5'. By 5–6 years most children can hop distance of 16'; use arms in opposition to feet; use either foot. By 6–7 years most children can hop onto small squares. By 7–8 years most children can hop in an alternate rhythmic pattern (2–2, 2–3, or 3–3 pattern).
Galloping: Step (walk) leap with same foot leading. **Skipping:** Step (walk) hop in rhythmic alternation. Watch for: patterned use of the feet; use of arms (should move smoothly, no flailing); coordination; balance; ability to sustain the pattern.	By 2–3 years a few children attempt a gallop. By 3–4 years most children perform a shuffle step (side step). By 4–5 years most children step hop on one foot. Some gallop fairly well with preferred foot. By 5–6 years most children gallop fairly well (not proficiently). Some children can skip. By 6–7 years most children can skip with ease.
Kicking: Moving an object by striking it with the foot. *Watch for:* stance; standing on two feet, stepping forward with balance (older children may be able to move forward several steps and kick); movement of kicking leg; balance on contact with ball and follow-through; placement of arms (no flailing); fluidity; coordination of nonkicking side (no extraneous movements). Early kicking with stationary ball, then ball rolling directly to child (can't shift position), then ball rolling and child meets it.	By 2–3 years most children kick with leg stiff, straight leg, and little body movement. By 3–4 years most children kick with lower leg bent on backward lift and straight on forward swing. By 4–5 years most children kick with greater backward and forward swing; use arms in opposition to legs; step into ball. By 5–6 years most children kick using mature pattern; kick through ball with arms synchronized; kick ball tossed into air with straight leg. By 6–7 years most children run and kick in stride. By 7–8 years most children kick proficiently and accurately; intercept a ball; adjust kicking to height of ball; can aim ball.
Throwing: Using hands and arm to propel a object through the air—overhand or underhand. *Watch for:* smooth fluid motion of throwing arm; coordination of nonthrowing arm (no extraneous movements); balance; stance; rotation of body (older children also lean slightly backwards); step forward as object is released; follow-through of throwing arm; whipping motion of the arm on release; arc of throw. Early throwing, no weight transfer. Smaller balls are easier to throw.	By 2–3 years most children face target and use both forearms to push; throw with little or no footwork or body rotation; may lose balance while throwing. By 3–4 years most children throw overhand or underhand with one arm fairly well; use some body rotation; may release ball too early or late. By 4–5 years most children throw proficiently for longer distances, with more mature overhand motion (at elbow); may prefer overhand or underhand. By 5–6 years most children throw in a mature pattern; step forward; improved accuracy; fluid follow-through. By 7–8 years most children throw overhand with whipping motion (lean body back in preparation); underhand with explosive release.

continued

Figure A–1   *continued*

Examples of Things to Look For	Developmental Pattern
Catching: Using hands to grasp or capture an object thrown through air. *Watch for:* stance (balanced, can move and catch); placement of the arms (trap against body or grasped with hands); following of object's path with eyes; positioning self under object; adjusting hand position to size of object. At the beginning, catches involve a ball rolling on ground. Large balls are easier to catch. Child may show more mature catching with large balls.	By 2–3 years most children stop rolling object with hands; stand with arms stiff; may close eyes, arch body away; close arms after object hits body. By 3–4 years most children hold arms out straight, stiff with hands facing object; trap against body. Catches bounced ball. By 4–5 years most children hold arms flexed at elbows; trap against body. Some children catch with hands. By 5–6 years most children try catching with hands; may still trap; follow trajectory of ball better. About half of the children can catch with hands. By 6–7 years most children are moderately proficient; flex elbows with hands forward; make contact with hands; may juggle object. By 7–8 years most children can catch with hands, little juggling; judge trajectory fairly well; move into position; adjust hand position to size of object.
Perceptual Motor Abilities: Body, time and time awareness, directional awareness, ability to move based on watching and listening to a model. *Watch for:* ability to clap to a steady beat; walk, jump, hop, gallop, or skip to a beat or to music; control of body when moving (no extraneous movements); sense of external space (doesn't walk into things, bump into people when moving); mimic movements of another person; perform a movement after listening to verbal directions.	By preschool most children can identify parts of the body; clap a simple rhythm; still lack spatial and directional awareness. By 6–7 years some children can mimic demonstrated movements presented in a sequence (clapping pattern); use verbal directions to execute a simple movement sequence; walk to the beat of a musical selection. Most children have trouble memorizing a sequence of movements.
Physical Fitness: The child's physical state after vigorous exercise and the ability to sustain vigorous exercise. *Watch for:* sustained enthusiastic performance of the movements; the amount of time a child spends in vigorous exercise; child's reaction to being tired (shortness of breath, absence of strength).	By 5 years most children can exercise vigorously for 10–15 minutes without needing to stop. By 8 years most children can exercise vigorously for 15–20 minutes.

Adapted from: Berk, 1994; Corbin, 1980; Gallahue, 1982; Kaplan, 1991; Poest, Williams, Witt, & Atwood, 1990; Schiamberg, 1988; Schirmer, 1974; Sinclair, 1973; Thomas, Lee, & Thomas, 1988; Weeks & Ewer-Jones, 1991; Weikert, 1987; Wickstrom, 1983; Williams, 1991.

Figure A–2   *Assessment and Analysis Guide: Small Muscle Development*

Examples of Things to Look For	Developmental Pattern
Manipulation/Manipulatives: Ability to manipulate with hand and fingers. *Watch for:* dexterity; flexibility; precision and control; coordination; sensory perceptual integration; how child stacks, moves, and rotates objects; which fingers are used; fluid finger movements (no false starts, no using chest or table to aid in manipulation, one finger or group of fingers not sticking out in an awkward manner); preference for right or left hand (one hand will be more coordinated).	By 2–3 years most children place simple geometric shapes in puzzle; string large beads; turn pages of book; work 4-piece puzzle; use pegboard with large pegs; stack small wooden blocks; do a fingerplay (fingers not independent); roll, squeeze, and pound modeling clay. By 4–5 years most children can string small wooden beads; work a 5-piece puzzle; use pegboard with small pegs; use fingers more independently; make balls and use tools with modeling clay (use cookie cutter). By 5–6 years most children can work a 12-piece puzzle; build complex structures with small blocks; braid; use fingers independently in fingerplays; attempt a pinch pot, coil pot, or "sculpture." By 6–7 years most children can build complex structures with small interlocking blocks; make a pinch, coil pot, or sculpture. By 7–8 years most children can swing a hammer accurately; sew and knit.
Self-Help Skills: Ability to eat, dress, and take care of self. *Watch for:* grasp of eating utensil; eating without dropping or getting food all over clothes/face; size of buttons, how many fingers used, ability to button/unbutton; zipping/unzipping.	By 2–3 years most children can eat with spoon; hold cup in one hand; put on a coat (unassisted); unbutton clothes. By 4–5 years most children can eat correctly with fork; button and unbutton clothes; zip zippers haltingly; put coat on hanger. By 5–6 years most children can button/unbutton clothes; zip zippers; eat with knife and fork; dress/undress; comb and brush hair; tie shoelaces.
Scissors, Paste, and Glue: Ability to use scissors, paste, and glue. *Watch for:* dexterity; precision and control; coordination; sensory perceptual integration; thumbs-up grasp of scissors; thumbs-up grasp of paper; scissors held straight as cut is made, no twisting or tearing of paper, straight not jagged edges, hand holding paper moves along as other hand cuts; control of amount of paste (no excessive globs); use of fingers or stick to spread paste.	By 2–3 years most children snip paper easily (cuts at edge of paper); scissors and paper held incorrectly; use large globs of paste or glue with little control. By 3–4 years most children make one full cut with scissors (cuts one length of scissors); hand position may be incorrect; make two full cuts (two lengths of scissors); have trouble cutting on straight line; use globs of paste or glue but have more control; use index finger to apply paste. By 4–5 years most children cut on a straight line and a corner (90-degree angle) moving paper hand forward; use correct hand position; keep paste and glue in right spot and use reasonable amount. By 5–6 years most children can cut on a curve; cut out simple geometric figure; cut interior angles (inside angle less than 90 degrees); cut out obtuse and acute angles; cut out a complex figure from a magazine; use scissors and paste/glue to make designs.

continued

Figure A–2   *continued*

Examples of Things to Look For	Developmental Pattern
Use of Writing Instruments: Ability to hold and use pencils, pens, crayons, markers, and paint brushes. *Watch for:* dexterity; precision and control; coordination; sensory perceptual integration; grasp of instrument (whole hand or three-point finger grasp); grasp should be firm (should not be too tight or too loose); position of hand on instrument (should not be too close to the eraser/top of pencil/pen or too close to point/paper); type of marks (stabs at paper, fluid scribbles, or careful formation of lines, such as in letters or a figure with a stopping and starting place); child drawings (human face, stick figures, features placed correctly, detail in features, and addition of scenery, such as houses, animals, trees, grass, and the sky); proportionate size of figures in drawing (house should be bigger than child); repeated features in scribbles (do scribbles look random or like attempts at writing?).	By 2–3 years most children grasp writing implements with whole hand or fist; jab at paper; make scribbles with movement of whole arm; copy vertical and horizontal lines. By 3–4 years most children try a three-point grasp but position on instrument inconsistent; copy a cross and a circle; scribble with spots of intense color; use horizontal and vertical lines, crosses, and circles in pictures. By 4–5 years most children use correct hand grasp but position on instrument still inconsistent; copy a square and some letters (from first and last name); draw suns; draw human figures, a head with facial features (placement of eye, nose, mouth may not be correct); draw human figures with stick arms and legs and facial parts in correct place; scribble with repeated features and on a horizontal line (looks like writing); scribble leaving space between "words." By 5–6 years most children can form written letters (many inverted or mirror images); color between lines; draw buildings, cars, and boats (proportions incorrect—people are larger than the buildings); trees and flowers; draw with correct proportions; incorporate letters into scribbling; write letters of first name (may not write letters in a line); write letters of last name (may not write letters in a line); draw rectangle, circle, and square. By 6–7 years most children hold pencil with fingertips; draw triangles; follow simple mazes; copy most letters (some still inverted); form words with letters (words may run together; words may begin on one line and end on another); write upper- and lowercase letters and numbers 1–10. By 7–8 years most children can: space words when writing; print accurately and neatly; copy a diamond correctly; begin to use cursive writing.

Adapted from: Ashton-Lilo, 1987; Beaty, 1994; Berk, 1994; Guerin & Maier, 1983; Kaplan, 1991; Levine, 1995; Linder, 1993; Mowbray & Salisbury, 1975; Papalia & Olds, 1996; Schiamberg, 1988, Schickedanz, Hansen, & Forsyth, 1990; Schirmer, 1974; Schwartz & Robinson, 1982; Thompson, 1986; Weeks & Ewer-Jones, 1991.

Figure A–3   *Assessment and Analysis Guide: Cognitive Development—Knowledge Base*

Examples of Things to Look For	Developmental Pattern
Basic Concepts *Watch for:* how much a child knows prior to instruction; use of knowledge base when learning new information; quantity and quality of information; use of concept at receptive level (point to, place object, nod in response); concept used at expressive level (tell name of); spontaneous use.	By 4–5 years most children know the concepts big/little, tall/short, long/short, high/low, wide/narrow, thick/thin, deep/shallow, on, next to, in, outside, inside, down, and up. Most children likely to make errors on underneath, below, over and under. Some children know full/empty, light/heavy, bottom/top/middle; first, second, third; rectangle, triangle, circle, line.
Color Concepts *Watch for:* ability to point to a color when asked; state color name when asked; spontaneous use of color concepts and names. Infrequently used color concepts are acquired later than those frequently used.	By 4–5 years most children know red, green, black, white, orange, yellow, blue, pink, brown, purple; most color names by 5 years.
Math Concepts *Watch to see if child can:* match object for object (one-to-one correspondence); distinguish more/same/not as much as/less than (without counting) when comparing small groups such as three objects to a group of five objects; rote count (up to what number?); count meaningfully (up to what number?); count starting on a specific number; recognize written numbers. *Note:* There is disagreement about the benefits of rote counting or memorizing number charts.	By 4–5 years most children can match objects one to one; distinguish more/same/not as much as/less than (without counting); tell which of two objects is same/longer/shorter, lighter/heavier, full/less full. Some children have ordinal principle (smaller numbers first, larger last); cardinal principle (last number = total number); abstraction principle (can count any objects); understanding that order of objects counted does not matter; rote and meaningfully count to 6. By 5–6 years most children can count 20 objects; count on a number other than 1 (5, 6, 7, 8, 9, 10); recognize and write numbers from 1 to 10; use rulers, scales, cups to measure (but cannot state numerically which is longer/shorter, heavier/lighter). By 6–7 years have an intuitive grasp of number; formal instruction in mathematics has begun. Consult curriculum guides and texts on mathematics development.
Scientific Concepts *Watch for:* simple descriptions of scientific phenomena; use of scientific vocabulary; use of complexes and concepts.	By 5–6 years most children know simple scientific concepts based on observable world (people, animals, plants, seasons, and weather); something about the concepts of heat, levers, earth and heaven, gravity, gears, life, and death.
Social Studies concepts and complexes associated with geography, history, and economics.	Only geography and history are given as examples.

continued

Figure A–3   *continued*

Examples of Things to Look For	Developmental Pattern
Geographical Concepts *Watch for:* use of spatial concepts to describe position of objects relative to self; use of maps (recognize relative distances and map conventions—boundaries, roads, distance).	By 5–6 years most children can understand own position in space relative to another thing or person (near to me, far from me, etc.); knows words to express spatial relationships; knows what a map is; can identify roads and buildings on a simple map.
History: Concepts related to time *Watch to see if child can:* tell a story using pictures; tell time, use time concepts; distinguish between immediate past and long ago; identify concepts related to the continuity of human life.	By 4–5 years most children know before/after, yesterday/today/tomorrow; can identify or tell the sequence of events in a story; can arrange a picture sequence in order; can distinguish immediate past from long ago but cannot distinguish differences with the concept of "long ago"; can identify family tree (grandparents, parents, self, and siblings); is aware of family traditions for birthdays and holidays.

Adapted from: Baroody, 1993; Berk, 1994; Boehm, 1991; Castaneda, 1987; Clark & Clark, 1977; Cole & Cole, 1995; DeVilliers & DeVilliers, 1978; Dutton & Dutton, 1991; Flavell, 1963; Forman & Kaden, 1987; Hinitz, 1987; Kamii & Rosenblum, 1990; Kaplan, 1991; Mussen, Conger, Kagan, & Huston, 1990; National Council of Teachers of Mathematics, 1989; Papalia & Olds, 1996; Schiamberg, 1988; Schultz, Colarusso, & Strawderman, 1989; Seefeldt, 1977; Wadsworth, 1978.

Figure A–4   *Assessment and Analysis Guide: Cognitive Development—Memory*

Examples of Things to Look For	Developmental Pattern
Attention *Watch for:* ability to point to or identify differences between two pictures; confusion between letters (*b* and *d*); sense used to take in information (looking or listening); signs of attending; ability to block out distractions; ability to attend when asked; different levels of attention (concentrates more on certain tasks or at certain points in a task—is there a pattern?); ability to vary attention based on the material to be learned (focus more on items that are not known or that were missed); response to teacher cues to attend (verbal cues such as "Look up here," "Pay attention," or nonverbal cues such as pointing at something); the cues child notices (confusing "this" and "that" when reading).	Be aware of cultural differences in the way children signal they are paying attention. By 2–6 years most children can concentrate and attend when interested; scan something visually to search, but not systematically; discriminate letters with vertical and horizontal lines (*E* vs. *M*) and right side up versus upside down (*M* vs. *W*). Most have some trouble attending when asked (if task is not of inherent interest); recognizing and responding appropriately to the teacher's cues to attend ignoring distractions (color, movement, loudness); discriminating letters that are mirror images (*d* and *b*, *p* and *q*); shifting attention from one task to another or concentrating more on certain tasks or aspects of a task. By 7 years and older most children can control attention; scan systematically; vary attention (although not as well as 12-year-olds); discriminate between letters; recognize and respond to most teacher cues to attend. Some children may need significant teacher help to maintain and focus attention or need coaching on interpreting subtle teacher signals for attention.
Memory Strategies *Watch for:* amount of information remembered; number of spontaneous strategies used; response to suggested strategies; description of strategies. Strategies are: *Rehearsal*—repeats information over and over, copies it (older children only). *Organization*—sorts or groups items (rearrange the spelling list so that similar words are together). Organizing objects in semantic categories (using words) rather than associations (what goes with this) is more mature. *Elaboration*—makes connections and relationships between new information and prior knowledge and experience ("I saw a frog just like that one at the zoo"; "That word looks kind of like 'thin' except it has a *k* at the end").	By 2 years most have a memory span of two items, use naming and looking as early strategies. By 3–4 years most children show recognition for 50-plus items; know scripts of familiar routines; begin to use some rehearsal; memory span of 3 to 4 items. By 5–6 years some children can use rehearsal strategies; use simple organization; state when task is easy or hard to remember. By 7–8 years most children can use rehearsal strategies; use organization. A few children can use elaboration spontaneously. Training in rehearsal, organization, and elaboration will improve ability to remember even for 2-year-olds. The use of new strategies requires constant adult coaching (telling child which strategy to use).

Adapted from: Beihler & Snowman, 1991; Berk, 1994; Berliner & Rosenshine, 1987; Brown, 1991; Bukatko & Daehler, 1992; Clark & Clark, 1977; Corno, 1987; Gage & Berliner, 1992; Grabe, 1986; Kaplan, 1991; Mussen, Conger, Kagan, & Huston, 1990; Papalia & Olds, 1996; Phye & Andre, 1986; Resnick & Resnick, 1992; Schiamberg, 1988; Slavin, 1997; Steinberg & Belsky, 1991; Winne & Marx, 1987; Wittrock, 1986.

Figure A–5   *Assessment and Analysis Guide: Cognitive Development—Logical Thinking*

Examples of Things to Look For	Developmental Pattern
Symbolic thought: Ability to manipulate and use symbols in thinking. *Watch for:* use of language as a tool for thinking; use of an object to stand for something else (doll is a baby); plays different roles; representational drawings (drawing of a specific thing decided on in advance); use of written symbols as a tool for thinking (will make marks to signify a pattern, writes words); use of graphs to symbolize numbers.	Information about the manipulation of roles as a part of symbolic thought is in Figure A–9 under Sociodramatic Play. By 2–3 years most children can use language as a tool for thinking; engage in symbolic play (use object to stand for something else or play different roles). Some children can make representational drawings. By 4–5 years most children can engage in representational drawing. Some children can use written symbols (write name, some numbers); make and interpret graphs with help from teacher. By 6 years and older most children can use written symbols; make and interpret graphs.
Classification: Ability to sort and group objects. *Watch for:* ability to sort and re-sort spontaneously; with properties given by teacher; by a single property (size, color, shape); by many properties simultaneously; by similarity (all buttons, all blocks); by all–some (all same object but different color); into a series (big, bigger, biggest). Children may state attribute; use of same principle to add new objects; create a simple pattern; create a complex, extended pattern.	By 2–6 years some children are not systematic or consistent in use of attributes to form the group. Most can classify based on one attribute; place objects in a series by one attribute; make a simple line pattern (ABABAB). A few can classify based on two attributes simultaneously (large blue, small blue, large red, small red); classify subgroups once groups are formed; make a complete line pattern (AABBCCAABBCC or ABCCABCCABCC). By 6–8 years most children can classify based on multiple attributes; understand relationship between broader classes and subclasses (objects can belong to several classes at the same time); classify based on two attributes at the same time (2 x 2 matrix).
Problem Solving: Use of available information, resources and materials to achieve a goal. *Watch for:* scripts (expected sequences of events developed from past); analysis (identify components, features, processes, arguments, events); comparisons; inferences (draw conclusions, make predictions, pose hypotheses, make educated guesses); evaluation of ideas; identification of the problem. Children may use formulas (math formulas, specific "recipes"); rules of thumb (strategies or estimations that have worked in the past but don't	Children of all ages benefit from teacher guidance and help when solutions do not work. By 3–6 years most children can use scripts to solve everyday problems; generate hypotheses (may be intuitive, not logical); use analysis; make comparisons; evaluate ideas; identify problems; use formulas, rules of thumb, and trial and error spontaneously. By 6 years and older most children make inferences based on logical rules; tell if they need more information; make psychological inferences (8 and older); use formulas, rules of thumb, think aloud strategies, work backwards strategies; use trial and error, and break large problems into smaller ones. With teacher support children 5 years and older can engage in metacognitive skills such as thinking about the

Figure A–5 *continued*

Examples of Things to Look For	Developmental Pattern
guarantee a solution); think aloud strategy (talk problem through aloud); work backwards strategy (start with the end or a possible solution first and work backwards to see if this matches the givens); use trial and error (try one solution and when it fails try another); break problem into a number of smaller problems.	problem-solving process, asking clarifying questions, planning a solution, reflecting on learning, errors, and understandings.
Conservation: All conservation tasks involve objects with the same physical attributes (number, mass, weight, length, area, volume) that are rearranged in front of the child to look very different. *Watch for:* response to Piagetian tasks or way child plays with quantity or amount; justification for answer; number conservation (the number of objects does not change when objects are arranged differently—one set in a pile and one set in a row); length (the length does not change even though objects are arranged differently); liquid (the amount of liquid does not change even though the liquid is in containers that look different—one tall and thin and the other wide); mass (the amount of clay in two balls does not change even though the balls look different—one is a ball and the other rolled into a snake).	By 2–6 years most children cannot conserve; will state one object or group of objects is _____ (more, longer, bigger). Current research suggests that preoperational children can conserve number with four or fewer objects, but may not be able to justify or explain their answers. By 6–8 years most children can conserve number, length, liquid, and mass; typical justifications are: "You didn't add any or take any away"; "You just moved them and if you moved them back there would be the same _____"; "It doesn't matter how you arrange them"; "They just look different, but they are the same _____."

Adapted from: Beihler & Snowman, 1991; Berk, 1994; Charlesworth, 1992; Clark & Clark, 1977; Cole & Cole, 1995; DeVries & Kohlberg, 1987; Dutton & Dutton, 1991; Flavell, 1963; Gage & Berliner, 1992; Ginsberg & Opper, 1988; Kamii & Rosenblum, 1990; Kaplan, 1991; Mussen, Conger, Kagan, & Huston, 1990; Papalia & Olds, 1996; Phye & Andre, 1986; Schiamberg, 1988; Schultz, Colarusso, & Strawderman, 1989; Slavin, 1997; Steinberg & Belsky, 1991; Tharp & Gallimore, 1988; Wadsworth, 1978.

Figure A–6   *Assessment and Analysis Guide: Language Development—Oral Language*

Examples of Things to Look For	Developmental Pattern
Phonology: Ability to pronounce words and to understand speech sounds. *Watch for:* pronunciation and enunciation; deletion of sounds (*nana* for *banana*); substitution of sounds (*dis* for *this*).	By 2–3 years children may repeat initial consonant vowel in multisyllabic words (*gege* for *cookie*); delete unstressed syllables (*nana* for *banana*); replace fricatives' hissing sounds with stop consonants (*tea* for *sea*, *tay* for *say*); replace liquid sounds (*l* and *r*) with glides (*w* or *j*)—(*wed* for *red*, *yewwo* for *yellow*, *jap* for *lap*); reduce consonant clusters (*pay* for *play*, *tain* for *train*); pronounce vowel sounds and *p* (pin), *b* (big), *m* (mama), *w* (want), *h* (house) correctly. By 4–5 years most children have few mispronunciations; still replace liquid sounds; pronounce *d* (dog), *k* (cat), *g* (gone), *f* (feet), *n* (no), *ng* (swing). By 5–6 years most children are 90% intelligible; have mastered most sounds, including *sh* (ship), *s* (sit), *ch* (chip), *v* (very), *r* (run), *l* (lamp). By 7–8 years most children are 100% intelligible; can pronounce *z* (zip), *th* (this, thin), *j* (jump), *zh* (sure).
Semantics: Understanding word and sentence meaning. The type of concepts understood are discussed in Figure A–3. *Watch for:* Use and understanding of words and sentences; literal versus abstract meanings; use of jokes and humor.	Receptive level/comprehension vocabulary much larger (for example, 3–4 years receptive = 1,500 words, expressive = 600–1,000 words). By 2–3 years most children understand possessives, common verbs, adjectives; understand function of many common nouns ("What do you write with?") By 3–4 years most children follow complex three-step commands; interpret words literally ("She's a cold person," meaning she feels cold). By 4–5 years most children understand polite forms (Would you like to sit down?); passive voice. By 5–6 years most children understand indirect speech acts ("It's cold outside," meaning it's cold next to the window); words less literally ("She's a cold person," meaning she does not express affection); jokes based on phonological ambiguity—play on sounds ("What do you call a cow that eats grass? A lawn-moo-er"). By 6–7 years most children appreciate jokes based on puns or double meanings of words—lexical ambiguity ("What did the grape say when the elephant stepped on it? It just let out a little 'wine' "); understand the difference between *promise* and *tell*, *ask* and *tell*.
Syntax: Ability to use the rules of grammar to produce sentences. *Watch for:* number of words used in an utterance; types of words used (nouns, pronouns, verbs, adjectives, and adverbs); verb tenses used	By 2–3½ years most children use present progressive tense (-ing); prepositions (on, in); plural nouns (dog*s*); verb "be" with adjective ("He is fun"); prepositions (in, for, from, with, to); noun phrases ("The book of dogs"); articles (a, an, the); regular past tense (walk*ed*); third-person regular present tense (he read*s* it); irregular present tense (has, does); contractions with

Figure A–6 *continued*

Examples of Things to Look For	Developmental Pattern
(present, present progressive, simple past, complex past, future); use of negatives (not, -n't); types of questions asked (simple: "What are you doing?"; tag questions: "This is yours, isn't it?"); coordinating conjunctions such as *and* to join two sentences ("The car was red and it made a lot of noise"); verb phrases ("He wanted to eat dinner"); embedded clauses ("I know he went home"); indirect object–direct object constructions ("Taylor gave me the toy"); passive voice ("The gingerbread man was eaten by the fox"); infinitive phrases ("Marcia is easy to please"); pronoun and referent ("When he liked you, he was nice").	"be" (He's tall); overregularizations, such as went*ed*, fell*ded*, foot*es*, men*s*, and mouse*s*. Some children use negations (-n't, not); questions ("What is he doing?" "Where is she going?"). By 3–4 years some children can use complex sentences with *and* and *wh* clauses (what, who, why, where, or when) ("I don't know *where* it is"). Most children use question forms with inverted auxiliary verb ("What *are* you doing?"), negations (-n't, not). By 4–5 years most children use three- to four-syllable words; more adjectives, adverbs, and conjunctions; four- to six-word sentences. Ask meaning of words. By 5 years and older most children use long complex sentences (more than six words); clauses ("The man who lived next door"); pronouns with referent ("After he ate, Bill went home"); passive voice with more than one attribute ("This is taller and thinner"); indirect requests ("Can I interest you in some cake?"); a variety of semantic structures to express the same idea; use grammar consciously and can describe why something is or is not correct (metalinguistic awareness).
Pragmatics: Ability to engage in effective and appropriate conversations with others. *Watch for:* the number of times child takes turns talking; appropriate turn-taking (doesn't interrupt, distract); sensitivity to listener's needs (clarification of unclear utterances); adjustments in speech with context (peers, teacher, younger children, or when playing different roles); manner of introducing new conversation topics (gradually or abruptly); ability to understand humor, irony, and sarcasm; use of different forms of speech, such as polite forms ("May I please have some?"), indirect forms ("Would you mind if I looked at it?"), and slang ("Sure thing, radical dude").	By 2–3 years children can sustain conversations for two turns (respond to previous utterances); change tone of voice when playing "baby"; use language as a tool (i.e., make a request, get attention of others, assert rights). By 3–4 years most children sustain conversations for three to four turns; understand intent of indirect requests for action; revise speech when asked (primarily by pointing); ask others to clarify ambiguous sentences; change speech used when playing stereotypic roles (doctor, mother, father); use some slang; more adept at using language as a tool; use polite forms; monitor conversations and intrude comments; project beyond present and create images for play. By 5 years and older most children carry on complex conversations (six turns or more); change conversation by modifying topic gradually; use slang with peers; use deference when making requests from adults; use subtle cues in speech to adjust to, convey, and maintain social status; adjust speech depending on need of listener (can judge when to add more detail); are sophisticated at using language as a tool.

Adapted from: Berk, 1994; Blank, Rose, & Berlin, 1978; Bukatko & Daehler, 1992; Cazden, 1972; Charlesworth, 1992; Clark & Clark, 1977; DeVilliers & DeVilliers, 1978; Faw & Belkin, 1989; Gage & Berliner, 1992; Genishi, 1987, 1988, 1992; Kaplan, 1991; Lindfors, 1987; Locke, 1993; Locke, 1993; Menyuk, 1988; Messer, 1995; Mussen, Conger, Kagan, & Huston, 1990; Owens, 1992; Petty, Petty, & Salzer, 1989; Schaefer, Staab, & Smith, 1983; Schiamberg, 1988; Steinberg & Belsky, 1991; Tough, 1977.

Figure A–7   *Assessment and Analysis Guide: Language Development—Written Language*

Examples of Things to Look For	Developmental Pattern
Book Handling Skills: Use of books in an appropriate way. *Watch for:* book held right side up with front facing reader; ability to identify beginning and end; page turning without bending or ripping pages; requests to "Read me a story."	By 2 years most children hold a book right side up; identify the beginning/end; turn pages; elicit others to share and read books. By 3–8 years most children identify and "read" the cover; make comments about who "wrote" the book; try "reading" aloud/read aloud.
Understanding the Function of Print: Understanding that print stands for or means something. *Watch to see if child can:* identify print symbols (logos, trademarks, or symbols, such as "don't walk" sign); distinguish between pictures and words in a book; understand that words are being read (as opposed to pictures); explain the purpose of reading (to tell a story, tell you something); retell a story using the book as a prop.	By early preschool most children talk about "reading"; identify some print symbols in context (Coke logo on a can); retold stories may lack detail and correct sequence; may think you "read" pictures, not print. By late preschool most children talk about reading in greater depth; know one reads words, not pictures. By kindergarten and early elementary most children know reading occurs without pictures; identify print symbols out of context (McDonald's logo on a paper bag); retell stories with detail and accuracy (elaborate on the characters, provide details, such as dress, tone of voice; can "read" familiar books).
Knowledge of Letters and Words: Ability to identify letter names and the sounds letters make and read simple words. *Watch to see if child can:* identify letters in own name or in words; say the names of letters; identify uppercase and lowercase letters; identify the sound a letter makes (can pull words apart into component sounds, give a rhyming word or a word that begins with ____ sound, tap out the sounds); identify what a word is (tap out the words in a sentence, point to words); read simple words (own name, familiar logos, and concrete nouns); read simple books with repetitive word patterns.	By early preschool most children can recognize letters in own name, names of friends, or print symbols (Barbie logo); give the names of five to ten letters; confuse some letters, such as *d/b, m/n, p/q.* By late preschool most children can identify a rhyme or give a rhyming word; give the name of many letters; still confuse some letters. By kindergarten to early elementary most children identify and say the name of most letters but still confuse some letters; know letters have sounds and identify the sounds; identify words that are the same (*dog, dog*); identify words that begin with the same letter (tap, tip); identify beginning sounds; identify ending sounds; tap out sounds in a word; use sound skills to analyze unfamiliar words; have some sight words; can match spoken to written word; use context and picture cues to self correct words. By 7 years most children make automatic self corrections; begin to read silently; have a sight vocabulary of high frequency words; have improved fluency.
Sense of "Story": Ability to tell, retell, or complete a story. *Watch for:* lists of events recalled (isolated incidents or integrated story); story structure (introduction, number of characters, a problem to be solved); description of climax (was	By early preschool most children tell and retell stories that are a collection of arbitrary ideas, arranged arbitrarily; told in vignettes ("Goldilocks saw bears. She ate something. I don't like hot things."); a collection of actions in a repeated pattern ("He went outside, he went inside. He went to. . . ."); scripts of everyday events ("She wakes up and goes outside to play"); contains characters acting at random ("The fox liked grapes so he cooked them. The gingerbread man stood up and ran away.

Figure A–7 *continued*

Examples of Things to Look For	Developmental Pattern
goal attained?); accuracy (follows original exactly, partially).	The fox went to get the gingerbread man."). Retold stories are not always accurate, bearing some resemblance to original. By later preschool to early elementary most stories are sequences or descriptions centering on one character and children discuss all events relative to that character ("She went home, she walked around, she ate her dinner. Then she took some jewelry and put it on. The prince came and she got married."); about a character who has a problem and overcomes. Retold stories are much more accurate and come close to original.
Writing Forms: Attempts at producing writing. *Watch for:* differentiation of scribbles for drawing and writing; scribbles with repeated features and horizontal orientation; scribbles mixed with letters; use of pictures to illustrate story; writing own name; writing composed of letters (random letters or representing words); number of letters in invented spellings (one or more, such as *cn* for can, *nst* for nest); distinguishable words.	By 2–3 years some children make no distinction between scribbling for writing and drawing. Most children identify scribbling as writing versus as drawing; may ask adults to write on pictures—beginning dictation. By 3–4 years most children write letters in their name; make letters incorrectly (i.e., some *E*'s sideways or upside down, multi-legged *E*'s, *R*'s are lines and circles, *b* is written as a *d*); scribble with a pattern (repeated elements, horizontal organization, spaces for words); may make strings of letters from right to left or left to right, random strings of letters in drawings, scribbles and letters intermixed. By 4–7 years many children begin inventing spellings using one letter for each word; one letter per syllable; one letter per phoneme (letter sound) within the word. Some children become interested in conventional spelling (ask teachers to show them how to spell). By 6–9 years most children incorporate vowels into invented spellings; leave space between words; string words together (some string several phrases together); use lower- and uppercase letters; use some punctuation (not always correctly); use more conventional spelling; and use simple sentences, sentence fragments, and run-on sentences. Some children can write simple paragraphs and lengthier sentences.
Reading of Own Writing: Ability to read story dictated to an adult or written by child. *Watch for:* amount of language use when rereading (a clause or phrase, a description, letters, or a story/exact information); dialogue over the picture; ability to retell words (tells story again); ability to read words.	By early preschool many children state that they are not writing or may refuse to tell you what they are drawing. This is acceptable. By late preschool to early elementary many children don't use the writing strategies to reading writing; may use phrases ("from here") or describe picture ("That's my mom"); may have a dialogue over the picture (Teacher: "and what is this. . . ." Child: "He's a frog"); may retell story exactly from memory; track to print (name written letters or match printed words with speech); have trouble generating a strategy to read words they can't remember. Some read the actual words.

Adapted from: Applebee, 1978; Barbour, 1987; Berk, 1994; Bertelson, 1986; Clay, 1991; Daniels, 1992; Gentry, 1982; Goodman, Goodman, & Hood, 1989; Mason & Stewart, 1990; McGhee & Richgels, 1990; Morrow, 1990; Peterson, 1995; Petty, Petty, & Salzer, 1989; Raines, 1990; Rhodes & Shanklin, (1993); Schickedanz, 1986; Sulzby, 1990.

Figure A–8   *Assessment and Analysis Guide: Personal–Social Development—Personal Development*

Examples of Things to Look For	Developmental Pattern
Self-Concept: Child's description of self. *Watch for:* ability to distinguish between private thoughts and imaginings and public ones; descriptions of self in terms of concrete characteristics; descriptions of self in terms of psychological and emotional disposition.	By 4–7 years most children distinguish between inner self (private thoughts, imaginings accessible only to child) and outer world; describe self in terms of concrete characteristics (name, physical appearance, possessions, typical behaviors—what I can do, or temporary states—how I feel at this moment). By 8 years and older most children describe self in terms of: psychological characteristics and traits (honest, trusting), emotional characteristics and traits (happy, get angry easily, moody), increasingly complex combination of characteristics; use social comparisons; attribute stable personality characteristics to self and others.
Self-Esteem: Evaluation of self-concept. Can be high where child sees self in a positive light, is satisfied with own strengths and accepts own weaknesses. Can be low where child sees self in negative light. *Watch for:* descriptions of self in terms of social acceptance, competence, physical prowess, academic/cognitive competence, and social self-worth; positive or negative evaluations of own characteristics.	By 4–6 years most children evaluate self-esteem in terms of social acceptance ("Do people like me?") and competence ("I can do _____"); tend to rate selves extremely high on all aspects. By 7–8 years most children evaluate self-esteem in terms of cognitive/academic competence (i.e., math, reading), physical prowess (sports), and social self-worth (good person, funny person); display global sense of self-esteem; show a decline in overall self-esteem at this age because unrealistically high assessments are adjusted. After a period of decline, self-esteem rises again.
Achievement Motivation: Tendency to evaluate one's performance against a standard of excellence. Adaptive motivation style: strive for success, desire to do well, and select challenging but not impossibly difficult tasks. *Watch for:* efforts to achieve mastery; selection of challenging but not impossibly difficult tasks; mastery efforts in all subjects/areas.	By 3–5 most children recognize success and failure and begin to attribute causes; tend to choose easy tasks; are "learning optimists"—overestimate their own abilities and underestimate task difficulties; believe they can learn if they try harder; need help setting realistic, reasonable short-term goals. By 5 years and older many children more realistically view their abilities and other levels of achievement; compare own performance to that of other children by 5–6 years; set high levels of aspiration for selves; feel anxiety about failure; continue to be learning optimists until 7 years; need help setting realistic, reasonable short-term goals. Some have adaptive mastery-oriented styles (attribute success to high ability, failure to lack of effort, like challenges); can develop patterns of test anxiety.

Figure A–8 *continued*

Examples of Things to Look For	Developmental Pattern
Emotional Development: Child's ability to feel, describe, and regulate emotions. Ability to identify emotions in others. *Watch for:* feelings expressed in different situations (pleasant or stressful situations); ability to recognize and label the emotions of self and others with words: "I feel happy." "He looks sad."	By 3–5 years most children can describe basic emotions (happy, sad, scared); exhibit pride, envy, and guilt by 3 years; can learn through social referencing (reading the emotions of others); recognize facial expressions (sad, happy, angry, surprised, and fearful); begin to mask or hide emotions by 3; describe cause and consequences of emotions; decline in separation distress and other attachment behaviors. By 6 years and older most children use multiple cues to evaluate the emotions in others; recognize that the cause of feelings can be internal and not visible to another person; know that someone may hide feelings; can suppress feelings, such as anger; know emotions fade with time and can be controlled by thoughts; understand mixed emotions by 8 years (can feel happy and sad at the same time).

Adapted from: Barnett & Zucker, 1990; Berk, 1994; Bukatko & Daehler, 1992; Cole & Cole, 1995; Curry & Johnson, 1990; Damon, 1977; Eisenberg, 1982; Johnson, Christie, & Yawkey, 1987; Kaplan, 1991; Ladd, 1990; Masten, 1989; Mergendoller & Marchman, 1987; Mussen, Conger, Kagan, & Huston, 1990; Papalia & Olds, 1996; Rogers & Sawyers, 1988; Samuels, 1977; Selman, 1981; Steinberg & Belsky, 1991.

Figure A–9 *Assessment and Analysis Guide: Personal–Social Development—Social Development*

Examples of Things to Look For	Developmental Pattern
Peer Relations: The type of interactions children have with age-mates. *Watch for:* amount of positive interactions (turn-taking, sharing, conversations, initiations, and responses); negative interactions (aggression, rejecting the requests of others); parallel play (play next to but not with another child); solitary play (play alone); associative play (play with other child but theme of play and roles not coordinated); cooperative play (play with others with common theme and planned roles); rough-and-tumble play interactions (physical play that ends in a positive exchange and not aggression); helping behavior (do they ask first, or just jump in and start helping?).	For all ages, group size influences group interaction. Fewer than five is the optimal size for children under 5 years. Five is optimal size for children 5 years and older. Peer acceptance is associated with positive emotional adjustment at all ages. By 3–4 years most children have interactions marked by fairly high rates of positive and negative exchanges; engage in parallel, solitary, and some associative play; begin to balance leading with following others; engage in simple turn-taking. By 4–5 years most children have higher rates of positive than negative interactions; longer verbal exchanges (some turn-taking); reciprocal, coordinated interactions; engage primarily in associative play with some parallel, solitary, and cooperative play; engage in rough-and-tumble play. By 5 years and older most children have high levels of positive interaction; engage primarily in cooperative play with some parallel, solitary, and associative play; engage in rough-and-tumble play; have peer interactions governed by social norms such as sharing and helping; are better at sustaining conversations (turn-taking); are more sensitive to others' needs; are concerned about being lonely.
Friendships: Special sustained relationship with one or two other people. *Watch for:* children who seem to play together more often, choose each other, and talk about being friends; length of relationship. Is it momentary (for time children are next to each other) or stable (persists over weeks, months, years); child's understanding of what it means to be a friend. After being asked how to make friends, how does the child respond? Six social processes are related to friendship formation: communicate clearly (ask for clarification of unclear messages); exchange information (ask questions of each other, exchange information and ideas); establish common ground (find something both enjoy or can do); resolve conflicts successfully (compromise, negotiate); show positive reciprocity (respond to other's ideas and requests); disclose information about self (share inner feelings, solicit feelings from others).	Sensitivity and intimacy are features of all friendships but not verbalized by younger children. At all ages, children give more positive reinforcement, have more interactions, and are more emotionally expressive with friends. Children use all six processes of friendship formation by 4 years. By 2–6 years most children have friendships that are momentary and fleeting (whomever child is playing with at that time is a friend); have disagreements over territory and space; solve disagreements by leaving or aggressive behavior. By 5–7 years most children describe friendship as concrete and activity based, affirmed by giving and sharing things (friends do the same thing); have friendships that are not fleeting, but not long-term either; have disagreements when one child will not compromise; solve disagreements by leaving or giving in; tend to have same-sex friends. By 8–12 years most children describe friendship as trust and intimacy, sharing of feelings, and providing mutual support (friends share personal problems); have longer-term relationships than earlier; have disagreements over jealousy, breaking trust, or gossiping behind back; have disagreements that do not end the friendship; must acknowledge trust was broken to repair friendship; are more likely to express disagreements with friends than other children.

Figure A–9   *continued*

Examples of Things to Look For	Developmental Pattern
Perspective Taking: Ability to take the role or position of another person and take more than one perspective at a time. *Watch for:* situations in which the child describes one or more perspectives ("He wanted the toy. I didn't want to give it to him"); responses showing child can take another's perspective; discussion of perspectives of characters in stories; recognition that others may think or feel differently; anticipation of another's thoughts and feelings; placing self in different roles and evaluating from each perspective.	By 3–5 years most children fail to distinguish between own interpretation and another person's (I like cookies so everyone likes cookies). By 4–7 years most children realize that other people have different perspectives, thoughts, and feelings because they are in different situations or have different information. By 6–12 years most children are aware that each person has different perspectives; know that what other people think influences their own perspective; can adopt another person's perspective and anticipate her reaction.
Empathy: Child's ability to feel the same feelings and respond to the feelings of another person. *Watch for:* situations in which child helps another person; situations in which child talks about needs of another; child's response to empathetic statements made by adults or other children; child's response to questions about "why we help other people"; response to stories about empathy.	Modeling and direct teaching all have a positive influence on empathy at all ages. By 3–5 years most children respond empathetically to others based on self-interest or simple empathetic feelings (without adopting other's perspective, but just feeling for other person); offer help to another person and give it even if it is not wanted. By 6 years and older most children have feelings of empathy based on stereotypic images of good and bad and concern for approval (people will think I am a good person); have empathetic responses imagining what another person is feeling; respond to the intensity of others' feelings; ask if help is needed before acting.
Social Problem-Solving Skills: Ability to generate and implement a number of possible solutions for social problems. *Watch for:* situations in which children have disagreements and how conflicts are handled; responses to typical classroom problems; number and type of strategies (mainly meet own or consider other's needs); ability to merge with rather than disrupt social interaction.	By 2–5 years most children use some strategies, but these are impulsive and based primarily on own needs; By 6 years and older most children generate more solutions than younger children do; have strategies that take into account the needs of others; generate solutions based on coordination of needs; can interpret social cues better than younger children do; evaluate probable effectiveness of a strategy better than younger children do; enter social group by merging with others (observe what others are doing, copy members of group, make positive comments, enter social group).
Aggression: *physical*—hitting, pushing, kicking; *verbal*—name calling, teasing, putting down; *instrumental*—fighting over a toy,	Extreme aggression is a highly stable trait for both boys and girls (likely to be highly aggressive at 10 years, associated with peer rejection, poor achievement levels, school dropouts, and delinquent behavior). Highly aggressive children may

continued

Figure A–9   *continued*

Examples of Things to Look For	Developmental Pattern
territory, or attention; *hostile*—designed to injure another person. *Watch for:* type of aggression; a pattern to behavior (with whom and when aggression occurs); reasons for the aggression.	misinterpret social cues and read aggressive intent into most social interactions (neutral or friendly). By 2–3 years most children exhibit primarily physical, instrumental aggression; are aggressive with children they are interacting with. Boys instigate and receive more aggression than girls. By 4–5 years most children engage in some verbal and physical aggression; engage in less instrumental aggression. Some engage in hostile aggression. By 6 years and older most children engage in less aggressive behavior than younger children; are verbally aggressive (teasing, name calling, taunting); engage in some hostile aggression.
Functioning in Learning Groups *Watch for:* General social skills and ability to form cooperative group; stay with the group, volunteer ideas to others; support and acceptance of others' ideas (use praise, no criticism of individuals); give diplomatic reasons for not using ideas; take responsibility for own work; resist dominating group or doing other's tasks; energize group when motivation is low; set/call attention to time limits; summarize ideas (seek accuracy, ask for elaboration, discuss reasoning).	There is no known developmental pattern for this area. However, many of the behaviors are related to advanced levels of perspective taking, empathy, peer relations, and social problem solving described above. In addition, the child's cognitive level and level of language development also influence the child's ability to learn in cooperative groups. The quality of cooperative learning in preschool will be very different from that found in elementary school. Younger children will require much more coaching in exactly how to state criticisms, for example, because they may not know how to word their opinions in an acceptable manner.
Sociodramatic Play: Acting out everyday and imaginary roles. *Watch for:* number and type of roles; number and type of actions performed; number and manner of use of objects (uses one object to be another—a block becomes an airplane; imaginary play—pretends to sweep with a broom); discussion of play (makes statements, describes actions, tells story, prompts action, proposes pretending); expression of emotions (enacting forbidden actions, unpleasant scenes, or actions and consequences—hurts people and goes to prison); use of rules in games (plays tag with rules).	Less mature sociodramatic play has a few roles with a few actions and objects; children use statements and descriptions of play when talking about and during play ("I'm washing the dishes"; "This is my house"). More mature play has more roles (several at the same time, switching back and forth—plays the mother and the baby); actions (intricate, series of actions—goes outside, hunts for berries, comes back, makes dinner); objects (more props are used or "pretended"); complex discussions (tell story—"We live in another time, like the future. They don't use cars"); prompting of actions, and proposals about pretending ("Let's say you're the good guy and you have a best friend, that's me"); changes in emotional tenor (more forbidden, unpleasant situations and action—consequence sequences—"She steals the jewels because she is very bad and then she gets caught by the police"). Rule-based games and play appear at about 6–11 years.

Adapted from: Arends, 1988; Asher & Renshaw, 1981; Barnett & Zucker, 1990; Berk, 1994; Bukatko & Daehler, 1992; Cole & Cole, 1995; Damon, 1977; Eisenberg, 1982; Gottman, 1983; Howes, 1980; Johnson, Christie, & Yawkey, 1987; Johnson, Johnson, Holubec, & Roy, 1984; Kaplan, 1991; Ladd, 1990; Masten, 1989; Mergendoller & Marchman, 1987; Mussen, Conger, Kagan, & Huston, 1990; Nourot & Van Hoorn, 1991; Papalia & Olds, 1996; Pepler & Rubin, 1991; Rogers & Sawyers, 1988; Selman, 1981; Slavin, 1997; Steinberg & Belsky, 1991; Trawick-Smith, 1988.

APPENDIX B

*Developmental Red Flags for Children of Ages 3 to 5**

What Are Red Flags?

Red flags are behaviors that should warn you to **stop, look,** and **think.** Having done so, you may decide there is nothing to worry about, or that a cluster of behaviors signals a possible problem. These guidelines will help you use red flags more effectively.

- Behavior descriptions are sometimes repeated under different areas of development. It is difficult to categorize children's behavior. Your job is to notice and describe what you see that concerns you. Do not try to decide into which category it fits.
- Look for **patterns** or **clusters** of red flags. One, or a few in isolation, may not be significant.
- Observe a child in a variety of situations in order to watch for the behaviors that concern you.
- Compare the child's behavior to the "norm," which should include children who are 6 months younger or 6 months older as well as the same age.
- Note how the child has grown during the past 3 to 6 months. Be concerned if you feel the child has not progressed.
- **Know normal patterns of growth and development.** What may be a red flag at one age can be a perfectly normal behavior at another.
- Keep in mind that each child's development is affected by personality, temperament, family structure and dynamics, culture, experiences, physical characteristics, and the match of child and family to your program.
- Use a detailed skills list to develop a skills profile for the child.

---

*Adapted from Kendrick, Kaufman, & Messenger, (1988) *Healthy Young Children: A Manual for Programs.* Used with permission of the publisher, the National Association for the Education of Young Children. The list is a joint effort of the Administration for Children, Youth, and Families; U.S. Department of Health and Human Services; Georgetown University Child Development Center; Massachusetts Department of Public Health; and the National Association for the Education of Young Children.

Consultation and Referral

None of us knows all there is to know about normal growth and development. Use all of your area resources to help you think about a child.

- Describe in detail what you see that concerns you. Do not try to conclude what it means or to label it. It is much more helpful to parents, consultants, and to the child to have descriptions, not conclusions.
- Talk with the child's parent(s).
- Wait and watch for a while **if** you have observed growth in the past 3 to 6 months. If no growth in the area of concern can be described, then it is time to ask for help.
- Know that if you recommend further evaluation of a problem and your concerns are confirmed, you have helped a child and family begin to solve a problem.

NOTE: These categories are intended to guide your observation of children ages 3 to 5 only. For older children, consult state or school district guidelines.

Major Developmental Areas

Social–Emotional Development, Which Includes

- Relationships
- Separations
- Involvement
- Focusing
- Affect
- Self-image
- Anxiety level
- Impulse control
- Transitions

Red Flags.   Be alert to a child who, compared with other children the same age or 6 months older or younger, exhibits these behaviors:

- Does not seem to recognize self as a separate person, or does not refer to self as "I"
- Has great difficulty separating from parent or separates too easily
- Is anxious, tense, restless, compulsive, cannot get dirty or messy, has many fears, engages in excessive self-stimulation
- Seems preoccupied with own inner world; conversations do not make sense
- Shows little or no impulse control; hits or bites as first response; cannot follow a classroom routine
- Expresses emotions inappropriately (laughs when sad, denies feelings); facial expressions do not match emotions

- Cannot focus on activities (short attention span, cannot complete anything, flits from toy to toy)
- Relates only to adults; cannot share adult attention, consistently sets up power struggle, or is physically abusive to adults
- Consistently withdraws from people, prefers to be alone; no depth to relationships; does not seek or accept affection or touching
- Treats people as objects; has no empathy for other children; cannot play on another child's terms
- Is consistently aggressive, frequently hurts others deliberately; shows no remorse or is deceitful in hurting others

How to Screen

1. Observe child.
   - Note overall behavior. What does the child do all day? With whom? With what does child play?
   - Note when, where, how frequently, and with whom problem behaviors occur.
   - Describe behavior through clear observations. Do not diagnose.
2. Note family history.
   - Makeup of family: Who cares for the child?
   - Has there been a recent move, death, new sibling, or long or traumatic separations?
   - What support does the family have—extended family, friends?
3. Note developmental history and child's temperament since infancy.
   - Activity level
   - Regularity of child's routine—sleeping, eating
   - Distractibility
   - Intensity of child's responses
   - Persistence/attention span
   - Positive or negative mood
   - Adaptability to changes in routine
   - Level of sensitivity to noise, light, touch

Motor Development—Fine Motor, Gross Motor, and Perceptual—Which Includes

- Quality of movement
- Level of development
- Sensory integration

Red Flags.   Pay extra attention to children with these behaviors:

- The child who is particularly uncoordinated and who
  —has lots of accidents
  —trips, bumps into things
  —is awkward getting down/up, climbing, jumping, getting around toys and people
  —stands out from the group in structured motor tasks—walking, climbing stairs, jumping, standing on one foot
  —avoids the more physical games

- The child who relies heavily on watching own or other peoples' movements in order to do them and who
  —may frequently misjudge distances
  —may become particularly uncoordinated or off balance with eyes closed
- The child who, compared to peers, uses much more of her or his body to do the task than the task requires and who
  —dives into the ball (as though to cover the fact that she or he cannot coordinate a response)
  —uses tongue, feet, or other body parts excessively to help in coloring, cutting, tracing, or with other concentration
  —produces extremely heavy coloring
  —leans over the table when concentrating on a fine motor project
  —when doing wheelbarrows, keeps pulling the knees and feet under the body, or thrusts rump up in the air
- The child with extraneous and involuntary movements, who
  —while painting with one hand, holds the other hand in the air or waves
  —does chronic toe walking
  —shows twirling or rocking movements
  —shakes hands or taps fingers
- The child who involuntarily finds touching uncomfortable and who
  —flinches or tenses when touched or hugged
  —avoids activities that require touching or close contact
  —may be uncomfortable lying down, particularly on the back
  —reacts as if attacked when unexpectedly bumped
  —blinks, protects self from a ball even when trying to catch it
- The child who compulsively craves being touched or hugged, or the older child who almost involuntarily has to feel things to understand them, who both may
  —cling to, or lightly brush, the teacher a lot
  —always sit close to or touch children in a circle
  —be strongly attracted to sensory experiences such as blankets, soft toys, water, dirt, sand, paste, hands in food
- The child who has a reasonable amount of experience with fine motor tools but whose skill does not improve proportionately, such as
  —an older child who can still only snip with scissors or whose cutting is extremely choppy
  —an older child who still cannot color within the lines on a simple project
  —an older child who frequently switches hands with crayon, scissors, paintbrush
  —an experienced child who tries but still gets paste, paint, sand, water everywhere
  —a child who is very awkward with, or chronically avoids, small manipulative materials
- The child who has exceptional difficulty with new but simple puzzles, coloring, structured art projects, and drawing a person, and who, for example, may

—take much longer to do the task, even when trying hard, and produce a final result that is still not as sophisticated compared to those of peers

—show a lot of trial-and-error behavior when trying to do a puzzle

—mix up top/bottom, left/right, front/back, on simple projects where a model is to be copied

—use blocks or small cubes to repeatedly build and crash tower structures and seem fascinated and genuinely delighted with the novelty of the crash (older child)

—still does a lot of scribbling (older child)

How to Screen

1. Note level and quality of development as compared with other children in the group.

Speech and Language Development, Which Includes

- Articulation (pronouncing sounds)
- Dysfluency (excessive stuttering—occasional stuttering may occur in the early years and is normal)
- Voice
- Language (ability to use and understand words)

Red Flags

- Articulation. Watch for the child
  —whose speech is difficult to understand, compared with peers
  —who mispronounces sounds
  —whose mouth seems abnormal (excessive under- or overbite; swallowing difficulty; poorly lined-up teeth)
  —who has difficulty putting words and sounds in proper sequence
  —who cannot be encouraged to produce age-appropriate sound
  —who has a history of ear infections or middle ear disorders

NOTE: Most children develop the following sounds correctly by the ages shown (i.e., don't worry about a 3-year-old who mispronounces *t*).

2 years—all vowel sounds
3 years—*p, b, m, w, h*
4 years—*t, d, n, k, h, ng*
5 years—*f, j, sh*
6 years—*ch, v, r, l*
7 years—*s, z,* voiceless or voiced *th*

- Dysfluency (stuttering). Note the child who, compared with others of the same age,
  —shows excessive amounts of these behaviors:
  repetitions of sounds, words (m-m-m; I-I-I-I-)
  prolongations of sounds (mmmmmmmmmmmmmmm)

      hesitations or long blocks during speech, usually accompanied
         by tension or struggle behavior
      putting in extra words (um, uh, well)
  —shows two or more of these behaviors while speaking:
      hand clenching
      eye blinking
      swaying of body
      pill rolling with fingers
      no eye contact
      body tension or struggle
      breathing irregularity
      tremors
      pitch rise
      frustration
      avoidance of talking
  —is labeled a stutterer by parents
  —is aware of her or his dysfluencies

- Voice. Note the child whose
  —rate of speech is extremely fast or slow
  —voice is breathy or hoarse
  —voice is very loud or soft
  —voice is very high or low
  —voice sounds very nasal

- Language (ability to use and understand words). Note the child who
  —does not appear to understand when others speak, even though hearing is normal
  —is unable to follow one- or two-step directions
  —communicates by pointing, gesturing
  —makes no attempt to communicate with words
  —has small vocabulary for age
  —uses parrot-like speech (imitates what others say)
  —has difficulty putting words together in a sentence
  —uses words inaccurately
  —demonstrates difficulty with three or more of these skills:
      making a word plural
      changing tenses of verb
      using pronouns
      using negatives
      using possessives
      naming common objects
      telling function of common objects
      using prepositions

NOTE: Two-year-olds use mostly nouns, few verbs. Three-year-olds use nouns, verbs, some adverbs, adjectives, prepositions. Four-year-olds use all parts of speech.

How to Screen

1. Observe child. Note when, where, how frequently, and with whom problem occurs.
2. Check developmental history—both heredity and environment play an important part in speech development.
3. Look at motor development, which is closely associated with speech.
4. Look at social–emotional status, which can affect speech and language.
5. Write down or record speech samples.
6. Check hearing status.
7. Note number of speech sounds or uses of language.

Hearing

Even a mild or temporary hearing loss in a child may interfere with speech, language, or social and academic progress. If more than one of these red flag behaviors is observed, it is likely that a problem exists.

Red Flags

- Speech and language. Look for the child
  —whose speech is not easily understood by people outside the family
  —whose grammar is less accurate than other children of the same age
  —who does not use speech as much as other children of the same age
  —who has an unusual voice (hoarseness, stuffy quality, lack of inflection, or voice that is usually too loud or soft)
- Social behavior (at home and in school). Look for the child who
  —is shy or hesitant in answering questions or joining in conversation
  —misunderstands questions or directions; frequently says "huh?" or "what?" in response to questions
  —appears to ignore speech; hears "only what he wants to"
  —is unusually attentive to speaker's face or unusually inattentive to speaker, turns one ear to speaker
  —has difficulty with listening activities such as storytime and following directions
  —has short attention span
  —is distractible and restless; tends to shift quickly from one activity to another
  —is generally lethargic or disinterested in most day-to-day activities
  —is considered a behavior problem—too active or aggressive, or too quiet and withdrawn
- Medical indications. Look for the child who
  —has frequent or constant upper respiratory tract infections, congestion that appears related to allergies, or a cold for several weeks or months

—has frequent earaches, ear infections, throat infections, or middle ear problems

—has had draining ears on one or more occasions

—is mouth breather and snorer

—is generally lethargic; has poor color

How to Screen

1. Observe current behavior related to speech and hearing.
2. Consult behavioral and medical history.
3. Consult audiologist or communication disorders specialist.

Vision, Which Includes

- Skills
- Acuity (ability to see at a given distance)
- Disease

Red Flags

- Eyes
  —are watery
  —have discharge
  —lack coordination in directing gaze of both eyes
  —are red
  —are sensitive to light
  —appear to cross or wander, especially when child is tired
- Eyelids
  —have crusts on lids or among lashes
  —are red
  —have recurring sties or swelling
- Behavior and complaints
  —rubs eyes excessively
  —experiences dizziness, headaches, nausea on close work
  —attempts to brush away blur
  —has itchy, burning, scratchy eyes
  —contorts face or body when looking at distant objects, or thrusts head forward; squints or widens eyes
  —blinks eyes excessively; holds book too close or too far; inattentive during visual tasks
  —shuts or covers one eye; tilts head

How to Screen

1. Note child's medical history. Has child had an eye exam? If not, recommend one.
2. Screen using a screening tool appropriate for young children, such as the Snellen E chart or Broken Wheel cards.

Glossary

Accountability: Being held responsible for something, such as holding schools, administrators, and teachers responsible for student achievement.

Alternative Assessment: Almost any kind of assessment approach other than conventional standardized tests, inventories, and instruments.

Amplification: Assisting the emergence of behavior and understanding that are *within* a child's Zone of Proximal Development, rather than accelerating beyond the child's ability to understand and perform.

Assessment: A term used loosely to refer to any type of appraisal of young children. In a narrower sense it refers to information from multiple indicators and sources of evidence, which is then synthesized, integrated, interpreted, and evaluated to make an assessment.

Assessment Instruments, or Assessment Tools: Checklists, inventories, structured observation guides, rating scales, and other systematic means of collecting and recording information about young children.

Assessment Procedures: Methods and techniques used in the assessment process, such as observation, interviews, work sampling, collection and analysis of children's work products, and tests of various kinds.

Authentic, Direct, or Performance Assessment: Type of assessment that uses tasks as close as possible to real-life practical and intellectual challenges. *Performance assessment* refers to the type of pupil response. If motor coordination is to be measured, the child performs an appropriate action. If writing is of concern, the child writes. *Authentic assessment* refers to the situation or context in which the task is performed. In authentic assessment the child completes the desired behavior in a context as close to real life as possible.

Benchmark: A point of reference for measurement and evaluation. Used especially in connection with content standards. For example, standards may state that "by the end of second [or fourth, or eighth] grade, children should be able to . . . "

Classroom Assessment: Assessments developed and used by teachers in their classrooms on a day-to-day basis.

Continuous Assessment: Type of assessment embedded within the daily processes of instruction so that appraisal of children's responses and actions—and subsequent adjustment of curriculum and teaching—is ongoing.

Criterion Referencing: A means of determining where an individual stands in relation to a criterion or performance standard rather than to other individuals. The meaning comes from comparison to an expected standard or criterion.

Curriculum-Embedded Assessment: A process of assessment that is an integral part of the curriculum, in contrast to tests or assessments that are given apart from daily teaching and instruction.

Diagnostic Assessment or Evaluation: An in-depth appraisal of an individual child by a specialist, frequently after a child has been identified by a screening process or a teacher.

Documentation: The process of classroom observation and record keeping over time and across learning modalities to keep track of children's learning.

Dynamic Assessment: Type of assessment in which adults give clues, leads, and hints or ask questions or pose problems to see what the person being assessed can do, both with and without assistance. It builds on conceptions of children's learning based on insights from Vygotsky and cognitive psychologists.

Evaluation: The establishment of specific values by which to judge whatever is being considered.

Formative Evaluation: Type of evaluation that provides necessary information to facilitate children's progress toward identified goals and objectives. It is concerned both with student learning and with the curriculum's responsiveness to children's needs.

"High-Stakes" Assessment: Any assessment that has the potential to influence educational opportunities for children, such as placement in special programs, ability grouping, or retention in grade.

Inclusion: Including children with disabilities or developmental delays in the educational setting where they would have been if they did not have a disability or delay.

Interdisciplinary Assessment: Type of assessment in which specialists from several disciplines work together with school personnel and parents outside the classroom to integrate their separate findings, reports, and perspectives.

Measurement: Quantification of some kind.

Multidisciplinary Assessment: Type of assessment in which specialists from several disciplines assess and evaluate a child independently and submit separate reports.

Norm Referencing: A means of determining an individual's performance in relation to the performance of others on the same measure. The meaning of the score emerges from comparison with the group of children, who constitute the norm.

Observational Measurement: The process of observing and assessing behavior in ways that yield descriptions and quantitative measures of individuals, groups, and settings.

Portfolio: A purposeful collection of children's work and other indicators of learning, collected over time, that demonstrates to the student and others the student's efforts, progress, or achievement in a particular developmental or subject area(s).

Portfolio Assessment: Type of assessment that evaluates the child's performance based on evidence that teachers and children have selected and compiled in a portfolio.

Reflection: A process by which an individual or group thoughtfully considers an experience, idea, work product, or learning. It is a "looking back" and reconstruction that usually involves language and may lead to revision based on the reflection.

Reliability: The extent to which any assessment technique yields results that are accurate and consistent over time.

Rubric: A rule or guide presenting clear criteria by which a complex performance can be judged.

Scaffolding: Providing, then gradually removing, external support for learning.

Scoring Rubric: A fixed scale and a list of characteristics describing performance for each of the points on the scale. Usually one level of the rubric is considered the acceptable level of performance.

Screening: Brief, relatively inexpensive, standardized procedures designed to quickly appraise a large number of children to find out which ones should be referred for further assessment.

Social Context: Everything in the environment that has been directly or indirectly influenced by the culture, including people (parents, teachers, peers) and materials (books, learning materials and supplies, equipment).

Standardized Tests: Published tests that specify what the tester says and does, the materials to be used, and the scoring processes, so that scores collected at different times and places will be comparable.

Standards: Outcome statements that specify what children should know and be able to do at different points in their school learning. Some statements of standards also address attitudes, values, and dispositions toward learning. In child assessment, standards are often used as a way of expressing expectations about intent and outcomes. *Content standards* state what every child should know and be able to do. *Performance standards* state how well a child should demonstrate knowledge and skills. They gauge the degree to which children have met the content standards.

Summative or Summary Evaluation: An evaluation that takes place at the end of a unit, course of study, year, or unit of schooling, and determines the degree of children's attainment of objectives. Results are often used for reporting to others.

Tests: Systematic procedures for observing a person's behavior and describing it with the aid of numerical scales or fixed categories.

Transdisciplinary Assessment: Type of assessment in which appropriate specialists and classroom personnel work together in regular classroom activities to conduct a child assessment.

Triangulation: As used in assessment, a term that refers to merging information from several sources and several techniques to reach a conclusion, rather than relying on one direct measure.

Validity: The extent to which any assessment technique fulfills the purpose for which it is intended.

Zone of Proximal Development: A concept from the Vygotskian theory of child development and learning. The zone encompasses the area of development that is emerging. The lower level of the zone is what a child can do independently. The higher level is what a child can do with maximum assistance.

References

Abbott, C. F., & Gold, S. (1991). Conferring with parents when you're concerned that their child needs special services. *Young Children, 46*(4), 10–14.

Administration for Children, Youth, and Families (1986). *Easing the transition from preschool to kindergarten: A guide for early childhood teachers and administrators.* Washington, DC: U.S. Department of Health and Human Services.

Airasian, P. W. (1994). *Classroom assessment* (2nd ed.). New York: McGraw-Hill.

Alexander, S. (1993, January 5). School room shuffle, grades 1 through 3 become one class with no texts, desks or "report cards": Some parents and principals balk. *The Wall Street Journal,* pp. A1, A6.

Almy, M. (1969). *Ways of studying children: A manual for teachers.* New York: Teachers College Press.

Almy, M., & Genishi, C. (1979). *Ways of studying children.* New York: Teachers College Press.

American Association for the Advancement of Science. (1993). *Benchmarks for science literacy.* Washington, DC: Author.

American Federation of Teachers, National Council on Measurement in Education, & National Education Association. (1990). *Standards for teacher competence in education assessment of students.* Washington, DC: Author.

American Psychological Association, American Educational Research Association, & National Council on Measurement in Education. (1985). *Standards for educational and psychological testing.* Washington, DC: Author.

Applebee, A. N. (1978). *The child's concept of story.* Chicago, IL: University of Chicago Press.

Arends, R. (1988). *Learning to teach.* New York: Random House.

Armstrong, T. (1995). *The myth of the A.D.D. child: 50 ways to improve your child's behavior and attention span without drugs, labels, or coercion.* New York: Dutton.

Arter, J. A. (1990). *Using portfolios in instruction and assessment.* Portland, OR: Northwest Regional Educational Laboratory.

Arter, J. A. (1994). *Integrating assessment and instruction.* Portland, OR: Northwest Regional Educational Laboratory.

Arter, J. A., & Paulson, P. (1991). *Composite portfolio work group summaries.* Portland, OR: Northwest Regional Educational Laboratory.

Arter, J. A., & Spandel, V. (1992, Spring). Using portfolios of student work in instruction and assessment. *Educational Measurement: Issues and Practice, 11*(1), 36–44.

Asher, R. S., & Renshaw, P. D. (1981). Children without friends: Social knowledge and social skill training. In S. R. Asher & J. M. Gottman (Eds.), *The development of children's friendships* (pp. 273–296). Cambridge, England: Cambridge University Press.

Ashton-Lilo, J. (1987). *Pencil grasp developmental sequence checklist*. Unpublished manuscript.

Athey, I. (1990). The construct of emergent literacy: Putting it all together. In L. M. Morrow & J. K. Smith (Eds.), *Assessment for instruction in early literacy* (pp. 45–61). Englewood Cliffs, NJ: Prentice-Hall.

Au, K. A. (1993). *Literacy instruction in multicultural settings*. Chicago: Harcourt Brace.

Bagnato, S. J., & Neisworth, J. T. (1991). *Assessment for early intervention*. New York: Guilford Press.

Bagnato, S. J., Neisworth, J. T., & Munson, S. M. (1989). *Linking developmental assessment and early intervention: Curriculum-based prescriptions* (2nd ed.). Rockville, MD: Aspen.

Bailey, D. B., & Simeonsson, R. J. (1988). *Family assessment in early intervention*. Columbus, OH: Merrill.

Barbour, N. (1987). Learning to read. In C. Seefeldt (Ed.), *The early childhood curriculum: A review of current research* (pp. 107–140). New York: Teachers College Press.

Barker, R. G. (1968). *Ecological psychology*. Stanford, CA: Stanford University Press.

Barnett, D. W., & Zucker, K. B. (1990). *The personal and social assessment of children: An analysis of current status and professional practice issues*. Boston: Allyn and Bacon.

Barona, A. (1991). Assessment of multi-cultural preschool children. In B. A. Bracken (Ed.), *The psychoeducational assessment of preschool children* (2nd ed., pp. 379–391). Boston: Allyn and Bacon.

Baroody, A. J. (1993). *Problem solving, reasoning, and communciation, K–8: Helping children to think mathematically*. New York: Macmillan.

Beaty, J. J. (1994). *Observing development of the young child* (3rd. ed.). New York: Macmillan.

Beihler, R. F., & Snowman, J. (1991). *Psychology applied to teaching* (6th ed.). Boston: Houghton Mifflin.

Bell, D. R., & Low, R. M. (1977). *Observing and recording children's behavior*. Spokane, WA: Performance Associates.

Belmont, J. M. (1989). Cognitive strategies and strategic learning: The socio-instructional approach. In F. D. Horowitz & M. O'Brien (Eds.), Children and their development: Knowledge base, research agenda, and social policy application [Special issue] (pp. 142–148). *American Psychologist, 44*(2).

Bennett, J. (1992). Seeing is believing: Videotaping reading development. In L. Rhodes & N. Shanklin (Eds.), *Literacy assessment in whole language classrooms K–8*. Portsmouth, NH: Heinemann.

Bentzen, W. R. (1992). *Seeing young children: A guide to observing and recording behavior* (2nd ed.). New York: Delmar Publishers.

Berger, K. S., & Thompson, R. A. (1995). *The developing person through childhood and adolescence* (4th ed.). New York: Worth Publishers.

Berk, L. E. (1994). *Child development* (3rd ed.). Boston: Allyn and Bacon.

Berk, L. E., & Winsler, A. (1995). *Scaffolding children's learning: Vygotsky and early childhood education.* Washington, DC: National Association for the Education of Young Children.

Berk, R. A. (1982). *Handbook of methods for detecting test bias.* Baltimore, MD: The Johns Hopkins University Press.

Berliner, D. C. (1987). But do they understand? In V. Richardson-Koehler (Ed.), *Educator's handbook: A research perspective.* New York: Longman.

Berliner, D. C., & Rosenshine, B. V. (Eds.). (1987). *Talks to teachers.* New York: Random House.

Bertelson, P. (Ed.). (1986). *The onset of literacy: Cognitive processes in reading acquisition.* Cambridge, MA: MIT Press.

Billups, L. R., & Rauth, M. (1987). Teachers and research. In V. Richardson-Koehler (Ed.), *Educators' handbook* (pp. 328–376). New York: Longman.

Blank, M., Rose, S. A., & Berlin, L. J. (1978). *The language of learning: The preschool years.* Boston: Allyn and Bacon.

Bloom, B. S., Englehart, M. B., Furst, E. J., Hill, W. H., & Krathwhol, D. R. (1956). *Taxonomy of educational objectives: The classification of educational goals: Handbook 1, cognitive domain.* New York: McKay.

Bodrova, E., & Leong, D. J. (1996). *Tools of the mind: The Vygotskian approach to early childhood education.* Englewood Cliffs, NJ: Merrill.

Boehm, A. E. (1991). Assessment of basic relational concepts. In B. A. Bracken (Ed.), *The psychoeducational assessment of preschool children* (2nd ed., pp. 241–258). Boston: Allyn and Bacon.

Boehm, A. E., & Weinberg, R. A. (1987). *The classroom observer: A guide for developing observation skills.* New York: Teachers College Press.

Bowman, B. (1992). Reaching potentials of minority children through developmentally and culturally appropriate programs. In S. Bredekamp & T. Rosegrant (Eds.), *Reaching potentials: Appropriate curriculum and assessment for young children* (Vol. 1). Washington, DC: National Association for the Education of Young Children.

Brandt, R. S. (Ed.). (1991). The reflective educator. *Educational Leadership, 48*(6).

Bredekamp, S. (Ed.). (1987). *Developmentally appropriate practice in early childhood programs serving children from birth through age 8.* Washington, DC: National Association for the Education of Young Children.

Bredekamp, S., & Rosegrant, T. (Eds.). (1992). *Reaching potentials: Appropriate curriculum and assessment for young children* (Vol. 1). Washington, DC: National Association for the Education of Young Children.

Bredekamp, S., & Rosegrant, T. (Eds.). (1995). *Reaching potentials: Transforming early childhood curriculum and assessment* (Vol. 2). Washington, DC: National Association for the Education of Young Children.

Brown, A. L. (1991). Knowing when, where, and how to remember: A problem of metacognition. In R. Glaser (Ed.), Advances in instructional psychology (Vol. 1, pp. 77–165). Hillsdale, NJ: Lawrence Erlbaum Associates.

Bukatko, D., & Daehler, M. W. (1992). *Child development: A topical approach.* Boston: Houghton Mifflin.

Burns, R. C. (Ed.). (1993). *Parents and schools: From visitors to partners.* Washington, DC: National Education Association.

California State Department of Education (1989). *CAP Generalized Rubric.* Sacramento, CA: Author.

Cambourne, B., & Turbill, J. (1990). Assessment in whole-language classrooms: Theory into practice. *The Elementary School Journal, 90,* 337–349.

Campione, J. C., & Brown, A. L. (1985). Linking dynamic assessment with school achievement. In C. S. Lidz (Ed.), *Dynamic assessment: An interactional approach to evaluating learning potential* (pp. 82–195). New York: Guilford Press.

Campione, J. C., Brown, A. L., Reeve, R. A., Ferrara, R. A., & Palinscar, A. S. (1991). Interactive learning and individual understanding: The case of reading and mathematics. In L. T. Landsmann (Ed.), *Culture, schooling, and psychological development* (pp. 136–170). Norwood, NJ: Ablex Publishing.

Cartwright, C. A., & Cartwright, G. P. (1984). *Developing observation skills* (2nd ed). New York: McGraw-Hill.

Casey, M. B. (1986). Individual differences in selective attention among pre-readers: A key to mirror-image confusion. *Developmental Psychology, 22,* 58–66.

Castaneda, A. M. (1987). Early mathematics education. In C. Seefeldt (Ed.), *The early childhood curriculum: A review of current research* (pp. 165–184). New York: Teachers College Press.

Cazden, C. B. (1972). *Child language and education.* New York: Holt, Rinehart & Winston.

Cazden, C. B. (1988). *Classroom discourse.* Portsmouth, NH: Heinemann.

Ceci, S. J. (1991). How does schooling influence general intelligence and its cognitive components? A reassessment of evidence. *Developmental Psychology, 27*(5), 703–722.

Chandler, P. D. (1994). *A place for me: Including children with special needs in early care and education settings.* Washington, DC: National Association for the Education of Young Children.

Charlesworth, R. (1992). *Understanding child development* (2nd ed.). Albany, NY: Delmar Publishers.

Chittenden, E., & Courtney, R. (1989). Assessment of young children's reading: Documentation as an alternative to testing. In D. S. Strickland & L. M. Morrow (Eds.), *Emerging literacy: Young children learn to read and write* (pp. 107–120). Newark, DE: International Reading Association.

Cizek, G. J. (1995). The big picture in assessment and who ought to have it. *Phi Delta Kappan, 77*(3), 246–249.

Clark, C. M., & Yinger, R. H. (1987). Teacher planning. In D. C. Berliner & B. V. Rosenshine (Eds.), *Talks to teachers* (pp. 342–365). New York: Random House.

Clark, H. H., & Clark, E. V. (1977). *Psychology and language: An introduction to psycholinguistics.* New York: Harcourt Brace Jovanovich.

Clay, M. M. (1985). *The early detection of reading difficulties* (3rd ed.). Auckland, New Zealand: Heinemann.

Clay, M. M. (1991). *Becoming literate: The construction of inner control.* Portsmouth, NH: Heinemann.

Clemmons, J., Laase, L., & Cooper, D. L. (1993). *Portfolios in the classroom: A teacher's sourcebook.* Jefferson City, MO: Scholastic, Inc.

Clift, R., Houston, W., & Pugach, M. (Eds.). (1990). *Encouraging reflective practice in education.* New York: Teachers College Press.

Cohen, D. (1995). What standard for national standards? *Phi Delta Kappan, 76*(10), 751–757.

Cole, M., & Cole., S. (1995). *The development of children* (2nd ed.). New York: W. H. Freeman.

Coleman, J. S. (1991). *Parent involvement in education.* (OERI, Order No. 065-000-00459-3). Washington, DC: U.S. Government Printing Office.

Colorado Department of Education. (1995). *Colorado model content standards for reading and writing.* Denver, CO: Author.

Committee for Economic Development. (1985). *Investing in our children: Business and the public schools.* New York: Author.

Committee for Economic Development. (1991). *The unfinished agenda: A new vision for child development and education.* New York: Author.

Corbin, C. B. (1980). *A textbook of motor development* (3rd ed.). Dubuque, IA: Wm. C. Brown Publishers.

Corno, L. (1987). Teaching and self-regulated learning. In D. C. Berliner & B. V. Rosenshine (Eds.), *Talks to teachers* (pp. 249–266). New York: Random House.

Cronbach, L. J. (1990). *Essentials of psychological testing* (5th ed.). New York: Harper & Row.

Curry, N. E., & Johnson, C. N. (1990). *Beyond self-esteem: Developing a genuine sense of human value.* Washington, DC: National Association for the Education of Young Children.

Damon, W. (1977). *The social world of the child.* San Francisco: Jossey-Bass.

Daniels, J. B. (1992). *A handbook for assessing student writing using a K–6 writing assessment portfolio developed by teachers at Rayan Elementary and Foothill Elementary Schools.* (Available from Jane Daniels, 1488 Greenbriar, Boulder, Colorado, 80303).

Derman-Sparks, L., & A.B.C. Task Force. (1989). *Anti-bias curriculum: Tools for empowering young children.* Washington, DC: National Association for the Education of Young Children.

DeVilliers, J. G., & DeVilliers, P. A. (1978). *Language acquisition.* Cambridge, MA: Harvard University Press.

DeVries, R., & Kohlberg, L. (1987). *Constructivist early education.* Washington, DC: National Association for the Education of Young Children.

Diana v. *California State Board of Education, et al.* No. C-70-37 (N.D.Cal., filed Jan. 7, 1970).

Diffily, D. (1994). *What parents think about alternative assessment and narrative reporting: One school's findings.* (ERIC Document Reproduction Service No. ED 381230).

Dodge, K. A., Pettit, G. S., McClaskey, C. L., & Brown, M. M. (1986). Social competence in children. *Monographs of the Society for Research in Child Development, 51* (2, Serial No. 213).

Dodge, K. A., & Somberg, D. R. (1987). Hostile attributional biases among aggressive boys are exacerbated under conditions of threats to the self. *Child Development, 58,* 213–224.

Dutton, W. H., & Dutton, A. (1991). *Mathematics children use and understand: Preschool through third grade.* Mountain View, CA: Mayfield Publishing.

Education and Human Services Consortium. (1991). *What it takes: Structuring interagency partnerships to connect children and families with comprehensive services.* Washington, DC: Institute for Educational Leadership.

Education for All Handicapped Children Act of 1975. 20 U.S.C. 1401 (P.L. 94-142).

Education of the Handicapped Act Amendments of 1986. 20 U.S.C. 1400 (P.L. 99-457).

Education Week/Special Report. (1995, April 12). *Struggling for standards.*

Eisenberg, N. (1982). The development of reasoning regarding prosocial behavior. In N. Eisenberg (Ed.), *The development of prosocial behavior* (pp. 219–249). New York: Academic Press.

Eisner, E. (1995). Standards for American schools: Help or hindrance? *Phi Delta Kappan, 76*(10), pp. 758–764.

Eisner, E. (1991). What really counts in schools. *Educational Leadership, 48*(5), 10–17.

Elkind, D. (1979). *The child and society: Essays in applied child development.* New York: Oxford University Press.

Engel, B. (1990). An approach to assessment in early literacy. In C. Kamii (Ed.), *Achievement testing in the early grades: The games grown-ups play* (pp. 119–134). Washington, DC: National Association for the Education of Young Children.

Epstein, J. L. (1987). Parent involvement: What research says to administrators. In E. E. Gotts & R. F. Purnell (Eds.), *Education and urban society: School–family relations* (pp. 119–136). Newbury Park, CA: Sage Publications.

ERIC Clearinghouse on Disabilities and Gifted Education. (1994). *Rights and Responsibilities of Parents of Children with Disabilities.* Reston, VA: Author.

Evans, C. (1991). Support for teachers studying their own work. *Educational Leadership, 48*(6), 11–13.

FairTest. (1990). What's wrong with standardized tests? *Factsheet.* Cambridge, MA: National Center for Fair and Open Testing.

Family Educational Rights and Privacy Act of 1974, 513(b) (1). 20 U.S.C. 1232 (P.L. 93-380).

Faw, T., & Belkin, G. S. (1989). *Child psychology.* New York: McGraw-Hill.

Feuer, M. J., Fulton, K., & Morison, P. Better tests and testing practices. *Phi Delta Kappan 74*(7), 530–533.

Feuerstein, R. (1979). *The dynamic assessment of retarded performers: The Learning Potential Assessment Device, theory, instruments, techniques.* Baltimore, MD: University Park Press.

Finn, C. E., Jr. (1991, March 11). National testing, no longer a foreign idea. *Wall Street Journal,* p. 10A.

Flavell, J. H. (1963). *The developmental psychology of Jean Piaget.* New York: Van Nostrand.

Forman, G., & Kaden, M. (1987). Research on science education for young children. In C. Seefeldt (Ed.), *The early childhood curriculum: A review of current research* (pp. 141–164). New York: Teachers College Press.

Gage, N. L., & Berliner, D. C. (1992). *Educational psychology* (5th ed.). Boston: Houghton Mifflin.

Gallahue, D. L. (1982). *Developmental movement exercises for young children*. New York: John Wiley and Sons.

Gallahue, D. L. (1993). Motor development and movement skill acquisition in early childhood education. In B. Spodek (Ed.), *Handbook of research on the education of young children* (pp. 24–41). New York: Macmillan.

Gardner, H. (1985). *Frames of mind: The theory of multiple intelligences.* New York: Basic Books.

Gardner, H. (1991). *The unschooled mind.* New York: Harper & Row.

Genishi, C. (1987). Acquiring oral language and communicative competence. In C. Seefeldt (Ed.), *The early childhood curriculum: A review of current research* (pp. 75–106). New York: Teachers College Press.

Genishi, C. (1988). Children's language: Learning words from experience. *Young Children, 44*(1), 16–23.

Genishi, C. (1992). *Ways of assessing children and curriculum: Stories of early childhood practice.* New York: Teachers College Press.

Gentry, J. R. (1982). An analysis of developmental spelling in GYNS AT WRK. *The Reading Teacher, 36*(2), 192–200.

Geography Education Standards Project. (1994). *Geography for life: National geography standards.* Washington, DC: National Geographic Research & Evaluation.

Ginsberg, H., & Opper, S. (1988). *Piaget's theory of intellectual development* (3rd ed.). Englewood Cliffs, NJ: Prentice-Hall.

Glaser, R. (1987). The integration of instruction and testing: Implications from the study of human cognition. In D. C. Berliner & B. V. Rosenshine (Eds.), *Talks to teachers* (pp. 329–343). New York: Random House.

Golden, D. B., & Kutner, C. G. (1986). *The play development progress scale.* Unpublished manuscript.

Goodenow, C. (1992). Strengthening the links between educational psychology and the study of social contexts. *Educational Psychologist, 27*(2), 177–196.

Goodman, K. S., Goodman, Y. M., & Hood, W. J. (Eds.). (1989). *The whole language evaluation book.* Portsmouth, NH: Heinemann.

Goodman, Y. M. (1978). Kid watching: An alternative to testing. *National Elementary School Principal, 57*(4), 41–51.

Goodwin, W. R., & Driscoll, L. A. (1980). *Handbook for measurement and evaluation in early childhood education.* San Francisco: Jossey-Bass.

Goodwin, W. R., & Goodwin, L. D. (1993). Young children and measurement: Standardized and nonstandardized instruments in early childhood education. In B. Spodek (Ed.), *Handbook of research on the education of young children* (pp. 441–463). New York: Macmillan.

Gottman, J. M. (1983). How children become friends. *Monographs of the Society for Research in Child Development, 48* (Serial No. 201).

Gotts, E. E. (1984). Using academic guidance sheets. In O. McAfee (Ed.), *School–home communications: A resource notebook.* Charleston, WV: Appalachia Educational Laboratory.

Gough, P. B. (Ed.). (1993). Feature section on alternative assessment. *Phi Delta Kappan, 74*(6), 444–479.

Grabe, M. (1986). Attentional processes in education. In G. D. Phye & T. Andre (Eds.), *Cognitive classroom learning: Understanding, thinking, and problem solving.* Orlando, FL: Academic Press.

Grace, C., & Shores, E. F. (1991). *The portfolio and its use: Developmentally appropriate assessment of young children.* Little Rock, AR: Southern Association on Children under Six.

Grant, C. A. (1984). *Preparing for reflective teaching.* Boston: Allyn and Bacon.

Guerin, G. R., & Maier, A. S. (1983). *Informal assessment in education.* Palo Alto, CA: Mayfield Publishing.

Gumperz, J. J., & Gumperz, J. C. (1981). Ethnic differences in communicative style. In C. A. Ferguson & S. B. Heath (Eds.), *Language in the USA.* Cambridge, England: Cambridge University Press.

Hakuta, K., & Garcia, E. E. (1989). Bilingualism and education. Children and their development: Knowledge base, research agenda, and social policy applications, [Special issue]. *American Psychologist, 44*(2), 374–379.

Haney, W., & Madaus, G. (1989). Searching for alternatives to standardized tests: Whys, whats, and whithers. *Phi Delta Kappan, 70,* 683–687.

Hanfmann, F., & Kasanin, J. (1937). A method of study of concept formation. *Journal of Psychology, 3,* 521–540.

Hebert, E. A. (1992, May). Portfolios invite reflection—from students and staff. *Educational Leadership, 49*(8), 58–61.

Hendrick, J. (1994). *Total learning: Curriculum for the whole child* (4th ed.). Columbus, OH: Merrill.

Herman, J. L., Aschbacher, P. R., & Winters, L. (1992). *A practical guide to alternative assessment.* Alexandria, VA: Association for Supervision and Curriculum Development.

Hiebert, E. F., & Calfee, R. C. (1989). Advancing academic literacy through teachers' assessments. *Educational Leadership, 47*(3), 50–54.

High/Scope Educational Research Foundation. (1992). *Child observation record.* Ypsilanti, MI: Author.

Hills, T. W. (1992). Reaching potentials through appropriate assessment. In S. Bredekamp & T. Rosegrant (Eds.), *Reaching potentials: Appropriate curriculum and assessment for young children* (Vol. 1). Washington, DC: National Association for the Education of Young Children.

Hinitz, B. F. (1987). Social studies in early childhood education. In C. Seefeldt (Ed.), *The early childhood curriculum: A review of current research* (pp. 237–270). New York: Teachers College Press.

Hollifield, J. (1989). *Children learning in groups and other trends in elementary and early childhood education.* Urbana, IL: ERIC/EECE.

Holmes, C. T., & Matthews, K. M. (1984). The effects of nonpromotion on elementary and junior high school pupils: A meta-analysis. *Review of Educational Research, 54,* 225–236.

Hopkins, K. D., Stanley, J.C., & Hopkins, B. R. (1990). *Educational and psychological measurement and evaluation* (7th ed.). Englewood Cliffs, NJ: Prentice-Hall.

Howes, C. (1980). Play scale as an index of complexity of peer interaction. *Developmental Psychology, 16,* 371–381.

Humphrey, S. (1989). The case of myself. *Young Children, 45*(1), 17–22.

Irwin, D. M., & Bushnell, M. M. (1980). *Observational strategies for child study.* New York: Holt, Rinehart & Winston.

Jackson, N. E., Robinson, H. B., & Dale, P. S. (1977). *Cognitive development in young children*. Monterey, CA: Brooks/Cole Publishing.

Jagger, A. M. (1985). Introduction and overview. In A. M. Jagger & M. T. Smith-Burke (Eds.), *Observing the language learner* (pp. 1–7). Newark, DE: International Reading Association.

Jersild, A. T. (1955). *When teachers face themselves*. New York: Teachers College Press.

Jewett, J. (1992, February). *Effective strategies for school-based early childhood centers*. Portland, OR: Northwest Regional Educational Laboratory.

Johnson, D. W., & Johnson, R. T. (1991). *Learning together and alone: Cooperative, competitive, and individualistic learning*. Englewood Cliffs, NJ: Prentice-Hall.

Johnson, D. W., Johnson, R. T., & Holubec, E. J. (1986). *Circles of learning: Cooperation in the classroom* (Rev. ed.). Edina, MN: Interaction Book Company.

Johnson, D. W., Johnson, R. T., Holubec, E. J., & Roy, P. (1984). *Circles of learning: Cooperation in the classroom*. Alexandria, VA: Association for Supervision and Curriculum Development.

Johnson, J. E., Christie, J. F., & Yawkey, T. D. (1987). *Play and early childhood development*. Glenview, IL: Scott, Foresman.

Jones, E., & Derman-Sparks, L. (1992). Meeting the challenge of diversity. *Young Children, 47*(2), 12–18.

Jones, R. L. (1988). *Psychoeducational assessment of minority group children: A casebook* (2nd ed.). Boston: Allyn and Bacon.

Juarez, T. (1996). Why any grades at all, Father? *Phi Delta Kappan, 77*(5), 374–377.

Kagan, S. L., Moore, E., & Bredekamp, S. (Eds.). (1995). *Reconsidering children's early development and learning: Toward common views and vocabulary*. Washington, DC: National Educational Goals Panel.

Kamii, C. (Ed.). (1990). *Achievement testing in the early grades*. Washington, DC: National Association for the Education of Young Children.

Kamii, C., & Rosenblum, V. (1990). An approach to assessment in mathematics. In C. Kamii (Ed.), *Achievement testing in the early grades: The games grown-ups play* (pp. 146–162). Washington, DC: National Association for the Education of Young Children.

Kane, M. B., & Khattri, N. (1995). Assessment reform: A work in progress. *Phi Delta Kappan, 77*(1), 30–32.

Kaplan, P. S. (1991). *A child's odyssey* (2nd ed). St. Paul, MN: West Publications.

Katz, L. G. (1992). *Approaches to learning: Dispositions as a dimension of school readiness*. Manuscript prepared for the Goal 1 Resource Group on School Readiness, National Education Goals Panel.

Katz, L. G., & Chard, S. C. (1989). *Engaging children's minds: The project approach*. Norwood, NJ: Ablex Publishing.

Katz, L. G., Evangelou, D., & Hartman, J. A. (1990). *The case for mixed-age grouping in early education*. Washington, DC: National Association for the Education of Young Children.

Kendall, F. (1996). *Diversity in the classroom: New approaches to the education of young children*. New York: Teachers College Press.

Kendall, J. S., & Marzano, R. J. (1994). *The systematic identification and articulation of content standards and benchmarks.* Aurora, CO: Midcontinent Regional Educational Laboratory. (on-line). Available: http://www.mcrel.org

Kendrick, S. K., Kaufman, R., & Messenger, K. P. (Eds.). (1988). *Healthy young children: A manual for programs.* Washington, DC: National Association for the Education of Young Children.

Kingore, B. (1993). *Portfolios: Enriching and assessing all students.* Des Moines, IA: Leadership Publishers, Inc.

Kneidek, T. (1991, October). *Reflections on portfolios: Northwest report.* Portland, OR: Northwest Regional Educational Laboratory, pp. 5–6.

Kounin, J. S. (1970). *Discipline and group management in classrooms.* New York: Holt, Rinehart & Winston.

Krechevsky, M. (1991). Project spectrum: An innovative assessment alternative. *Educational Leadership, 48*(5), 45–48.

Kuschner, D. (1989). "Put your name on your painting, but . . . the blocks go back on the shelves." *Young Children, 45*(1), 49–56.

Ladd, G. W. (1990). Having friends, keeping friends, making friends, and being liked by peers in the classroom: Predictors of children's early school adjustment? *Child Development, 61,* 1081–1100.

Lau v. Nichols, 414 U.S. 563 (1974).

Lawler, S. D. (1991). *Parent–teacher conferencing in early childhood education.* Washington, DC: National Education Association.

Lawson, J. (1986). A study of the frequency of analogical responses to questions in black and white preschool-age children. *Early Childhood Research Quarterly, 1*(4), 379–386.

Lay-Dopyera, M., & Dopyera, J. E. (1987). *Becoming a teacher of young children* (2nd ed.). Lexington, MA: D. C. Heath.

Leong, D. J., McAfee, O., & Swedlow, R. (1992). Assessment and planning in early childhood classrooms. *The Journal of Early Childhood Teacher Education, 13*(40), 20–21.

Levine, K. (1995). *Development of prewriting and scissor skills: A visual analysis.* Boston: Communication Skill Builders.

Lewis, A. (1991). America 2000: What kind of a nation? *Phi Delta Kappan, 72*(10), 734–735.

Lewis, A. (1995). An overview of the standards movement. *Phi Delta Kappan, 76*(10), 745–750.

Lidz, C. S. (1991). *Practitioner's guide to dynamic assessment.* New York: Guilford Press.

Linder, T. W. (1993). *Transdisciplinary play-based assessment: A functional approach to working with young children.* Baltimore: Paul H. Brooks.

Lindfors, J. W. (1987). *Children's language and learning* (2nd ed.). Englewood Cliffs, NJ: Prentice-Hall.

Locke, J. L. (1993). *The child's path to spoken language.* Cambridge, MA: Harvard University Press.

Love, J. M. (1991, November 9). *Transition activities in American schools.* Paper presented at the National Association for the Education of Young Children Conference, Denver, CO.

Love, J. M., Logue, M. E., Trudeau, J. V., & Thayer, K. (1992). *Transitions to kindergarten in American schools. Final report to the Office of Policy and Planning, U.S. Department of Education* (Contract LC88089001). Portsmouth, NH: RMC Research Corporation.

Love, J. M., & Yelton, B. (1989). Smoothing the road from preschool to kindergarten. *Principal, 68*(5), 26–27.

Maeroff, G. I. (1991). Assessing alternative assessment. *Phi Delta Kappan, 73,* 272–281.

Manning, M. L., & Lucking, R. (1990). Ability grouping: Realities and alternatives. *Childhood Education, 66*(7), 254–256.

Marzano, R. J., Pickering, D., & McTighe, J. (1993). *Assessing student outcomes: Performance assessment using the dimensions of learning model.* Alexandria, VA: Association for Supervision and Curriculum Development.

Mason J. M., & Stewart, J. J. (1990). Emergent literacy assessment for instructional use in kindergarten. In L. M. Morrow & J. K. Smith (Eds.), *Assessment for instruction in early literacy* (pp. 155–175). Englewood Cliffs, NJ: Prentice-Hall.

Masten, A. S. (1989). Resilience in development: Implications of the study of successful adaptation for developmental psychopathology. In D. Cicchetti (Ed.), *The emergence of a discipline: Rochester symposium on developmental psychopathology* (Vol. 1, pp. 261–294). Hillsdale, NJ: Lawrence Erlbaum Associates.

Mayer, R. E. (1992). Cognition and instruction: Their historic meeting within educational psychology. *Journal of Educational Psychology, 84*(4), 405–412.

McAfee, O. (1985). Circle time: Getting past "two little pumpkins." *Young Children, 40*(6), 24–29.

McAfee, O. (1987). Improving home–school relations: Implications for staff development. In R. F. Purnell & E. E. Gotts (Eds.), *Education and urban society: School–family relations* (pp. 185–200). Newbury Park, CA: Sage Publications.

McCracken, J. B. (1993). *Valuing diversity: The early years.* Washington, DC: National Association for the Education of Young Children.

McGhee, L. M., & Richgels, D. J. (1990). *Literacy's beginnings.* Boston: Allyn and Bacon.

Mehrens, W. (1991, April). *Using performance assessment for accountability purposes: Some problems.* Paper presented at the annual meeting of the American Educational Research Association, Chicago, IL.

Meisels, S. J., Jablon, J. R., Marsden, D. B., Dichtelmiller, M. L., Dorfman, A. B., & Steele, D. M. (1994). *The work sampling system: An overview* (3rd ed.). Ann Arbor, MI: Rebus Planning Associates, Inc.

Meisels, S. J., & Steele, D. (1991). The early childhood portfolio collection process. *Center for Human Growth and Development.* Ann Arbor, MI: University of Michigan.

Meisels, S. J., Steele, D. M., & Quinn-Leering, K. (1993). Testing, tracking, and retaining young children: An analysis of research and social policy. In B. Spodek (Ed.), *Handbook of research on the education of young children* (pp. 279–292). New York: Macmillan.

Mendelson, A., & Atlas, R. (1973). Early childhood assessment: Paper and pencil for whom? *Childhood Education, 49,* 357–361.

Menyuk, P. (1988). *Language development: Knowledge and use.* Boston: Scott, Foresman.

Mercer, J. (1972). *Labeling the mentally retarded.* Berkeley, CA: University of California Press.

Mergendoller, J. R., & Marchman, V. A. (1987). Friends and associates. In V. Richardson-Koehler (Ed.), *Educators' handbook: A research perspective* (pp. 279–328). New York: Longman.

Messer, D. J. (1995). *The development of communication from social interaction to language.* New York: John Wiley and Sons.

Meyer, C. A. (1992, May). What's the difference between authentic and performance assessment? *Educational Leadership, 49*(8), 39–40.

Morine-Dershimer, G. (1990, November 12). Paper presented at the meeting of the National Association of Early Childhood Teacher Educators, Washington, DC.

Morrow, L. M. (1990). Assessing children's understanding of story through their construction and reconstruction of narrative. In L. M. Morrow & J. K. Smith (Eds.), *Assessment for instruction in early literacy* (pp. 110–134). Englewood Cliffs, NJ: Prentice-Hall.

Morrow, L. M., & Smith, J. K. (Eds.). (1990). *Assessment for instruction in early literacy.* Englewood Cliffs, NJ: Prentice-Hall.

Mowbray, J. K., & Salisbury, H. H. (1975). *Diagnosing individual needs for early childhood education.* Columbus, OH: Merrill.

Murphy, S., & Smith, M. A. (1990, Spring). Talking about portfolios. *The quarterly of the national writing project and the center for the study of writing.* Berkeley, CA: University of California.

Mussen, P. H., Conger, J. J., Kagan, J., & Huston, A. C. (1990). *Child development and personality* (7th ed). New York: Harper & Row.

National Association for Sport and Physical Education (NASPE). (1995). *Moving into the future: National physical education standards: A guide to content and assessment.* Reston, VA: Author.

National Association for the Education of Young Children. (1988). Position statement on standardized testing of young children 3 through 8 years of age. *Young Children, 43*(3), 42–47.

National Association for the Education of Young Children. (1982). *Early childhood teacher education guidelines.* Washington, DC: Author.

National Association for the Education of Young Children & National Association of Early Childhood Specialists of State Departments of Education. (1991). Guidelines for appropriate curriculum content and assessment in programs serving children ages 3 through 8. *Young Children, 46,* 21–38.

National Association of State Boards of Education (1988). *Right from the start: The report of the NASBE task force on early childhood education.* Alexandria, VA: Author.

National Council of Teachers of Mathematics. (1989). *Curriculum and evaluation standards for school mathematics.* Reston, VA: Author.

National Education Association. (1993). *Student portfolios.* West Haven, CT: Author.

National Education Goals Panel. (1991). *Measuring progress toward the national education goals: Potential indicators and measurement strategies.* Interim Resource Group Reports. Washington, DC: Author.

National Governors' Association. (1990). *America in transition: Report of the Task Force on Children.* Washington, DC: Author.

New, D. A. (1991). Teaching in the fourth world. *Phi Delta Kappan, 73*(5), 396–398.

Northwest Regional Educational Laboratory. (1991, June). New rules, roles, relationships explored. *Northwest Report,* pp. 1–2.

Northwest Regional Educational Laboratory. (1994). *Portfolio resources bibliography.* Portland, OR: Author.

Nourot, P. M., & Van Hoorn, J. L. (1991). Symbolic play in preschool and primary settings. *Young Children, 46*(6), 40–51.

Oakes, J. (1991). *Can tracking research influence school practice?* Paper presented at the meetings of the American Educational Research Association, Chicago, IL.

Owens, R. L. (1992). *Language development: An introduction.* New York: Macmillan.

Papalia, D. E., & Olds, S. W. (1996). *A child's world: Infancy through adolescence* (7th ed.). New York: McGraw-Hill.

Parten, M. B. (1933). Social participation among preschool children. *Journal of Abnormal and Social Psychology, 27,* 243–269.

Patterson, K., & Wright, A. (1990). Speech, language, or hearing impaired children: At risk academically. *Childhood Education, 64*(2), 91–95.

Paulson, F., Paulson, P., & Meyer, C. (1991). What makes a portfolio a portfolio? *Educational Leadership, 48,* 60–63.

Pepler, D. J., & Rubin, K. H. (1991). *The development and treatment of childhood aggression.* Hillsdale, NJ: Lawrence Erlbaum Associates.

Perrone, V. (1991). *On standardized testing: A position paper of the Association for Childhood Education International.* Wheaton, MD: Association for Childhood Education International.

Peterson, M. (1995). Research analysis of primary children's writing. ERIC Document ED-382-986.

Petty, W. T., Petty, D. C., & Salzer, R. T. (1989). *Experience in language* (5th ed.). Boston: Allyn and Bacon.

Phillips, S. U. (1983). *The invisible culture: Communication in classroom and community on the Warm Springs Indian Reservation.* White Plains, NY: Longman.

Phinney, J. S. (1982). Observing children: Ideas for teachers. *Young Children, 37,* 14–17.

Phye, G. D., & Andre, T. (Eds.). (1986). *Cognitive classroom learning: Understanding, thinking, and problem solving.* Orlando, FL: Academic Press.

Poest, C. A., Williams, J. R., Witt, D. D., & Atwood, M. E. (1990). Challenge me to move: Large muscle development in young children. *Young Children 45*(5), 4–10.

Powell, D. (1989). *Families and early childhood programs.* Washington, DC: National Association for the Education of Young Children.

Raines, S. C. (1990). Representational competence: (Re)presenting experience through words, actions, and images. *Childhood Education, 66,* 139–144.

Ravitch, D. (1995). *National standards in American education.* Washington, DC: Brookings Institution.

Regional Educational Laboratories' Early Childhood Collaboration Network. (1995). *Continuity in early childhood: A framework for home, school, and community linkages.* Charleston, WV: Appalachia Educational Laboratory.

Resnick, L. B., & Resnick, D. L. (1992). Assessing the thinking curriculum: New tools for educational reform. In B. R. Gifford & M. C. O'Connor (Eds.), *Future assessments: Changing views of aptitude, achievement, and instruction* (pp. 37–750). Boston: Kluwer.

Rhodes, L., & Shanklin, N. (1992). *Literacy assessment in whole language classrooms K–8.* Portsmouth, NH: Heinemann.

Rhodes, L., & Shanklin, N. (1993). *Windows into literacy: Assessing learners K–8.* Portsmouth, NH: Heinemann.

Richarz, A. S. (1980). *Understanding children through observation.* New York: West Publishing.

Rogers, C. S., & Sawyers, J. K. (1988). *Play in the lives of children.* Washington, DC: National Association for the Education of Young Children.

Rogoff, B. (1990). *Apprenticeship in thinking: Cognitive development in social context.* New York: Oxford University Press.

Rogoff, B., & Gardner, W. (1984). Adult guidance of cognitive development. In B. Rogoff & J. Lave (Eds.), *Everyday cognition: Its development in social context* (pp. 95–116). Cambridge, MA: Harvard University Press.

Sakharov, L. S. (1990). Methods for investigating concepts. *Soviet Psychology, 28*(4), 35–66.

Salvia, J., & Yesseldyke, J. E. (1995). *Assessment* (6th ed.). Boston: Houghton Mifflin.

Samuels, S. C. (1977). *Enhancing self-concept in early childhood.* New York: Human Sciences Press.

Sandoval, J., & Irvin, M. G. (1990). Legal and ethical issues in assessment of children. In C. R. Reynolds & R. W. Kamphaus (Eds.), *Handbook of psychological and educational assessment of children: Intelligence and achievement* (pp. 239–252). New York: Guilford Press.

Sattler, J. M. (1992). *Assessment of children* (3rd ed.). San Diego, CA: Jerome M. Sattler.

Schaefer, R. E., Staub, C., & Smith, K. (1983). *Language functions and school success.* Glenview, IL: Scott Foresman.

Schiamberg, L. B. (1988). *Child and adolescent development.* New York: Macmillan.

Schickedanz, J. A. (1986). *More than the ABC's: The early stages of reading and writing.* Washington, DC: National Association for the Education of Young Children.

Schickedanz, J. A., Hansen, K., & Forsyth, P. D. (1990). *Understanding children.* Mountain View, CA: Mayfield Publishing.

Schirmer, G. J. (1974). *Performance objectives for preschool children.* New York: Adapt Press.

Schultz, K. A., Colarusso, R. P., & Strawderman, V. W. (1989). *Mathematics for every young child.* Columbus, OH: Merrill.

Schultz, T. (1989). Testing and retention of young children: Moving from controversy to reform. *Phi Delta Kappan, 71*(2), 125–129.

Schwartz, S. L., & Robinson, H. F. (1982). *Designing curriculum for early childhood.* Boston: Allyn & Bacon.

Seefeldt, C. (1977). *Social studies for the preschool–primary child.* Columbus, OH: Merrill.

Seifert, K. L. (1993). Cognitive development and early childhood education. In B. Spodek (Ed.), *Handbook of research on the education of young children* (pp. 9–23). New York: Macmillan.

Selman, R. L. (1981). The child as a friendship philosopher. In S. R. Asher & J. M. Gottman (Eds.), *The development of children's friendships* (pp. 242–272). Cambridge, England: Cambridge University Press.

Shepard, L. A. (1982). Definition of bias. In R. A. Berk (Ed.), *Handbook of methods for detecting test bias* (pp. 9–30). Baltimore: The Johns Hopkins University Press.

Shepard, L. A. (1989). Why we need better assessments. *Educational Leadership, 46*(7), 4–9.

Shepard, L. A. (1991a). Readiness testing in local school districts: An analysis of backdoor policies. In S. H. Fuhrman & B. Molen (Eds.), *Politics of curriculum and testing: 1990 Yearbook of the Politics of Education Association* (pp. 159–179).

Shepard, L. A. (1991b). Will national tests improve student learning? *Phi Delta Kappan, 73,* 232–238.

Shepard, L. A., & C. L. Bliem. (1993). *Parent opinions about standardized tests, teacher's information, and performance assessments: A case study of the effects of alternative assessment in instruction, student learning, and accountability practices.* Los Angeles, CA: National center for research on evaluation, standards, and student testing. (ERIC Document Reproduction Service No. ED 378227).

Shepard, L. A., & Graue, M. E. (1993). The morass of school readiness screening: Research on test use and test validity. In B. Spodek (Ed.), *Handbook of research on the education of young children* (pp. 293–305). New York: Macmillan.

Sinclair, C. B. (1973). *Movement of the young child: Ages two to six.* Columbus, OH: Merrill.

Slavin, R. E. (1987). Ability grouping and student achievement in elementary schools: A best-evidence synthesis. *Review of Educational Research, 57,* 293–336.

Slavin, R. E. (1997). *Educational Psychology,* (5th ed.). Boston: Allyn & Bacon.

Smilanski, S., & Shefatya, L. (1990). *Facilitating play: A medium for promoting cognitive, socio-emotional, and academic development in young children.* Gaithersburg, MD: Psychosocial and Educational Publications.

Smith, J. K. (1990). Measurement issues in early literacy development. In L. M. Morrow & J. K. Smith (Eds.), *Assessment for instruction in early literacy* (pp. 62–74). Englewood Cliffs, NJ: Prentice-Hall.

Smith, M. L., & Shepard, L. A. (1988). Kindergarten readiness and retention: A qualitative study of teachers' beliefs and practices. *American Educational Research Journal, 25,* 307–333.

Smith-Burke, M. T. (1985). Reading and talking: Learning through interaction. In A. Jaggar & M. T. Smith-Burke (Eds.), *Observing the language learner.* New York: International Reading Association.

Spector, J. E. (1992). Predicting progress in beginning reading: Dynamic assessment of phonemic awareness. *Journal of Educational Psychology, 84*(3), 353–363.

Staff. (1989, January/February). Unpopular children. *The Harvard Education Letter.* 5(1), 1–3.

Stallman, A. C., & Pearson, P. D. (1990). Formal measures of early literacy. In L. M. Morrow & J. M. Smith (Eds.), *Assessment for instruction in early literacy* (pp. 7–44). Englewood Cliffs, NJ: Prentice-Hall.

Stanley, N. V. (1996). Vygotsky and multicultural assessment and instruction. In L. Dixon-Krauss (Ed.), *Vygotsky in the classroom: Mediated literacy instruction and assessment* (pp. 133–148). White Plains, NY: Longman.

Steinberg, L., & Belsky, J. (1991). *Infancy, childhood, and adolescence: Development in context.* New York: McGraw-Hill.

Stenmark, J. K. (1991). *Mathematics assessment: Myths, models, good questions, and practical suggestions.* Reston, VA: National Council of Teachers of Mathematics.

Stiggins, R. J. (1994). *Student-centered assessment.* New York: Merrill.

Stiggins, R. J. (1995). Assessment literacy for the 21st century. *Phi Delta Kappan, 77*(3), 238–245.

Stiggins, R. J., & Conklin, N. J. (1992). *In teachers' hands: Investigating the practices of classroom assessment.* Albany, NY: State University of New York Press.

Stone, S. J. (1995). Portfolios: Interactive and dynamic instructional tool. *Childhood Education, 71*(4), 232–234.

Stone, S. J. (1995). *Understanding portfolio assessment: A guide for parents.* Reston, VA: Association for Childhood Education International.

Sulzby, E. (1990). Assessment of writing and children's language while writing. In L. M. Morrow & J. K. Smith (Eds.), *Assessment for instruction in early literacy* (pp. 83–109). Englewood Cliffs, NJ: Prentice-Hall.

Suro, R. (1992, December 15). Poll finds Hispanic desire to assimilate: National Hispanic Political Survey. *The New York Times,* p. 1.

Taylor, R. T., Willits, P., & Lieberman, N. (1990). Identification of preschool children with mild handicaps: The importance of cooperative effort. *Childhood Education, 67,* 26–31.

Tharp, R. G., & Gallimore, R. (1988). *Rousing minds to life: Teaching, learning, and schooling in social context.* New York: Cambridge University Press.

Thomas, J. R., Lee, A. M., & Thomas, K. T. (1988). *Physical education for children: Concepts into practice.* Champaign, IL: Human Kinetics Books.

Thompson, C. (1986). *Scissors cutting program.* Unpublished manuscript. University of Kansas, Dept. of Human Development and Family Life.

Tough, J. (1977). *The development of meaning.* London: Allen & Unwin.

Trawick-Smith, J. (1988). Play leadership and following behavior of young children. *Young Children, 54,* 51–59.

Tuma, J. M., & Elbert, J. C. (1990). Critical issues and current practice in personality assessment of children. In C. R. Reynolds & R. W. Kamphaus (Eds.), *Handbook of psychological and educational assessment of children: Intelligence and achievement* (pp. 239–252). New York: Guilford Press.

Tyler, R. W., & Wolf, R. M. (1974). *Crucial issues in testing.* Berkeley, CA: McCutcheon.

U.S. Department of Health and Human Services. (1978). *Mainstreaming preschoolers.* Washington, DC: U.S. Government Printing Office.

Valencia, S. (1989). *Assessing reading and writing: Building a more complete picture.* Seattle, WA: University of Washington Press.

Valencia, S. (1990). A portfolio approach to classroom reading assessment: The whys, whats, and hows. *The Reading Teacher, 43*(4), 338–340.

Valencia, S. W., Hiebert, E. F., & Afflerbach, P. P. (Eds.). (1994). *Authentic reading assessment: Practices and possibilities.* Newark, DE: International Reading Association.

Valencia, S. W., & Place, N. A. (1994). Literacy portfolios for teaching, learning, and accountability: The Bellevue Literacy Assessment Project. In S. W. Valencia, E. F. Hiebert, & P. P. Afflerbach (Eds.), *Authentic reading assessment: Practices and possibilities* (pp. 134–156). Newark, DE: International Reading Association.

Villegas, A. M. (1991). *Culturally responsive pedagogy for the 1990's and beyond* (Report). Princeton, NJ: Educational Testing Service.

Vygotsky, L. S. (1962). *Thought and language.* Cambridge, MA: MIT Press.

Vygotsky, L. S. (1978). *Mind and society: The development of higher mental processes.* Cambridge, MA: Harvard University Press [Original works published 1930, 1933, 1935.]

Wadsworth, B. J. (1978). *Piaget for the classroom teacher.* New York: Longman.

Warger, C. (Ed.). (1988). *A resource guide to public school early childhood programs.* Alexandria, VA: Association for Supervision and Curriculum Development.

Webb, N. (1983). Predicting learning from student interaction: Defining the interaction variables. *Educational Psychologist, 18,* 33–41.

Weeks, Z. R., & Ewer-Jones, B. (1991). Assessment of perceptual motor and fine motor functioning. In B. A. Bracken (Ed.), *The psychoeducational assessment of preschool children* (2nd ed., pp. 259–283). Boston: Allyn & Bacon.

Weikert, P. S. (1987). *Round the circle: Key experiences in movement for children ages 3 to 5.* Ypsilanti, MI: High/Scope Press.

West, B. (1992). Children are caught between home school, and culture and school. In B. Neugebauer (Ed.), *Alike and different: Exploring our humanity with young children* (pp. 127–139). Washington, DC: National Association for the Education of Young Children.

Wickstrom, R. L. (1983). *Fundamental motor patterns* (3rd ed.). Philadelphia: Lea and Febiger.

Williams, H. G. (1991). Assessment of gross motor functioning. In B. A. Bracken (Ed.), *The psychoeducational assessment of preschool children* (2nd ed., pp. 284–216). Boston: Allyn and Bacon.

Winne, P. H., & Marx, R. W. (1987). The best tool teachers have—their students' thinking. In D. C. Berliner & B. V. Rosenshine (Eds.), *Talks to teachers* (pp. 267–306). New York: Random House.

Wittmer, D. S., & Honig, A. S. (1994). Encouraging positive social development in young children. *Young Children, 49*(5), 4–12.

Wittrock, M. C. (Ed.). (1986). *Handbook of research on teaching* (3rd ed., pp. 255–296). New York: Macmillan.

Wolery, M. (1994). Assessing children with special needs. In M. Wolery & J. M. Wilbers (Eds.), *Including children with special needs in early childhood programs* (pp. 71–96). Washington, DC: National Association for the Education of Young Children.

Wolery, M., & Dyk, L. (1984). Arena assessment: Description and preliminary social validity data. *Journal of the Association for Persons with Severe Handicaps, 9,* 231–235.

Wolery, M. P., Strain, P. S., and Bailey, D. B. (1992). Reaching potentials of children with special needs. In S. Bredekamp & T. Rosegrant (Eds.), *Reaching potentials: Appropriate curriculum and assessment for young children.* (Vol. 1, pp. 92–111). Washington, DC: National Association for the Education of Young Children.

Wolery, M., & Wilbers, J. M. (Eds.). (1994). *Including children with special needs in early childhood programs.* Washington, DC: National Association for the Education of Young Children.

Wolf, D. P. (1989). Portfolio assessment: Sampling student work. *Educational Leadership, 46*(7), 35–39.

Workman, S., & Anziano, M. C. (1993). Curriculum webs: Weaving connections from children to teachers. *Young Children, 48*(2), 4–9.

Wortham, S. C. (1995). *Measurement and evaluation in early childhood education* (2nd ed.). Englewood Cliffs, NJ: Merrill.

Wortham, S. C. (1995). *The integrated classroom: Assessment–curriculum link in early childhood education.* New York: Macmillan.

Zaporozhets, A. V., & Elkonin, D. B. (1971). *The psychology of preschool children.* Cambridge, MA: MIT Press.

Zill, N., Collins, M., West, J., & Hausken, E. G. (1995). Approaching kindergarten: A look at preschoolers in the United States. *Young Children, 51*(1), 35–38.

AUTHOR INDEX

SUBJECT INDEX

The abbreviation f stands for figure.

6986